MAKING A LANDSCAPE SACRED
Outlying Churches and Icon Stands in Sphakia, Southwestern Crete

BY

Lucia Nixon

Oxbow Books

Published by
Oxbow Books, Park End Place, Oxford OX1 1HN

ISBN 1 84217 206 9   978 1 84217 206 3

A CIP record for this book is available from the British Library

This book is available direct from
Oxbow Books, Park End Place, Oxford OX1 1HN
(Phone: 01865–241249; Fax: 01865–794449)

and

The David Brown Book Company
PO Box 511, Oakville, CT 06779, USA
(Phone: 860–945–9329; Fax: 860–945–9468)

or from our website

www.oxbowbooks.com

Printed in Great Britain by
Short Run Press, Exeter

To Simon

sine quo non

Anecdote of the Jar

I placed a jar in Tennessee,
And round it was, upon a hill.
It made a slovenly wilderness
    Surround that hill.

The wilderness rose up to it,
And sprawled around, no longer wild.
The jar was round upon the ground
    And tall and of a port in air.

It took dominion everywhere.
    The jar was gray and bare.
It did not give of bird or bush,
Like nothing else in Tennessee.

Wallace Stevens

CONTENTS

LIST OF FIGURES, TABLES AND COLOUR PLATES

List of Figures

List of Tables

List of Colour Plates

ACKNOWLEDGEMENTS

In Sphakia, thanks are due especially to Khrysi and Thodhori Athitakis; Anna Kantounaki; Georgios Saviolis, priest (Anopoli); and to Spiro Vranakis and the Koukounarakis family, particularly Pinelopi Koukounaraki and her granddaughter Zampia; Papageorgi Khiotakis, area priest of Sphakia in Nomikiana; Papanikolao Papadhosipho, priest in Patsianos (Frangokastello). Kanakis Geronymakis of Vouvas provided useful information about the practice of xekatharisma. In the Mesara, Manolis Kadhianakis of Pitsidhia contributed once again to my understanding of Cretan landscapes. In Khania, I thank the staff of the funeral parlour Axion Esti, for providing information about the cost of building icon stands and churches. I intend to find some way of reporting the results of this research to my informants, but particularly those in Sphakia; Nixon 2001 explains the thinking behind this decision.

I would like to thank the Greek Ministry of Culture and Sciences and the Greek Archaeological Service, particularly Maria Andreadhaki-Vlazaki, Vanna Niniou-Kindeli, and Stavroula Markoulaki of the KE' Ephoreia of Prehistoric and Classical Antiquities in Khania, for granting us the permits and giving us the practical assistance that have made the work of the Sphakia Survey possible. I thank also the Canadian Archaeological Institute in Athens for processing our permits. I am most grateful for financial support for all members of the project, from Queen's University at Kingston; the Social Sciences and Humanities Research Council of Canada; the Institute for Aegean Prehistory; the University of New Brunswick at Saint John; the Arts and Humanities Research Council; in Oxford, Lady Margaret Hall, Magdalen College, the Faculty of Literae Humaniores, the Research and Equipment Committee, and the Craven Committee; and Baylor University. I would like to thank all the students and specialists working on the Sphakia Survey for their dedicated participation.

In the course of the research for this book, I have received additional grants for field visits from the Craven Committee. The colour plates were made possible by two further grants from the Craven and Jowett Funds; I am most grateful to them. I have made use of Byzantine–Venetian–Turkish (BVT) pottery dates done by Margrete Hahn (Odense) and Pamela Armstrong (Oxford), and documents made available by other senior members of the Sphakia Survey, Simon Price (Oxford), and Oliver Rackham (Cambridge). I have been especially lucky to have access to Simon Price's BVT entries in the site catalogue, and to his summary chapter on the BVT epoch. Rosemary Bancroft-Marcus (Oxford, now Brussels) has worked on some of the relevant Greek MSS, while Machiel Kiel (Utrecht) has located and translated Ottoman records for us.

I would like also to thank the Greek Ministry of Land Use, Settlement, and the Environment (Athens) for furnishing excellent aerial photographs and giving us permission to publish them, and again the Canadian Archaeological Institute at Athens for helping us to obtain that permission.

Various libraries in Oxford helped with books and other information: the Ashmolean (now Sackler) Library (archaeology); the Slavonic, East European, and Modern Greek Annexe of the Taylorian Institution; the Oriental Institute (Arabs in Crete); the Tylor and Balfour Libraries (anthropology); and the Map Room, Bodleian Library.

I received much technical help and expertise in preparing the final MS of the book. Ina Döttinger, Sphakia Survey research assistant, patiently and meticulously helped with formatting the bibliography and preparing the maps; Charles Crowther and Maggy Sasanow (Centre for the Study of Ancient Documents, Oxford) provided essential helping with scanning.

I am also grateful to Val Lamb and Clare Litt at Oxbow for their help in seeing the book through to publication.

I thank my students in Archaeology and Anthropology at Oxford for their help with this book. Teaching this subject requires a broad approach to many different landscapes, and giving undergraduate tutorials has given me much helpful stimulus to my own thought. Andrew Sherratt, who died prematurely in February 2006, embodied the breadth of enquiry and generosity of spirit which characterises this degree at its best. I thank also Naomi Freud who replaced me for four terms as Director of Studies at St Peter's College, including the crucial term when the MS was completed. I will be forever grateful to my former colleague Thomas H. Tarver III, who in 1998 arranged for me to have the room in Magdalen, St Swithun's I.8, in which I wrote this book. I thank also St Hilda's College for granting me the research time in 2005–2006 when I was dealing with final revisions and proofs.

Versions of various sections of this book were given to various conferences and seminars: Intersecting Times: The Work of Memory in South Eastern Europe, 26.6.00, held at Clyne Castle, Swansea, University of Wales Centre for the Study of South Eastern Europe; Courtauld Institute of Art, London, 16.11.00; Byzantine Studies Seminar, Oxford, 16.1.01; Greek Archaeology Group, Oxford, 24.5.01; Ancient History seminar, Oxford, 20.1.04; Classics Colloquium, Department of Classics, University of Texas at Austin, 22.1.05. I am grateful to members of all these audiences for their useful comments. Some of the material on the grammar of location was included in an interview for the radio programme 'Baptizing the Gods', which explored the possibility of links between ancient Greek religion and Modern Greek Orthodoxy (broadcast 20.7.03 on BBC 3).

I thank many helpful and perceptive colleagues. Two of the other senior members of the Sphakia Survey, Jennifer Moody and Oliver Rackham, took part in many discussions of landscape, sacred and otherwise. Renée Hirschon and Olga Demetriou read and commented usefully on an earlier version of the MS, as well as providing additional references. Marina Pyrovolaki, whose family is from Anopoli, helped me with additional local information. Jim Coulton provided me with the reference to the ancient altar from the Kibyra-Olbasa Survey, published by Nicholas Milner. Mark Whittow found me the all-important footnote which led me to the information about wayside crosses and crucifixes in France. Peter Mackridge improved my translations of crucial Modern Greek texts. John Bennet helped me to see that location and explanation were the spatial and social sides of the same coin. Philip Pullman told me about Wallace Stevens' poem 'Ancedote of the Jar', which describes the effects of something made by people on the surrounding landscape; the poem appears on p. 76 of his *Collected Poems*, published by Faber and Faber. I am grateful to Julia Sleeper, who helped. Both Elizabeth Nixon and Miranda Nixon made usefully forthright comments on the MS; Elizabeth Nixon also improved the final version of the book title (suggesting the more dynamic Making a Landscape Sacred, instead of Making a Sacred Land-scape). I thank also my teachers, both official and inadvertent, especially Machteld Mellink, who did not live to receive her copy of this book, and Mabel Lang, who I hope will.

In the words of the mantinadha, I have had wonderful friends and colleagues, as many as the swallows (eikha parea omorphi, osa ta khelidhonia, εἴχα παϱέα ὅμοϱφη, ὅσα τα χελιδόνια!); they have provided good company and support, often much-needed, at various stages. Among them, and in addition to those already named, are Fleur Benest, Sue Bottigheimer, Laurence Brockliss, Hugh Brody, Bojan Bujic, Rosemary Burch, Katherine Clarke, Anne Compton, Felicity Cooke, Alison Etheridge, Christine Ferdinand, Lawrence Goldman, Suzie Hancock, Clare Harris, Kevin Hilliard, Chris Howgego, Margaret Kean, Henrietta Leyser, Susan Lisk, Rebecca Nestor, Alice Niwinski, Joy Parr, Helen Piddington, Mark Pobjoy, Pamela Rumball Rogers, Lyndal Roper, Judith Secker, Cynthia Shelmerdine, Richard Sheppard, Sue Sherratt, Tony Smith, Eric Southworth, Nicholas Stravroulakis, Sarah Thompson, Ralph Walker, and Michael Wheeler-Booth. And finally, Simon Price, senior member of the Sphakia Survey and husband extraordinaire, helped me at every stage of producing the MS, and remained interested and enthusiastic to the end. A final thank you to everyone mentioned here, and to those whose names I may inadvertently have left out. For the faults that undoubtedly remain in this book, despite everyone's help, I remain responsible.

ABBREVIATIONS

Throughout the book:

Ag. (Agia, Agios, Agioi) = Saint(s) in modern Greek

In the catalogue only:

B	Byzantine
E	east
H	Height
LR	Late Roman
N, NE, NW	north, northeast, northwest
PH	Prehistoric
R	Roman
S, SE, SW	south, southeast, southwest
T	Turkish
V	Venetian
W	west

Note on the Transliteration of Greek

It is well-known that there is no consistent way of transliterating Greek. This book uses a modified version of the system proposed for Modern Greek by the Annual of the British School at Athens. But the usual inconsistencies will be found here: Athens rather than Athina; Frangokastello rather than Phrangokastello. It is hoped that readers will be able to cope with these divergences.

1

INTRODUCTION

Greek sacred landscapes, much studied for classical antiquity, can also be investigated for more recent periods. Outlying churches and icon stands constitute a sacred system which provides a rich opportunity for studying the Byzantine, Venetian, and Turkish periods, and by extension, earlier epochs as well. The discussion here draws on the approaches used by others working in the Greek world, and also makes use of the spatial and diachronic perspective of archaeological survey. In particular, this study of outlying church and icon stands in the eparchy of Sphakia is embedded in, and depends on, a much larger project, the Sphakia Survey. The overall objective of the Survey is to investigate how humans have interacted with this rugged landscape since people first arrived ca 3000 B.C. until the end of the Turkish period in ca A.D. 1900. Without all the other data collected by the Survey, it would not have been possible to contextualise a book focused on these religious structures within the landscape of Sphakia.[1]

---

[1] Sphakia is an adminstrative district (deme, dhimos, δήμος; formerly eparchy, eparkhia, επαρχία) in southwestern Crete covering some 472 km². I have used the term eparchy in this book as it was the official term for the area until the late 1990s. The Sphakia Survey is co-directed by Jennifer Moody and the author, with senior participation of Simon Price (project historian) and Oliver Rackham (botanist and historical ecologist). Sphakia is a rugged area with considerable altitudinal compression: in only 16 km, the landscape changes from palm trees on the coast to elevations of ca. 2,400 m at the top of the White Mountains, where there is snow even in summer. The area is dissected by about 12 gorges running south to the Libyan Sea, of which the most famous is the Samaria Gorge. The Sphakia Survey has worked at every elevation and in every environmental zone. We selected areas for investigation on a stratified random basis and transected sets of quarter kilometer squares. We walked line transects where such squares were impractical (gorges, mountaintops), engaged in focused extensive exploration, and revisited all the sites. Our fieldwork revealed 315 sites spanning 5,000 years which we have divided into three major epochs (Prehistoric, Graeco-Roman, and Byzantine–Venetian–Turkish).

From the beginning, the Sphakia Survey aimed to collect and synthesise all possible types of evidence. Data were categorised in four groups: environmental (e.g. pollen cores, taxonomic botany, land use, climate); archaeological (sherds, stone tools, coins, bone, metal objects, glass, buildings, and standing structures); documentary (ancient and later inscriptions; Byzantine, Venetian, and Ottoman manuscripts and texts; Cretan poetry, both written and oral; novels such as those of Kondylakis [1987] and Waugh [1955]); and anthropological. For anthropological references see Tumasonis 1983, Vogelsang unpub. pers. comm.; Damer 1988, 1989; and Fielding 1953.

In the first field season of the Sphakia Survey in 1987, I noticed two icon stands (AN IK 16 and 17, PLATE 15) close together on the old kaldirimi (stone-paved mule-track) from Khora Sphakion to Anopoli, and wondered why they were there. After further fieldwork, I realised that I had learnt unconsciously to orient myself in relation to the outlying churches, by land and by sea: they were conspicuous landmarks, and they made it possible for me always to know where I was in a confusing and sometimes dangerous landscape. Again, I wondered why the churches had been built in those locations, and what this landmark aspect had to do with their function as churches. When I realised that the outlying churches and icon stands, together with the villages and their religious structures, constituted a set of markers for the sacred landscape of Byzantine–Venetian– Turkish Sphakia, I then began to make a separate study of them.

Outlying churches (exokklisia, εξωκκλήσια) are small churches outside settlements; they are similar to most small churches within settlements. They can have a monastery attached, and they can have cemeteries, but they need have neither, and most in Sphakia do not. Icon stands (in Sphakia, eikonostasia, εικονοστάσια) seem mainly to be linked with settlements, though they can be outside them as well. They are boxes or containers for icons, on supports or stands, built of stone, metal or concrete, large enough to contain two or three icons. All churches of the period under consideration also contain (or originally contained) icons.

Both outlying churches and icon stands can appear to be in the middle of nowhere, yet it is clear that people chose their location, and that therefore their placement cannot be random.

The earliest outlying church in Sphakia dates to the 10th–11th c.; icon stands may begin only in the 19th c. New examples of both outlying churches and icon stands are still being constructed in Sphakia, as in other parts of Greece. This study begins in A.D. 1000 with the first Sphakiote exokklisi and continues to A.D. 2000.[2]

After an exploratory pilot season in 1986, fieldwork was conducted from 1987 to 1992. Analysis of finds began in 1989 and continued until 1998 in conjunction with other specialist work. The Survey website was launched in October 2000 (Nixon and Moody et al. 2000); it is intended to complement the final paper publication in two volumes on which our efforts are now focused. Relevant Sphakia publications to date: Nixon and Moody et al. 1988, 1989, 1990, 1994; Moody and Nixon et al. 1998; Nixon et al. 2000; Francis et al. 2000; Nixon 2001; Nixon and Price 2001; Price et al. 2002; Moody et al. 2003; Price and Nixon 2005.

The site numbers used in this book, e.g. 4.21, are also used on the website, where they can help to locate images and other information.

[2] Ag. Pavlos, on the shore below the village of Ag. Ioannis, is the earliest exokklisi in Sphakia; see discussion, p. 62 and n. 70, which gives details of the church (architecture, dating, legends). This study includes both the entire Byzantine–Venetian–Turkish epoch in Sphakia, which was included in the work of the Sphakia Survey, and the 20th c., which was not. Here Byzantine is 962–1204; Venetian is 1204–1645; and Turkish is 1645–1898, or 1900 to be tidy. (Herakleion fell to the Turks later than Sphakia, in 1669.)

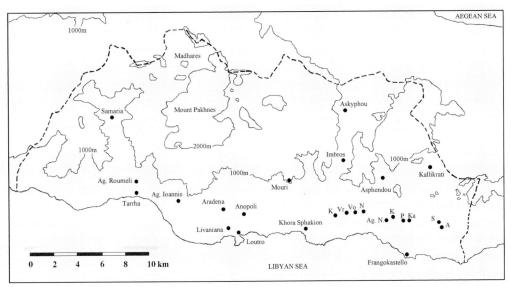

FIG 1 Map of Sphakia with villages and other places mentioned in the text. Abbreviated village names, from west to east: K(omitadhes), Vr(askas), Vo(uvas), N(omikiana), Ag. N(ektarios), K(olokasia), P(atsianos), K(apsodhasos), S(kaloti), and A(rgoule).

Information about the Byzantine–Venetian–Turkish (BVT) landscape of Sphakia, collected and analysed by the Survey from the beginning of the project in 1987, provides the general background for the study of outlying churches and icon stands. In addition, I made a detailed study of outlying churches and icon stands in the two areas where the Sphakia Survey has concentrated its efforts, the Anopolis (PLATES 1 and 2; TABLE 1) and Frangokastello Plains (PLATES 3 and 4; TABLE 2), and I have re-examined the evidence for outlying churches and icon stands in other parts of Sphakia (FIG 1). For all of this work I was able to draw on the entire timespan investigated by the Survey, roughly 3300 B.C. – A.D. 1900, as well as collecting information for the 20th c. I was also able to talk to people about their reasons for building new outlying churches and icon stands, and their criteria for choosing somewhere to construct them, and to compare my perception of their landscape with their own.

Outlying churches (and to a lesser extent, icon stands) mark the location of routes, resources (often at the time when they were first used), and boundaries. In the dissected terrain of Sphakia, these sacred structures make routes, resources, and boundaries conspicuous and visible over varying distances. The outlying churches provide a key to understanding how people have defined and used resources, and how their exploitation of the landscape has changed and developed over the millennium examined here; knowledge of settlement locations alone is not enough to track the changing use of local resources. While the areas marked by outlying churches and icon stands have tended to become smaller over time, the general function of marking remains more or less the same.

But I would argue that the primary function of outlying churches and icon stands is symbolic. These monuments mark, protect, and preserve the memory of significant loci in the landscape of Sphakia, loci not only important but also vulnerable enough to require the divine protection provided by icons. There are different reasons for remembering particular points in the landscape; in recent times, outlying churches and icon stands have been built to remind local inhabitants of their immediate ancestors.

I conclude that from the beginning, outlying churches in Sphakia added important local stories to the grand narrative of Greek Orthodoxy; and that one of their enduring functions was (and is) to mark the presence and boundaries of Hellenic Christianity, in a conspicuously memorable form. They also make a positive and visible declaration of the boundaries of Hellenic Christianity, sufficient to counter all threats from invasions, beginning with the expulsion in A.D. 962 of the Arabs from Crete.[3]

Several aspects of my study build on previous work, and constitute new contributions to the post-processual study of landscapes in general, and sacred landscapes in particular.[4]

First, I develop the concept of the predisposition of a landscape through earlier human use. Tilley's *Phenomenology of Landscape* focussed on the transition from the non-monumental Mesolithic to the often highly monumentalised Neolithic in Britain. The three landscapes he considers were used, but not conspicuously marked, in the Mesolithic period (Tilley 1994). The Byzantine–Venetian–Turkish epoch in the Greek world comes after several monumental periods, notably the Roman period with its pagan and Christian phases. In Sphakia, this epoch comes immediately after a period of Late Roman church-building which left conspicuous traces in the landscape. The Late Roman churches could be abandoned or adapted for later use, but they were too visible to be ignored. It is

---

[3] For a discussion of various definitions of Hellenism and its boundaries see Leontis 1995; cf. Sbonias 2005.

[4] Renfrew and Bahn (2000, 16) define the difference between processualism and post-processualism as follows:

> 'Processual archaeology moves forward by asking a series of questions, just as any scientific study proceeds by defining aims of study – formulating questions – and then proceeding to answer them. The symbolic and cognitive aspects of societies are also important areas emphasised by recent approaches, often grouped together under the term *postprocessual* or *interpretive archaeology* [authors' emphases], although the apparent unity of this perspective has now diversified into a variety of concerns.' Among recent post-processual methods, they say later on (2000, 42) is the phenomenological approach, 'where the archaeologist sets out to experience or to re-experience the humanly shaped landscape as it has been modified by … human activities…'

possible therefore to examine the effects of the Late Roman predisposition of the Sphakiote landscape on the new, Hellenic Christianity which then developed in the Byzantine period.

Similarly, it is possible, and crucial, to look at different grammars of location for each sacred landscape in a particular place. Successive sacred landscapes can differ wildly, even without a change of religion, as the briefest comparison of Late Roman and Byzantine–Venetian–Turkish/20th c. Christian monuments in Sphakia will make clear, because each period has its own logic or grammar in terms of the nature and location of monuments. When two religious monuments are built in the same place at two different times, people are often quick to say that they are evidence for continuity of cult. But assuming religious continuity in such cases amounts to serious intellectual sloppiness. The study of the two monuments is important, and can, if done properly, show whether there was reuse or continuity; but only the study of complete landscapes can reveal the underlying grammars that produced each one. What needs to be marked, by whom, and why and when? And with what effect on the landscape and on its inhabitants? An understanding of the grammar of location is needed to define the various 'somewheres' selected for individual monuments.

Third, Tilley's work on landscape discusses Prehistoric small-scale societies in Britain, using modern small-scale societies in Australia, Canada, Melanesia, and the U.S. to get at human perceptions of, and relationships with, landscapes elsewhere. This kind of comparison is useful if carefully done, but will always involve a dislocation in space as well as time. In studying Byzantine–Venetian–Turkish/20th c. Sphakia, I have been able both to look at a succession of larger-scale societies, and to use archaeological, documentary, and oral evidence, all from one area (though the oral information pertains only to the latest phase of the study area, there are many Early Venetian documents for the earlier ones). Studying the same place diachronically eliminates the problems of dislocation mentioned above. And investigating the more recent past has obviated the difficulties of reconstructing the details of Prehistoric landscapes (cited as a problem by Tilley 1994, 73), and it has also made it possible to compare local perceptions of landscape with my own.

Fourth, I have also been able to compare information about location – the spatial/material data obtained through conventional archaeological means – with information about explanation – that is, oral and written information about outlying churches and icon stands, in terms of the hermeneutic value of the latter to archaeologists. Oral information, consisting of interviews and conversations, is certainly useful, and indeed essential to collect when possible; it adds a great deal in terms of range of explanation, and in terms of nuance and history of specific monuments. In this case I have been fortunate to have written evidence, both documents and maps, to exploit as well. But the comparison confirms that significant phenomenological patterns in sacred landscapes can be derived through non-oral, archaeological analysis alone – that is from location. The unexpectedly strong validation of conventional archaeological spatial analysis – particularly when it can be tested against various kinds of oral and written sources – is perhaps one of the most significant aspects of my work. Moreover, it is possible to work in a rigorous way from location to explanation, that is, to make suggestions based on spatial analysis about the social reality of the landscape in question, because in general there are only so many kinds of location and explanation (see chapter 3). Or to put it another way, while oral and written evidence do make it possible to add more social information, purely archaeological information, properly analysed, can produce a reliable interpretation of landscape with social as well as spatial content.

Finally, my conclusions and methodological suggestions can be applied to outlying churches and icon stands elsewhere in the Byzantine–Venetian–Turkish and later Greek world, and also to sacred landscapes in other periods and places, including the Prehistoric Aegean. I explore some of these applications at the end of the book.

2

INTELLECTUAL BACKGROUND

The general intellectual context for this study is the phenomenological approach taken by Tilley (1994), among others (Bender 1993; Ashmore and Knapp; Ucko and Layton 1999), which argues that 'space is socially produced', and that accounts of ancient or other landscapes that fail to take this into account are by definition incomplete and two-dimensional (Tilley 1994, 3, 10).

In other words, there is no such thing as a monument in the middle of nowhere; all parts of any human landscape are always in the middle of somewhere (even if that somewhere turns out to be liminal), as Stevens suggests in his 'Anecdote of the Jar', reproduced at the beginning of this book. Indeed, some particularly important monuments are in the middle of everywhere. The task of the post-processual landscape researcher is to identify and contextualise the 'somewhere' of each monument, and to consider the whole of which they are a part.

Two questions identified as 'deceptively simple' by Tilley and Bradley have also helped to frame my own enquiry. Tilley began his study of three landscapes in Neolithic Britain with this question: 'Why were particular locations chosen for habitation and the erection of monuments as opposed to others?' (Tilley 1994, 1). Bradley used another deceptively simple question in his discussion of sacred landscapes in Neolithic and Bronze Age Europe: 'What do monuments do to the places where they are built?' (Bradley 2000, 140).

Two groups of concepts are important. First is the concept of sacred landscapes. It is important not only to study individual sacred structures, of whatever kind, but also to consider them together: the total set of material expressions of religious behaviour in a particular landscape will usually add up to something that is more than the sum of its parts. Or to put it another way, it is not possible to assess the meaning and importance of indivudual sacred structures without knowing how they relate to others in the locality. In addition, it is crucial to see how sacred landscapes develop and change over time.[5] Which features in a particular landscape are to be sacralised, and how? Which features are never marked by sacred structures? What do different sacred structures have

---

[5] For sacred landscapes, see Bradley 1996, 1998, 2000; Horden and Purcell 2000, 403–460.

in common, however different their form? How does the meaning of individual structures change, if new ways of sacralising landscapes are introduced?

The second important concept is that of liminality, particularly in exploring the function of sacred monuments as boundary markers. 'Liminal' is a term used by anthropologists to label different stages in transformational rituals such as rites of passage (van Gennep 1960). Here I use it spatially, for example to discuss the liminal space along the boundaries of different villages and communes (koinotites, κοινότητες). (Such space cannot be marginal, because more than one spatial entity is under discussion.) I also use liminal in a temporal sense, e.g. to describe the liminal period during which Late Roman Christianity in Sphakia was transformed into something else.

In this book I also make use of and draw together a number of different intellectual strands and traditions, relating mainly to work on the Byzantine–Venetian–Turkish/20th c. landscapes of the Greek world.

Historians of the period have reconstructed sequences of important events based mainly on texts, including the development of icons, the period of iconoclasm, and the establishment of icons as crucial to Greek Orthodoxy; understandably they tend to talk about territory only on a large scale (Whittow 1996). Until recently they tended not to talk about mentality, though travellers of the 19th c. (notably Pashley) did do so.

Scholars studying the art and architecture of the Byzantine and later periods traditionally focussed on icons and wall-paintings, and the churches in which they were displayed; other forms of material culture and settlements were seldom studied (Gerola 1905–32 and 1961, Lassithiotakis 1971, Gallas et al. 1983; Bissinger 1995; Spatharakis 2001). Moreover, it was mainly the 'good' icons, wall-paintings, and churches of some quality and complexity that were investigated, and therefore dated; Faure (1979) was unusual in studying 'rock' churches (built under overhangs) and his background was in any case archaeological. Thus 'inferior' examples are not anchored chronologically, unless they happen to be mentioned in texts. Cormack (1985) was exceptional in looking at the cultural context of icons; more recently he has written about icons as a cultural phenomenon in Crete, and how they were influenced by the presence of the Venetians (1997).

But no scholar of Greek churches, to my knowledge, has considered the setting of the churches considered 'significant' to the period; indeed it is difficult even to find photographs that show the position of churches relative to their village, town, or landscape. Byzantinists on the whole do not take offical scholarly notice of icon stands, partly because most of them are relatively recent, but partly because the icons they contain are not up to art historical standards.

On the other hand, archaeologists working on periods earlier than Byzantine–Venetian–Turkish have been greatly interested in the formation and functioning of sacred landscapes. For example, Peatfield (1992) has studied the location of Minoan peak sanctuaries.[6] And for a later period de Polignac (1984) provoked major interest in the role of extraurban Greek sanctuaries as, among other things, boundary markers for newly emergent poleis; it is all the more astonishing that his book contains no maps. Others such as Alcock and Osborne (1994) have since developed some of de Polignac's ideas. Nixon (1991) has discussed how sanctuaries marking the borders of early Greek cities on Crete often made use of the visible remains of Minoan settlements; Prent (2003) and Wallace (2003) have further explored Iron Age cult places at Bronze Age monuments. Morgan has investigated the 'evolution of a sacral "landscape" ' in the early Corinthian state (C. Morgan 1994 and cf. also 2003).

This archaeological interest has carried over into multi-period archaeological field surveys (of which the Sphakia Survey is one). Alcock (1994) has looked generally at evidence for cult outside cities in Hellenistic and Roman Greece, while Carter (1994) has done a fine-grained analysis of rural sanctuaries in the territory of the Greek colony of Metaponto.

But even archaeologists doing diachronic survey have been slow to recognise the potential of outlying churches and icon stands for landscape analysis. In a special study done in the context of the Southern Argolid Survey, Murray and Kardulias mapped outlying churches and icon stands in the Pikrodhafni Valley; to my knowledge they remain the only archaeologists to mention the latter type of religious monument. Whitelaw in his ethnoarchaeological study of part of Northwest Keos maps isolated churches, but does not comment on their odd distribution in the landscape, nor does he make it possible to correlate chapel names with locations, because no site numbers or labels are given (as with other Keos site maps). In his discussion of the Western Mesara from A.D. 961–1900, Vallianos mentions churches as boundary markers and commemorative structures without discussing individual examples. Koukoulis wrote a substantial catalogue of the churches in the Methana Survey area, but their role in the development of that landscape was not discussed in detail. In her article on agriculture and rural settlement in the Ottoman period, Brumfield notes the position and date for two monasteries in the Vrokastro survey area, but does not mention any other outlying churches. As a participant in the Pylos Regional Archaeological Project, Lee made a focussed study of the landscape around one village in the time since 1829. He described how people from two older settlements created a new village, in order to be closer to the new car roads built in the 1960s. The area selected was already cultivated and had its own outlying church, dedicated to Ag. Apostoloi, which has given the new village its name. What Lee does not explore is the connection between the church as marker for resources that would help to make a new settlement viable on the one hand, and the choice of that particular location for the new settlement on the other. Two surveys on the island of Kythira have paid an unusual amount of attention to

---

[6] Peatfield 1992, on the coincidence of Minoan peak sanctuaries and churches to Prophitis Ilias.

churches and their place in the landscape. The Australian Paliochora-Kythera Archaeological Survey (APKAS) has combined data from the many standing churches in the area with information in census records, in order to track the development of the mediaeval and later landscape. The Kythera Island Project has analysed the post-mediaeval landscape in its research area; exokklisia are included in this work. Both projects have made use of Geographic Information Systems to investigate the mediaeval and later uses of the landscape, as well as human exploitation of Kythira in earlier periods.[7]

For anthropologists working in Greece, icons and churches constitute material signs of the general Orthodox belief system, visible in the particular Greek community being studied. The power of icons and the importance of the Orthodox church as an institution are well understood, but symbolically, and not, in most cases, spatially. Thus discussions of icon stands or churches are usually couched in rather vague terms, as though the placement of real examples had no importance. For example, du Boulay does comment on the two icon stands at the eastern and western entrances to the village of Ambeli, but says nothing about the location of the village church in relation to the square and the fountain (1974, 13–14). Similarly, Herzfeld discusses legends associated with a miraculous icon in 'the lonely chapel of St George of Karidhi on the north coast'; he emphasises, rightly, the 'localist flavour' of such stories which are focussed on very particular landscapes; but he does not speculate on why that church was built there.[8]

Stewart's otherwise excellent book on exotika (malign spirits) is another good example; he rightly notices the placement of icon stands, or 'shrines' in his terminology, at liminal points such as crossroads, and he suggests that outlying churches might have something to do with taming the wilderness, but the actual location of these sacred structures in real space is of no interest to him, and most of the maps he produces are conceptual ones (Stewart 1991, 161, 165). Furthermore, because his study focusses on one village, he calls its edges 'marginal'. In real (as opposed to conceptual) space, every village has a 'margin'

---

[7] *Southern Argolid*: Murray and Kardulias 1986 and 2000; *Kea*: Whitelaw 1991, 414, 426–427; *Western Mesara*: Vallianos 1993 and cf. now Tsougarakis and Angelomatis-Tsougarakis 2004; *Methana*: Koukoulis 1997; *Vrokastro*: Brumfield 2000, 52, 54. *Pylos Regional Archaeological Project*: Lee 2001; for outlying churches and resources as a package, see pp. 53–57 below. *Australian Palichora-Kythera Archaeological Survey*: Gregory n.d., Diacopoulos 2004 (which also includes relevant discussion of the Eastern Korinthia Archaeological Survey). *Kythera Island Project*: Bevan et al. 2003, 220; James Conolly pers. comm. 2004. For other relevant uses of GIS, see Llobera 2001 (assessing the perception of topographic prominence); Soetens et al. 2003 (GIS and Minoan peak sanctuaries); J. Coleman Carter has been using GIS to analyse the sacred landscape of Metaponto (pers. comm. 2005). Note also that in their general book on Crete, Rackham and Moody discuss sacred landscapes in Crete (pre-Christian, Christian, Ottoman, but not Jewish) with useful maps of churches and monasteries throughout the island (1996, 179–188, with maps on pp. 183 and 186). For Jewish sites and synagogues on Crete, see Stavroulakis and DeVinney 1992.

[8] Herzfeld 1990a, 111, 116 and cf. pp. 81–83 below.

and these are often contiguous. For this reason the concept of liminality (rather than marginality) becomes important.

In fact, Stewart's discussion excludes two real dimensions, time as well as space: for him, icon stands and outlying churches exist only in the ethnographic present. The possibility of talking about the formation of the sacred landscape on Naxos – whether, for example, 'the wilderness' was tamed gradually, or all at once – is thus precluded. The same is true for the discussion in Hart (1992).[9]

Green and King do include time as a significant variable in their study of the Pogoni area in Northwest Greece, but they do not mention churches at all. This omission is striking for two reasons. First, they do discuss the difference between footpaths and car roads in terms of landscape perceptions, and second, they state that sectarian differences between local Christians and Muslims affect local 'constructions and perceptions of landscape' (Green and King 2001, 272, 275–283).[10]

There are two anthropologists, one Greek and one foreign, who have pushed the analysis of sacred landscapes in modern Greece forward. Kyriakidhou-Nestoros' 1975 article on icon stands in a northern Greek village, which I read after doing much of the work for this book, has confirmed many of my own ideas about the placement and significance of icon stands. Her article is important for two reasons. First, it confirms that icon stands are built for similar reasons and in similar locations in northern Greece. Second, her very title uses the phrase 'logic of landscape', which is similar to my own grammar of location, and reveals her perception that icon stands and churches are part of a sacred landscape which needs to be considered as a whole.[11]

Kenna (1976, 1991, 1994–95) is exceptional in suggesting that outlying churches are linked to patterns of land-ownership, and in noticing where, precisely,

---

[9] Some of the papers in Pavlides and Sutton 1994–95 do begin to look at the formation of sacred and other landscapes in the built environment of Greece, though the time depth is seldom very great; see papers by Dubisch and Kenna, as well as Pavlides' and Sutton's own introduction.
For an anthropological account of the metaphysical meanings of physical landscapes and monuments in Mongolia, see Humphrey 1995. But on the whole anthropologists studying landscapes inside and outside Greece tend to focus on the symbolic rather than the spatial; one index of this focus is the almost total lack of maps in such studies. For example, Stewart and Strathern 2003 is an edited book of 263 pages with ten papers, and ten illustrations. Only three papers are illustrated, with a total of ten illustrations. Only one paper has maps (two); the paper discussing maps includes none. The remaining eight illustrations are photographs, only one of which shows a landscape.
[10] In a conversation with Green (pers. comm. 2004) she said that many churches in the area had been restored by Pogoni people who had emigrated to the U.S. and other destinations, but she saw no significance in this phenomenon. See pp. 85–86 below on the restoration of churches by 'expatriates'.
[11] Kyriakidhou-Nestoros 1975: I owe this valuable reference to an anonymous scholar who attended the Byzantine Studies seminar presentation of this paper, and also to Panagiotis Dhoukellis. Kyriakidhou-Nestoros includes photographs of both churches and icon stands, mostly in villages in Khalkidhiki. Mikelakis (2005) has a similar perspective, but discusses only icon stands. I am grateful to Georgios Deligiannakis for this reference.

churches are located in village neighbourhoods. In other words, she acknowledges that the symbolic world of social relationships is sometimes very directly mapped in real space. I shall return to her work in chapter 5 below.

While exokklisia remain generally uninvestigated unless they are architecturally or iconographically interesting, several people have written about icon stands. Konstantinidhis publishes four icon stands in western Crete, without discussing their placement or date, at the end of an article on folk architecture. Khatziphoti looks at roadside icon stands in several parts of Greece. Plymakis has written a book about the icon stands of Crete; he includes older examples which are on footpaths as well as more recent icon stands by car roads. Both Khatziphoti and Plymakis include useful parallels from other countries and cultures, such as the calvaires of northwestern Europe. Saccopoulos looks only at Greek roadside icon stands; he suggests that though they are modern, they incorporate symbols and artifacts relating to the classical and Byzantine heritage of Greece.[12]

There is also important work on wider issues. Leontis' discussion of topographies of Hellenism (1995) cited above (in footnote 3) shows, on a larger spatial and chronological scale, how real and imagined topographies of Hellenism continue to be important in Greek landscapes, both inhabited and analysed. Alcock's work (2001, 2002) has shown definitively that people in the past selectively used and manipulated the landscape of the earlier past, both for commemoration and for 'willed forgetfulness', as part of the construction of new identities, especially at times of instability and social change. She has also coined the term 'memory theatre' in relation to the Agora at Athens in the Roman period. I suggest that the way monuments are treated often reflects very closely the selective chronology of desire that first constructed and later maintained or altered or destroyed them, in theatres both of memory and of oblivion (Nixon 2004).

And finally, Fakinou's novel *Astradheni* conveys the experience of outlying churches in the mid 20th c. Astradeni is a little girl who moves from Symi to Athens, and the church is a powerful symbol of memory and safety, providing a continuing and divine link to Symi as she and her family deal with the dangers of the city. Almost every time she remembers her island home, she remembers the monastery church of Ag. Constantine; everything that is good about her home

---

[12] Konstantinidhis 1975, 205–206 and pls 26 and 27; Khatziphoti 1986, 14–15 (Alsace, the former Yugoslavia), and Plymakis 2001b, 94, 142 (Alps, Japan, Thailand) give parallels for calvaires and similar markers in other countries and cultures; Saccopoulos 1986.
Further (rare) photographic documentation of icon stands comes from Papadhimou and Manousakis 1974, one of a number of Greek books with photographs of traditional Greek landscapes. This unpaginated book has pictures of nine icon stands in the Peloponnese (one); on Evvoia (two), in Attica (four), on Crete (one); in Larisa (one). Few further details of their location are given, and none for the Cretan example. Cf. also Trivizas and Dhimitriou 2005.

territory clusters around this small church, set high above her village with a beautiful view of hills and sea, surrounded by good land producing vines and flowers and abundant water. This experience is also part of the landscape of outlying churches and icon stands.[13]

---

[13] Fakinou 1991 [1982], 12, 24, 109–112, 137–138,142, 159, 224–225. Ag. Constantine is one of several outlying churches mentioned in the book; for others, see pp. 71; 76–77; 112; 163; 211.

3

INDIVIDUAL CHURCHES AND ICON STANDS: DESCRIPTION, LOCATION, EXPLAINED

3.1 Describing Churches and Icon Stands

3.1.1 Outlying Churches

Small (i.e. non-congregational) churches share the same features, whatever their location. Information in the description below therefore applies to all small Greek churches, whether they are inside or outside settlements, unless stated otherwise.

All small churches can be called ekklisies, or ekklisakia (little churches). A church outside a settlement is called an exokklisi, literally an outside church). But the word *esokklisi, literally an 'inside church' (i.e. physically part of a settlement) does not exist. One implication is that village churches are perceived as the norm, and that outlying churches are seen as a later addition to the repertoire of sacred architecture. This perception will be discussed and challenged below, particularly in the analysis of Anopoli and Frangokastello, where I contend that far from being later extras, outlying churches were integral to the development of the Byzantine–Venetian–Turkish settlement pattern from its earliest stages.

Like most village churches, most exokklisia are simple rectangular structures, and small. As usual with churches, they are set with their long sides running east-west. The eastern end may have an apse, often with a small opening, if not an actual window; the door is normally on the west or south sides. There need not be any other openings or windows; see PLATE 17 for an example.[14]

---

[14] Some measurements of simple structures: Samaria Osia Maria (site number 1.22): ca 2m50 x 3m40; Ag. Roumeli Panagia (1.28): 7m70 (inc. apse) x 5m90; Ag. Ioannis outside the village of Ag. Ioannis (3.03): original church ca 2m75 x 3m40, with later additions to west and south aisle (date of 1874 over door marks repair). Ag. Pavlos below the village of Ag. Ioannis (3.01) is unusual is having a more complex plan, but is still a relatively small structure, ca 6m50 x 8m30, plan in Gallas et al. 1983: 256 fig. 212. FK CH 8 Ag. Kharalampos in the Frangokastello Plain (8.50) has had a long and complex

The materials used for Byzantine–Venetian–Turkish churches were the same as those used for houses; it is their form that distinguishes sacred from secular structures. In this period, churches were built of local stone and plastered; at some point, it became common practice to whitewash them. Some outlying churches have their own lime kiln nearby, as in the case of the church of Ag. Nikolaos in the Samaria Gorge (1.17).[15] But it is not currently possible to date the practice of whitewashing churches, nor is it possible to date lime kilns (where the whitewash was produced). It is possible to say that whitewash makes outlying churches even more visible than they already were; see the discussion below (pp. 25–26) of visibility by land and sea as a factor in the location of these churches.[16]

The tiled roofs of the Byzantine–Venetian–Turkish period were often replaced by a solid concrete roof in the second half of the 20th c. In some cases the original roofing was of stone slabs. A small frame for a bell was often added in the 19th c., though some are as early as the Venetian period. In the Venetian and earlier Turkish periods, churches were sometimes decorated at the time of their construction with ceramic glazed bowls (bacini), commonly, but not always, arranged in a cross shape of five bacini over the door. Sometimes the bacini have been broken or removed, but the bowl-shaped depressions remain.

The church may have an enclosure around it, usually a low wall with a gate. Churches with cemeteries will always have such an enclosure, and may well have large trees as well (often cypresses, sometimes olives). Cemeteries may have two kinds of graves: older, unmarked arcosolium tombs built right against the church itself, or very close to it (see FIG 2 for an example); and freestanding family tombs. The latter are usually labelled with the names of the family and the birth and

---

history and was also a monastery; the actual church measures 11m60 x 8m20.)

[15] 1.17 is the permanent Sphakia Survey site number assigned to this church. Survey sites are grouped in eight regions. Ag. Nikolaos in the Samaria Gorge is therefore Site 17 in Region 1. These site numbers can be used to obtain further information from the Sphakia Survey web site (Nixon and Moody et al. 2000), at <http://sphakia.classics.ox.ac.uk>.

[16] There are words for whitewash in Byzantine and Mediaeval Greek but no examples connecting them with churches; the Byzantinists whom I have consulted know of no texts referring to whitewashing churches. Some early churches seem never to have been whitewashed, such as Ag. Pavlos below the village of Ag. Ioannis (3.01), and FK CH 10 Prophitis Ilias Skaloti. In the early 20th c. photograph taken by Gerola (1993, 246 fig. 298), Ag. Apostoloi in Khora Sphakion (6.18) is not obviously whitewashed, but it may simply have been very grubby (as well as neglected – there are major cracks in the façade); in the late 20th c. it was brilliantly whitewashed. In the 20th c. novel *Astradheni*, each family in Symi was responsible for one monastery or outlying church, so all the churches were all kept white (Fakinou 1991, 138). Unwhitewashed churches are still visible but whitewashing makes them visible over much greater distances; contrast the outlying church of St Catherine in Dorset, U.K., used as a landmark by sailors crossing Lyme Bay (Fair and Moxom 1993, frontispiece, 12, 14, 15) with whitewashed exokklisia of smaller size in Sphakia such as AN CH 19 Ag. Aikaterini or FK CH 2 Ag. Ioannis Prodhromos in PLATES 7, and 16 and 17. Cf. Spratt's reaction to a newly restored and whitewashed church on p. 75 below.

Fɪɢ 2   FK CH 10. Prophitis Ilias with tombs (arcosolia) and fallen roof tiles in front of west end of chapel. July 1990.

death dates of the most recently deceased family members buried inside them. These labels seem to be a feature of the later 20th c.

Near the church and usually within the enclosure, if there is one, can be found various types of ecclesiastical debris: remains of an old epitaphios (the symbolic bier carried around villages and eventually into churches at Easter); piles of the old ceramic tiles removed when the roof was replaced with concrete; old bottles used for oil; purple glass fragments.

Inside the church the most important items are the icons, which will include at least one icon of the deity or saint to whom the church is dedicated, as well as others, and the iconostasis (εικονόστασις), also decorated with sacred pictures, which separates the area of the altar from the rest of the church. The main icon can usually be recognised by the small metal votive plaques (tamata, τάματα) suspended below it, and, at the time of the saint's day, a garland of flowers. Some older churches have wall-paintings, but their absence in a plausibly old church may mean only that they were covered in whitewash. Inside the church it is easier to see the shape of the roof; a pointed (Gothic) arch can indicate a date either in the Venetian or Turkish period.

Near the door there will be candles of different sizes and money left to pay for them, and a metal stand with a container with sand in it for lit candles. Some churches may have a piece of furniture with rounded slots for the candles (the bagaz, μπαγκάζ), and a small slot for money (labelled in Greek riptete ton obolon, ρίπτετε τον όβολον literally 'throw the obol [money]'). Somewhere there will be an incense burner (thymiatirio, θυμιατήριο), and an oil lamp with a floating wick, plus a bottle of oil to replenish it as needed, often with a newspaper underneath it. There may also be a stand for the order of service, ecclesiastical chairs along the long sides of the church, and a chandelier. In the later 19 c./earlier 20th c., patterned encaustic tiles were often used for church floors.

Without documents it is virtually impossible to assign precise dates for the construction of earlier simple churches, as they seldom if ever have dated building inscriptions. Either a Gothic arch or the presence of bacini can indicate a date within the long Venetian-Turkish period, but bacini may offer a much more precise date than this, if as is usual they are integral to the original construction of the church.[17] Wall-paintings, which can be added after construction, may also suggest a fairly precise terminus ante quem for the construction of the church. Dated graffiti will give a terminus ante quem. 20th c. churches often have building inscriptions giving a date.

Outlying churches are of course still being built. Nowadays they can be built of concrete (beton), sometimes in combination with cinder/breeze blocks. A prefabricated concrete church can be placed on a prepared platform at the site; the cost in 1999 was 2.5 million drachmas (7,337 euros) including materials and labour, but exclusive of any church furnishings. Churches will still be whitewashed.

Churches can be commissioned or built by individuals, without consultation with the local diocese; such spontaneous construction can cause problems later on, when people want to celebrate the saint's day, and a priest is required, or when the family can no longer afford to maintain the church that they decided to build.

Outlying churches can be used for prayer and candle lighting by individuals at any time. There is usually only one actual service (leitourgia, λειτουργία) conducted by a priest for a congregation per year, on the saint's day. Anyone may attend, regardless of which village (or eparchy, or country!) they come from. Those present may move in and out of the church during the service. Physically being in the church during the service is not a requirement (as in village churches).[18]

---

[17] Atti XXVI Convegno internazionale della Ceramica, Albisola 28–30 May 1993 (1996) on 'I bacini murati medievali. Problemi e stato della ricerca'. Turkish bacini in Sphakia: 1.17 Samaria Gorge: Ag. Nikolaos; 3.20 Aradhena, bacini added on the tower of Mikhail Arkhangelos. We are grateful to Pamela Armstrong for dating the bowls.

[18] See for example the summary of the name day service held at FK CH 7 Ag. Nikitas in the catalogue.

3.1.2. Icon Stands

Icon stands are literally that, a box or container for icons, on a support or stand. On Crete, the words for icon stand are eikonostasi (εικονοστάσι) and ekklisaki (εκκλησάκι); outside Crete, the word proskynitari (προσκυνητάρι) is also used. There are three types, overlapping in age. The oldest of the three types, like churches and houses, is built of local stone, and whitewashed; a typical example is 2m00 tall, 1m44 wide, and 1m76 deep. The whitewash, combined with their position, can make them visible over long distances by day, despite their relatively small size. A stone icon stand looks like a shaped cairn until you see the little door/window, which opens to reveal the icons inside it. AN IK 9 is a good example of the type (PLATE 13).

Most newer icon stands are metal, painted white, blue, or green. These modern icon stands are literally a box on a stalk, set in cement; the box will usually be some 40–50 cm square, total height perhaps only 1m14. These are the icon stands most commonly seen, placed by the side of car roads to commemorate an accident (real or averted); they can also have other functions. See PLATE 9 for an example (AN IK 2).

The third and newest type is made of pre-cast concrete, in the shape of a little church, thus literally an 'ekklisaki'; the size of the little church being roughly the same size as a metal icon box. These were not seen in Sphakia (nor in other parts of Crete) until the 1990s. I have seen them placed immediately outside someone's house; I was told that they could be put alongside roads and outside hotels, and that the new church form had become fashionable (egine modha, έγινε μόδα). AN IK 11 (PLATE 14) is one of two examples in Sphakia seen by me before 2000; the other is the later of two successive icon stands described as AN IK 15.

Icon stands of all three types contain several icons; one figure, again either a member of the Holy Family saint or a saint, is the focus of the dedication, but other saints may also be depicted. All three types often have a cross on top. Stone and metal icon stands also typically contain an oil lamp with floating wick, an incense burner, candles, and money. Concrete 'church' icon stands may be equipped with a socket for a light bulb, plus an electrical cable to be plugged in to a house's electricity supply. Plate 11 shows the interior of AN IK 2, a metal icon stand.

Unlike churches, icon stands can face in any direction. I found it important to note their orientation, because of the visibility of the light within them, and because of their general location. For example, there is a clear difference between an icon stand facing outwards from a settlement, and one facing in; see or example AN IK 16 (out) and 17 (in) discussed below.

Dating the construction of icon stands is both easy and difficult. The material used to build icon stands is a rough guide to their relative date. Stone icon stands are usually, though not always, older than metal ones; I have seen no dated metal examples older than 30–40 years, which gives a very rough terminus post quem.

As already mentioned, the concrete church icon stands are a product of the 1990s and later. The general impossibility of dating older stone icon stands is a matter of no small frustration, as these are the oldest examples of all. AN IK 18 was built of stone in 1977 – it says so on its metal cross. But there is no obvious way to date stone icon stands such as AN IK 16, which is old enough to have gone out of use and to have been superseded by a metal icon stand (AN IK 17; see below for discussion).

Price and tradition figure in the choice of material nowadays. Stone is readily available and 'free'; metal and concrete stands have to be paid for with money, and seem therefore to be more prestigious. Nowadays, as with churches, anyone, male or female, can set up an icon stand; the various reasons for doing this will be discussed below. A metal icon stand will cost about 80,000 drachmas (235 euros), with perhaps another 10,000 drachmas (30 euros) for the cement platform to support it; again, these prices exclude the cost of the icons and other contents. In 2000 concrete church icon stands cost 70,000 drachmas (204 euros) for a small one, 80,000 (235 euros) for a large one, exclusive of the supporting platform. It is significant that the place of purchase observed by me was not a 'holy shop' but a pottery workshop.

But unlike the case of churches, there is never any ecclesiastical involvement: lighting a lamp or a candle or burning incense are the only actions needed; no priest is required to activate the power of the icons. The maintenance of an icon stand, similarly, can be done by anyone.

A rough date for the most recent use of an icon stand can be worked out from the date of the coins used to pay for oil or incense, and also from the date of the newspapers sometimes used to line the bottom of the box.[19]

3.2 The Locations of Individual Outlying Churches and Icon Stands

In this section I present the general or 'macro' evidence for patterns in the location of individual churches and icons stands, inside and outside villages, both in Sphakia and in other parts of the Greek world, before proceeding to the 'micro' section focusing on Anopoli and Frangokastello. Most of the examples included here are from Sphakia, with a few from other parts of Crete and Greece.

It is important to note that the same structure, outlying church or icon stand, can be built for more than one of the reasons discussed here.

I begin with a brief note on the location and dedication of churches. All churches, regardless of location, are dedicated to Christ, the Holy Ghost (Ag.

---

[19] Dates of coins in AN IK 17 on 11.4.99: 1976, 1990, 1992 (2), 1994; dates of coins in my pocket that day: 1986 (2), 1992 (3), 1994.

Pnevma), the Christian Trinity (Ag. Triadha), the Virgin Mary (Panagia), another member of the Holy Family, a saint, or, rarely, a figure from the Old Testament (Prophitis Ilias, the prophet Elijah, is almost the only one); the same is also true of icon stands.

There seems to be no connection between the gender of the saint and the type of location for churches and icon stands. In fact there is usually no connection between the specific saint and the type of location, with two kinds of exceptions for churches. First of all, Ag. Antonios and Prophitis Ilias do have churches in predictable locations. Churches to Agios Antonios are usually built onto areas where there is a useful rocky overhang; these are not caves but rather cave-like hollows (spilaiodeis koilotites), or 'rock shelters' in the Palaeolithic sense. The built wall necessary to enclose a space for the church is often whitewashed and therefore can make the church visible. In Sphakia there are several churches to Ag. Antonios, for example on the Loutro peninsula (5.11, Sector II); above the neighbourhood of Bros Gialos in Khora Sphakion (6.07); and below Komitadhes (8.02).[20]

Churches to Prophitis Ilias can be built inside villages. When they are built outside villages as exokklisia, they are positioned on relatively low peaks, either inside villages or within easy walking distance of at least one village. In Sphakia there are five churches to Prophitis Ilias, two in villages and three outside them, ranging in altitude from range from 100 to 700 m; thus in Sphakia Survey terms they occur at the 'down' and 'middle' altitudes.[21]

In dissected terrain like the karst landscapes of Sphakia there are many suitable clefts (Ag. Antonios) and low peaks (Prophitis Ilias). The task is therefore to determine why some hills and rock shelters are chosen for churches and not others, because the reasons for their selection are additional to the geography.

There is a second kind of significant topographic factor in the dedication of churches. Most dedicatees are saints whose names can be used for humans –

---

[20] In other words, the overhangs used for churches of Ag. Antonios are not the same kind of feature as the caves used for sacred purposes in earlier periods, such as the Graeco-Roman Agiasmatsi Cave in Sphakia, or the caves used in other parts of Crete during the Prehistoric epoch (Idaean, Kamares, Dictaean, etc.) Overhangs and caves are both features of the same karst landscape, but they are emphasised and used in different ways in different periods. For Agiasmatsi, see Francis et al. 2000, 451–456; and cf. Bradley 2000, 97–113. Platakis lists all the 'overhang' or 'rock shelter' churches in Crete by saint, with Ag. Antonios having one of the longest lists, Platakis 1979, 12–13. Faure 1979 lists them by eparchy; for Sphakia pp. 72–73. Cf. also Tomadhakis 1978.

[21] Churches to Prophitis Ilias in Sphakia: 1. P. Ilias above the deserted village of Peradoro, 404m (1.04), see Spratt 1865, II.215). 2. P. Ilias between Ag. Ioannis and Aradhena, 645m (3.14); 3. P. Ilias in Limnia, neighbourhood of Anopoli, 700m (4.33); 4. P. Ilias in Mesokhori, neighbourhood of Khora Sphakion, ca. 100m (6.18); 5. P. Ilias between Kapsodhasos and Skaloti, 125m (FK CH 10 in Catalogue below, and 8.59).

For definitions of these altitudes ('middle', 'down'), see Appendix 2.

For further discussion of which saints get churches and when, see Rackham and Moody 1996, 182, who point out that most mediaeval chapels are 'dedicated to saints who would have been well known in Crete during its Early Byzantine Period', i.e. before the Arab invasion.

Antonios, Ilias, Maria/Panagia (Maria, Panagiota/Panagiotis). The saint's day becomes the name day of those people, so that all Marias and all Iliases celebrate simultaneously and collectively; only very late in the 20th c. were birthdays celebrated, and then mainly in cities. The name day celebration includes the obligation to take part in the leitourgia at the nearest church dedicated to the relevant saint, inside or outside a village. Outlying churches in less accessible locations – on a higher hill than usual, for example – are sometimes dedicated to beings or entities after whom people cannot be named, such as Ag. Pnevma (the Holy Ghost) or Timios Stavros (the True Cross). The obligation to take part in the leitourgia therefore falls on everyone who is able to get to the church. The only Ag. Pnevma in Sphakia is at 2264 masl; the church of Timios Stavros at the top of Mt Kophinas in the Mesara Plain (south central Crete) is at 1231 masl; both of these are far higher than churches to Prophitis Ilias.[22]

It is interesting that although there are Sphakiote saints, Ag. Emmanouil and Ioannis, the only church in the eparchy dedicated to them was built in the 1980s; the church lies between the neighbourhoods of Kares and Ammoudhari in the Askyphou Plain.

3.3 Churches within Settlements: Slopes and Edges

There are two types of location for churches in villages or neighbourhoods, which I have named 'slope' and 'edge'. 'Slope' churches are usually built at the highest point of a settlement on a detached slope, often where the footpath comes in from outside the village. For example, in the village of Livaniana (5.08) above Loutro, the only church is at the top of the village; cf. also the church shown in the midst of houses at the top edge of the Lakkoi ridge, in the area north of Sphakia (Pashley 1837, II. 146 [picture], 156). In Georgitsi (6.17), a now deserted neighbourhood of Khora Sphakion, there is a variation on this theme. The houses occupied a roughly triangular area spread out over a slope, with one church at the top and two others, at the two lower 'corners'. These churches mark out the perimeter of the neighbourhood and together form a protective outline around it.

'Edge' churches are constructed at the least protected edge of a settlement built on flattish land, again where a route from somewhere enters the settlement. The church of Mikhail Arkhangelos has stood guard over Aradhena (3.20) since the

---

[22] For a discussion of the general shift from collective to individual in social and material life in the later 20th c. in Greece, of which the change from name days to birthdays is one aspect, please see pp. 78–79 and n. 106 below. For name days in general, see Gavrielides 1974. There are two churches to Timios Stavros in the periphery of Anopoli (AN CH 3, AN CH 5), both at lower altitudes. Their location may have something to do with boundaries; AN CH 5 is certainly on the commune boundary between Anopoli and Khora Sphakion.

14th c. when it was built at the top of the homonymous gorge at the edge of the village (Gallas et al. 1983, 253).[23]

Village churches on slopes and edges often have cemeteries, and it is true that people usually prefer to have cemeteries on the periphery of settlements. Nonetheless it remains true that people select the outermost 'dangerous' spot in a village for the churches themselves. Visibility is as important for village churches – they must be seen to protect their settlement – as it is for outlying churches, as will become clear in the discussion below.

3.4 Outlying Churches and Icon Stands: Location and Explanation

Outlying churches and icon stands need to be considered together as two elements in a single continuum of sacred structures. In analysing their physical and symbolic position in the landscape, I have found it essential to separate location and explanation.[24]

Location here means a distinct type of place or site in which outlying churches and icon stands can be built, which can be observed or deduced by spatial analysis alone, that is without recourse to any oral or written information. Some types of location are more frequently used for outlying churches, others for icon stands; for example, icon stands are usually found closer to settlements, and normally mark human rather than natural features of the landscape. There are also chronological differences in location types, which are discussed below.

All outlying churches and icon stands are on routes. Once these would all have been routes for pedestrians and pack animals, such as kaldirimia (built mule tracks, καλντιρίμια) or monopatia (footpaths, μονοπάτια); now car roads must also be taken into account. Single churches or icon stands can, and frequently do, mark more than one of these locations. By contrast, where explanations are available, normally only one explanation is given for each structure.

The four main types of location are discussed below.

Explanation here means the reasons given by people for building outlying churches and icon stands, discussed orally by those who know the relevant landscapes up to A.D. 2000; shown on maps; or supplied by written sources. Explanations are available mainly for more recent churches and icon stands. They are usually connected with commemoration, and fall into four major types, which

---

[23] The churches in Louis de Bernières' fictional town of Periboli follow this pattern: St Nicholas in the centre; St Minas at the bottom; and a tiny white frescoed chapel (nameless as to saint) at the top. Some distance away from the town there was an exokklisi on the top of a hill by the sea, 'a very small chapel that was used only once or twice a year, and of which no one knew the origin'; de Bernières 2004, 266–267, 574, 603.

[24] See Appendix 3 for a brief discussion of how Khatziphoti (1986) and Plymakis (2001b) try to account for locations and explanations.

are discussed below. Explanations are not usually deducible by spatial analysis; they are something which you must be told. For example, you might suspect that FK CH 2 Ag. Ioannis Prodhromos marked some kind of boundary between the villages of Ag. Georgios/Kolokasia and Patsianos, but only a map or a person could confirm that this church lies just west of the commune boundary separating the two.

The question of how well location and explanation fit together will be discussed in greater detail below in section 6.2. For now it is sufficient to make two points. First, each outlying church and icon stand will have a spatially observable specific location, but its specific explanation has to be determined through further work. For example, an outlying church or an icon stand built over an earlier sacred structure has a particular type of location, which then needs to be explained; the presence of an earlier sacred structure does not in and of itself constitute a sufficient explanation for why the church or icon stand was built just there.

Second, the location and explanation of specific structures may not always have obvious links. Some older churches located at liminal points in the landscape do in fact mark human boundaries. But where both location and explanation are available for more recent structures, they do not necessarily converge (see chapter 6 and TABLE 7).

For earlier outlying churches we cannot easily establish the explanation given at the time of their construction – why, precisely, they might have been built. But the discussion below will show that the choice of location for recent churches seems congruent with the choices made for earlier ones, in other words that the means of selecting where they were built seem to be consistent over time.

The churches and icon stands discussed here as examples for location and explanation were chosen because they are outside the two study areas. These exterior examples are intended to set up issues to be explored more fully in the chapter on the core areas of Anopoli and Frangokastello (chapter 4; TABLES 1 and 2; and the Catalogue).

3.4.1 Location

1. IMPORTANT RESOURCES (WATER, ARABLE LAND, ETC) AND NEW ACTIVITY

One of the best examples is also the earliest outlying church in Sphakia. Ag. Pavlos (3.01, PLATE 5) was built in the 10th–11th c. 'in the middle of nowhere' on the shore below Ag. Ioannis, on the path between the anchorage south of Ag. Roumeli, and Loutro. Ag. Pavlos is in fact very definitely in the middle of somewhere. It sits at the contact zone between salt and fresh water, and therefore marks the location of drinkable water, which can be found by digging in the gravel nearby. It is also near the path leading up to Ag. Ioannis which would otherwise be difficult to find, as the village is invisible from the sea (Gallas et al. 1983, 256–257, fig. 212).

Similarly, outlying churches can indicate good arable land. The church of Ag. Triadha (6.06) west of Khora Sphakion lies at the top of a large terraced enclosure on a SE-facing slope, well above the main footpath from Khora to Anopoli. The terraces were relatively broad and therefore easier to cultivate than most. The church is shown in Monanni's 1631 drawing of the area but its precise construction date is not known.[25]

It is rarer for icon stands to mark the location of important resources. I know of one instance where an icon stand may mark a natural feature: an icon stand on the footpath west of the mouth of the Trypiti Gorge, near a spring; it is undated (1.05; L. Wilson 2000, 183). Two Sphakiote exokklisia built in the 1990s reveal new uses of 'old' areas, and shed light on another dimension of the marking of important resources. One is the church built on a new dirt road east of Askyphou, in memory of a deceased family member, male in this case. The construction of the church and the road suggest that this is an area whose use has changed, in this case from arable farming to EU-subsidised shepherding.

The second is the church built at Ta Marmara, on the headland at the foot of the Aradhena Gorge (PLATE 6). In the Venetian–Turkish period there was a watermill at the foot of the gorge, now disused (see under 3.20). The builder of the church lives in Anopoli and keeps his sheep at Ta Marmara in winter; this is a well-known traditional-modern subsistence activity. But the local economy has changed. In summer, there are now significant numbers of tourists staying in Khora Sphakion and Loutro. The builder of the church takes tourists by kaïki to swim at the shore below it. Since he finished the church, he has added some rent rooms. Previously this area had been little used, but new economic activity has changed the way that people, including the owner, see previously worthless land at Ta Marmara. The church is now part of the set of landmarks visible by sea and by land in this area.[26] In these two cases, the construction date of the church indicates the date of the recognition and significant use of a particular resource, whether arable, pasture, water, or as in the case of Ta Marmara, touristic. Building a church sets a sacred seal on the possession and economic importance of an area, by making the builder's claim on it visible.

I suggest further that the two older churches discussed above, Ag. Pavlos (3.01) and Ag. Triadha (6.06), may also have functioned in the same way – that is, that these churches made visible someone's claim on their respective areas. In the analysis below of Anopoli and Frangokastello, I make the assumption that a church marking important resources also gives the date for the beginning of the

---

[25] For Monanni's picture of this area, see the final image in the site entry for Khora Sphakion (6.12). For outlying churches and icon stands as predictors for earlier sites using the resources which they mark, see the discussion in Appendix 4.

[26] When asked why he had built the church, informants in Anopoli said 'because he wanted to build a church' (!). This response marked the nadir of my efforts to collect useful oral explanations for the *locations* of churches.

use of those resources. Thus knowing the date of exokklisia marking resources can help us to reconstruct the history of the landscape, in terms of which resources came into use when, and in which order. I also suggest that it is important to get information about all churches in the periphery of a village, because remoter churches can be a crucial guide for deducing the nature and use of more distant resources. These issues are explored in greater detail in section 4.3 below (comparison of Anopoli and Frangokastello).

2. VISIBILITY, BY LAND AND SEA

Like other structures with sacred significance, icon stands and churches (outlying or in villages) are built to be seen. Strategies for making sacred structures visible vary with the landscape. In many landscapes, churches and mosques are made instantly recognisable by the addition of spires and minarets; often it is the spires and minarets which are visible before the rest of the settlement to which these structures typically belong.[27] In dissected terrain like that of Sphakia, well-positioned structures need be neither large nor tall to be seen over long distances. Furthermore, the custom of whitewashing churches and icon stands dramatically increases their visibility; unwhitewashed stone structures are not so easy to distinguish in a stony landscape.[28]

This enhanced visibility is important both by land and by sea. Nautical maps of Greece regularly mark churches as 'conspic.' (conspicuous) to show that they can be used as landmarks for navigation; similarly, temples in antiquity were used both to identify both harbours and anchorages and also to mark out dangerous shoals and rocks.[29]

All churches and icon stands can be seen from somewhere, but some churches are definitely more visible than others. Indeed some churches can be seen from everywhere, and I refer to these hypervisible churches as 'beacons'. Beacon churches, visible over long distances, often marking something of great importance, occur in settlements (as slope churches) as well as outside them. Ag. Georgios on Mt Lykavittos in Athens is an example of a beacon church within a city. Not all churches are so conspicuous: FK CH 9 Ag. Ioannis sto Lakko is far less visible than FK CH 2 Ag. Ioannis Prodhromos. There is thus a hierarchy of visibility, with some churches acting as 'beacons', identifying a specific location or territory from afar, and others serving as more local markers.

---

[27] In flat areas with few structures built by humans, landscape markers need not be very large, as in the case of the Arctic inuksuit, which typically measure four feet tall and are very seldom taller than a person (Hallendy 2000, 46). Stonehenge is another example of an extremely well-positioned structure, which is hypervisible from any number of viewpoints (Peters 2000; and cf. Watson 2001 on Avebury).

[28] See n. 16 above. Note also Spratt on the effects of whitewash, p. 75 below.

[29] See for example the chart for Corfu Harbour in Heikell 1982, 32, where the citadel and a church are labelled 'conspic.' as good landmarks for identifying and negotiating the harbour. For temples and other markers in antiquity, see Morton 2001, 197–201, 310–313.

Equally, churches are considered to 'look at' the terrain around and usually below them, and the viewshed of a church is often named after it. Outside Sphakia, one well-known example is the church of Prophitis Ilias on a low hill at ca 300m northeast of Knossos, which has given the name Aïlias to the area it 'sees'. There is also an Aïlias in Sphakia, the area below FK CH 10 Prophitis Ilias. Similarly, the area below and southwest of the church of Ag. Georgios in Kavros (6.01, north of Khora Sphakion) is called Ag. Georgios.

Although smaller, icon stands too can be visible from a distance: a whitewashed icon stand above Loutro marks an important junction in the path above the village, and is clearly visible by land and by sea.[30]

The date of construction of highly visible churches (and icon stands) is crucial to establish, as in the case of new activity involving important resources marked by churches. For example, the church of Ag. Georgios on the top of Mt Lykavittos in Athens is clearly a 'beacon church', and yet it is a relatively recent addition to the Athens skyline. Lykavittos was always outside the walls of the ancient city. Later there may have been a Byzantine church of Prophitis Ilias here. In the Ottoman period, the hills, of which Lykavittos is the southernmost peak, were known as the Tourkovounia; Athens by this time had dwindled to a small village. The new church of Ag. Georgios was built soon after the Kingdom of Greece was established (1832) and Athens became its capital (1833). Its construction showed clearly and conspicuously that Athens was no longer Turkish, and that the new capital had begun to expand, with new areas coming into use.[31]

3. LIMINAL LOCATIONS

Outlying churches are sometimes built in liminal places, such as entry points to geographic units. For example, the Monastery of Odhigitria in south central Crete is constructed on a low eminence at the northern end of the Agiopharango (Holy Gorge), where the scrubbier phrygana of gorge meets the flatter, more fertile Mesara Plain.[32]

Icon stands are often built at crossroads or intersections, whether of footpaths or of car roads. Machin commented on the number of icon stands near Asi Gonia (just outside Sphakia in the eparchy of Apokoronou), some of which appear to mark the places where side paths branch off from the main route into the village. The icon stand MS 18 in the southern Argolid recorded by Murray and Kardulias,

---

[30]Both churches and icon stands are equipped with lights. The floating oil lamps in icon stands makes them visible by night as well as by day. Some, in villages, are lit every night; more remote icon stands were lit when people left early in the morning, e.g. to pick olives (typically in October/November, in Sphakia).

[31] Freely 1991, 301–303; Tsigakou 1981, 121, for Thomas Hope's 1820 view of a strangely unadorned Lykavittos.

[32] Cameron 2003, 164–165 gives a useful summary about this monastery and its location. For photographs see Vasilakis 1992, figs 30.1 (ground) and 30.2 (aerial).

who were puzzled by its placement, is certainly at an intersection, and may well be there in order to mark the junction between the main road and the side road branching off from it.[33]

4. EARLIER SIGNIFICANT STRUCTURES

Sacred structures such as exokklisia and icon stands can be built over earlier structures which have some contemporary significance. These earlier structures may themselves have been sacred or significant in some other way when they were built, but they need not have been. It is a question of later meanings, and as discussed above, selection by the people building the later structure.

For example, the Greeks who built Iron Age temples and Hellenistic shrines on/near visible Minoan walls, and established hero-cults on/near Bronze Age tombs were taking the earlier structures to be significant for their own time, and making them important in their own, later chronologies of desire.[34]

The best example of a Byzantine–Venetian–Turkish church marking earlier sacred structures in Sphakia is the chapel of the Panagia, which lies slightly inland from, and north of, the Graeco-Roman city of Tarrha, which was deserted by the BVT period (church and Graeco-Roman city, 1.28). The church is very conspicuous from the sea, although it is not particularly high up. The chapel is very precisely positioned over the bema (sanctuary) of an earlier, larger basilica, itself built over (and reusing blocks from) a classical temple. In this case there is no doubt that the locations of the two later structures were both determined by the locations of the two earlier ones.[35]

In some cases, it may be that later sacred structures merely coincide with earlier ones. One example is the church of Ag. Georgios located just upslope of the Minoan peak sanctuary on the Cycladic island of Kythira. The church does not seem to have been positioned so as to mark the Bronze Age peak sanctuary, so it is unlikely that it represent any kind of cult continuity; instead it might be better to think of two grammars of location happening to pick the same spot.[36]

---

[33] Machin 1983, 114: '[Votive] offerings are often placed in small churches (*ekklisakia*, author's italics) which are located on the boundaries of the village at crossroads and gorges, i.e. at points which appear to correspond with potential points of intersection between the satanic and social worlds.' I saw icon stands at such locations in Asi Gonia in April 1999. Murray and Kardulias 1986, 29 and 31. Similarly, Stewart (1991, 84) has commented on the 'shrines' in his research area on Naxos, which simultaneouslsy mark crossroads and protect passersby from the dangers associated with them.

[34] See Alcock 2002 esp. 108ff for Hellenistic Crete (although she is wrong about Agiasmatsi, pp. 114–115; cf. Francis et al. 2000). Note also that earlier structures can be both up- and down-graded in terms of their later significance: this is a question of the prevailing chronology of desire, and whether people wish to establish a theatre of memory or of oblivion at the site of the earlier structures; cf. Nixon 2004.

[35] For a picture of this church, see the fourth image in the entry for Tarrha (1.28) on the Sphakia Survey website.

[36] Sakellarakis 1996 does not discuss the location of the church in relation to the peak sanctuary; see pl. 10a for a clear view of both. Determining continuity, or the lack thereof, is clearer in the case of Mt

Icon stands marking the location of ruined churches are common in Attica (Pamela Armstrong, pers. comm.). Plymakis gives several Cretan examples of this phenomenon. One of these is the icon stand set up near the ruins of the Late Roman East Basilica at Loutro (5.11A, Sector I), consisting of a metal icon box set on two ancient marble columns re-used from the basilica (Plymakis 2001b, 33–35; 132).

3.4.2 Explanation

1. HUMAN BOUNDARIES

This explanation seems like a location, and in a way it is – but human boundaries can be confirmed only by people and what they produce (oral accounts, documents, maps), and not by spatial analysis. 'Human boundaries' are thus classified as explanations.

There are many examples of churches and icon stands as formal boundary markers of different kinds.[37]

Ag. Pnevma (2.37, 2260 masl) lies on the borders between two eparchies, Sphakia and Apokoronas. It also marks the point where three communes (koinotites) of Apokoronas had their southwest, mountainous, ends (abutting the old eparchy boundary). This small structure provides a clear and unambiguous marker, in this case for land boundaries which could otherwise be disputed. It is worth noting that the view from the summit here is spectacular: Spratt describes how he saw the Libyan Sea and Gavdhos to the south, and islands of the Aegean to the north.[38] Ag. Pnevma is particularly significant because it is the only sacred structure found at the 'up' altitude described below in Appendix 2.

Similarly, the church of Prophitis Ilias (1.04) near the deserted village of Peradhoro sits on the old eparchy boundary between Sphakia and Selino; Pashley noted the position of the church on this boundary, though he did not investigate the gorge.[39]

Ioukhtas in central Crete. In this case, the Minoan peak sanctuary is at one end of the ridge, with an easy view north to Arkhanes and beyond, while the churches (Aphendi Khristos and three others) are some distance away with a dramatic view to the west, south, and east (site visit of September 2003). The only architecture at the actual peak sanctuary is an OTE communications centre; see Cameron 2003, 129–130.

[37] As noted by Vallianos (1993, 239) as a general phenomenon in his discussion of the western Mesara; he does not give examples.

[38] Spratt 1865, II. 155–159. On the view: '…it must be confessed by those who have been mountain-climbers, even for sport or pleasure, that few places produce more solemnity of thought and feeling, or impress the mind more strongly with devotional desire, than the serenity and solitude that in general pervade a lofty hill.' (p. 158).

[39] Pashley 1837, II. 101; the village was already long deserted and nameless when he visited it in 1834; cf. Spratt 1865, II. 244–245.

Dividing dissected terrain like this with a boundary running along high points is a fine old tradition, also known from Bronze Age Greece: the boundary separating the Hither and Further provinces of Pylos runs along the peaks of Mt Aigaleon. Similarly, de Polignac noted that extraurban sanctuaries in early Iron Age Greece were often located on the boundaries between polis territories; he assumed that the poleis came first and the outlying sanctuaries second, but it may be that the boundaries are marked out during the formative time when a settlement pattern crystallises.[40]

What is new and different in Byzantine–Venetian–Turkish Greece is the use of churches to make such boundaries visible over long distances. Given that churches make boundaries visible, and unequivocally so, it is also interesting that several churches in Sphakia were designated as places where cases of suspected perjury in the case of theft of animals or other property could be cleared up. The process was called xekathárisma, and is discussed in section 5.5 below on Sphakia in the Turkish period.

2. SUPERNATURAL CONTACT

Churches and icon stands can be built because of contact with the supernatural connected with a particular place. The contact can be with the benign world of God, the Panagia, and saints, or with the malign world of spirits –collectively called exotika (εξωτικά), literally 'things outside or beyond' – such as demons (dhaimones, δαίμονες or dangerous nymphs (neraïdhes, νεράϊδες), and is often made through dreams and visions.[41]

The 'here-ness' of this contact is of fundamental importance. The churches and icon stands declare to onlookers that they need look no further for the spot where it happened – it was here. As Herzfeld (1990a, 117) puts it, 'The formal tales of the saints pale into comparative insignificance before narrative evidence of their immanence in local experience and in the local landscape.'

Thus churches and icon stands mark the precise location of supernatural contact, whether it is good, or bad. Both kinds of contact need to be remembered; in the case of malign spirits, further contact also needs to be prevented.

An example of benign contact comes from Tinos, where in 1822 a nun had a vision of a woman surrounded by light, who instructed the nun to excavate a particular field, and to begin the building of her church (naos, ναός). Several miracles are associated with the excavation, including the discovery of an icon

---

[40] Provinces of Pylos: Chadwick 1976, 35 –60; Mt Aigaleon as boundary, p. 43 with map, p. 44. De Polignac 1995 (1984), and 1994 with maps, 14 and 17; cf. the map showing the location of archaic sanctuaries on Kephallinia in relation to polis boundaries in Randsborg 1995: 94–99. De Polignac has been criticised by Horden and Purcell 2000, 456–457. For a discussion of outlying churches being built during the establishment of the Byzantine–Venetian–Turkish settlement pattern in Sphakia, see pp. 62–74 below.

[41] For exotika, see Stewart 1991; translation of the term exotika is on p. xv. For dreams, Stewart 1997.

(Dubisch 1995, 134–136). In this case on Tinos, the church is a visual reminder of the vision, the link between the locality and the Panagia, and the miracles.[42]

As for malign contact, icon stands are frequently built at crossroads to prevent demons or other exotika from harming passers-by. Stewart records an icon stand at a tristrato (τρίστρατο), or place where three roads meet, after two separate accidents occurred there. The second one involved a man whose injury prevented him from entering the priesthood – 'final proof of the demonic forces at this [location]', which could be countered by the icon stand.[43]

Neraïdhes are one kind of exotika which make crossroads dangerous. One of Myrivilis' characters in *The Mermaid Madonna* (1959, 130–131) gives a good description of their power:

> The first kind [of nymphs] are those that inhabit valleys and streams, that go abroad at night under the moon, and lie in wait at crossroads as naked as on the day they were born. They are beautiful demonesses and easily ensnare wayfarers who know nothing about fairy folk. They sit in the middle of the road, set up their distaffs, and spin their thread. They draw wool from the moon when it's full, and that's why it wanes. They crisscross the oaths with threads, and that's why whoever comes along gets tangled in their moonskeins, falls under a spell, and either loses the power of speech or wastes away.

3. SPECIFIC EVENTS AND PLACES

The most frequent reason given nowadays for building an outlying church is to commemorate a deceased member of someone's kin group; the choice of saint, and of location, are up to the commissioner, but the church must be on land belonging to the kin group (Nixon, fieldwork; and cf. Kenna 1976). The notion of remembering dead relatives is built into the Greek way of death, with remembrance services at ever longer intervals after a person's death (mnimosyna, at 40 days, three months, six months, nine months, a year). Building a church can therefore be seen as a visible, and more permanent, way of commemorating someone.

I know of two icon stands in Sphakia built to commemorate a dead person, but there may be others. FK IK 3 commemorates a young man killed in a car accident in 1995. The second was set up some time within the last 15 years by a husband on the seashore south of the village of Skaloti, in memory of his wife who drowned there while helping to pull in their fishing nets.

---

[42] The tradition of using sacred structures to mark the place where a god or sacred being made contact can be seen in the Erekhtheion, where one small section of the North Porch was left open to show where Poseidon flung down his trident in the contest with Athene; Dinsmoor 1975, 187 n.1 and 188, fig. 70; cf. Travlos 1971, 217, fig. 280.

[43] See Stewart 1991, 84 for discussion, and fig. 13 on p. 86 for a picture of the icon stand (shrine in Stewart's terminology).

Explanations for churches and icon stands also mention the commemoration and marking of older structures. The church of Analipsi tou Khristos (8.05A), near the village of Vraskas in Sphakia, was built in the locality known as Ta Livadhia (the meadows), near an area called Ta Kataleimata, the ruins. From the evidence of the pottery seen here, these ruins seem to be the remains of Venetian houses which went out of use in the Turkish period, ca 1800. The local explanation is that church marks the location of a much earlier village which was destroyed by the Saracens.[44]

Icon stands frequently mark the spot where an accident either took place or was averted. Accidents can, and did, happen on kaldirimia or footpaths just as they do now on car roads, so one basic place for icon stands is on routes of various kinds and periods. 'Accident' icon stands are nowadays metal or sometimes cement. They are always placed by the side of a car road, facing onto it.[45]

4. PROMISE OR VOW (GREEK TASIMO)

Churches and icon stands can be built because someone vowed to build them. In some cases, people imply that they are thank-offerings, but the specific reason for the vow need not be given. In other cases, more details are given: Kenna notes that some outlying churches on Anaphi were built because of vows to saints thought to have some expertise or control over particular illnesses and diseases (1994–95, 454).[46]

---

[44] Interview with Kanakis Geronymakis, September 2004. Note also two other sites, nos. 260A. Tou Sarakinou o Volakas (on the coast), and 266. Kouloures (which he glosses 'here was the village before the Saracens'), Geronymakis 1996, 13.

[45] See Zinovieff 2004, 178–180 for an account of the decision-making involved in erecting an 'accident' icon stand.

[46] For churches as a way of fulfilling vows, see Vallianos 1993, 239; again, he does not give specific examples for the western Mesara. And cf. the story related in Dubisch 1994–95, 417 n. 24 of a church built into the rocks where villagers had taken refuge from invading Turks.

4

LANDSCAPE STUDY OF ANOPOLI
AND FRANGOKASTELLO

I hope to have shown that churches and icon stands, both in the two study areas and in other parts of the Greece, are placed according to similar principles, with more or less similar lines of development over time. Icon stands consistently function as protective markers (sometimes through commemoration, whether of individuals through accidents, or of churches), while outlying churches consistently function as declaratory markers, whether of useful resources, or boundaries, or both.

But listing the reasons for the location of outlying churches and icon stands gives only a partial account of these structures, because it does not consider them in relation to one another, either spatially or diachronically. In order to understand the full significance of outlying churches and icon stands it is necessary to consider them as elements of the sacred assemblage in particular landscapes, over time. The size of Sphakia has made it possible to test our ideas about changing cultural landscapes by contrasting different areas within the eparchy. Anopoli and Frangokastello are the two most studied areas within Sphakia, and have already yielded a number of interesting comparisons (Nixon and Moody et al. 1994). In the section below, I attempt to contextualise the study areas within Anopoli and Frangokastello by considering their long-term historical context.

4.1 Anopoli
(PLATES 1 and 2, TABLE 1)

4.1.1 Introduction

I discuss Anopoli first, because it provides a clear example of the continuing tradition of marking settlements and landscapes with icon stands and outlying churches, having older and newer examples of both. Furthermore, precisely because it has recent eikonostasia and exokklisia, the example of Anopoli permits us to compare the spatial pattern of their location with the explanations given for their construction and placement. The result should be satisfying for archaeologists studying landscape, because it is possible to show that the cumulative pattern which can be observed from material remains is real, even though it may seem different from the one-by-one accretion suggested by oral testimony.

The mountain plain of Anopoli lies at ca 600 masl; its area is approximately 12 km². The plain is bounded on the west by the Aradhena Gorge, where AN IK 1 is located; along the northeast by a line of hills rising sharply to approximately 1000m; on the east by the neighbourhood of Kampia, the low peak of Troulos at 541m and the crossroad where the old footpath up from Khora Sphakion divides (see AN IK 16 and 17); and on the south by the Anopolis Ridge, which renders the village invisible from the Libyan Sea below. During the Byzantine–Venetian–Turkish period the nearest villages were Aradhena, perched on the west side of the homonymous gorge; Khora Sphakion to the southeast, on the coast; and Mouri to the northeast, deserted since just after World War II. Near Mouri were two smaller settlements, Koutsoura to the north and Kavros to the south.

In form Anopoli is like other Sphakiote villages in mountain plains; instead of being nucleated, it consists of several neighbourhoods (geitonies), usually placed on rocky lumps so as to leave the alluvial floor of the basin free for agriculture. Askyphou, Impros, and Kallikrati are other examples. Anopoli has ten neighbourhoods, all on slopes except Kampos which is on the flat.[47] Up to the earlier 20th c., all ten were occupied. Since then emigration has meant that two neighbourhoods (Vadhiana, Pavliana) are now totally deserted, and some of the others are inhabited only by old people. Churches and icon stands in this area can be found in all four of the locations listed above: important resources and new activity; visibility; liminal locations; and earlier significant structures.

The altitude of the village of Anopoli is middle (as for Askyphou, Impros, and Kallikrati). Down in this area lies at Loutro (ancient Phoinix), the only safe winter harbour on the southcoast of Crete. This area was used during the Byzantine–Venetian–Turkish period, but had no permanent settlement; nowadays it is a touristic enclave. Up is in the Madhares or summer pastures in the White Mountains at ca 1800m, where people from Anopoli have their mitata (stone shepherd's huts, μητάτα; singular is mitato, μητάτο), which are grouped by neighbourhood, just as in the village. The old commune of Anopoli included land

---

[47] From west to east, the ten neighbourhoods of Anopoli are Ag. Dhimitrios, Gyro, Riza, Kampos, Limnia, Pavliana, Skala, Mariana, Vadhiana, and Kampia. Placing settlements on rocky outcrops so as to leave as much arable free for agriculture as possible is a sensible strategy which also underlies the distribution of the nuraghi of Sardinia. These stone towers were usually built on basalt plateaux, often near the better soils provided by alluvial plains or neogene marls; see Grove and Rackham 2002, 164–165.

TABLE 1: Outlying churches and icon stands in Anopoli, up to 2000, numbered from west to east.

NUMBER AND SAINT(S)	MATERIAL	DATE	LOCATION	EXPLANATION
AN CH 1 Ag. Aikaterini 4.21 Sector A	stone	VT (?V)	2. Visibility 4. Earlier significant structures	
AN CH 2 Ag. Nektarios	stone	1971-1974	3. Liminal location (outer edge of village)	3. Specific events and places
AN CH 3 T. Stavros (Loutro) 5.21	stone	VT (?V)	1. Resources 2. Visibility	
AN CH 4 Ag. Paraskevi, with later icon stand 5.22	stone (both)	VT (?V) church	1. Resources 2. Visibility	
AN CH 5 T. Stavros (Mouri) 6.03A	stone	VT, probably V	1. Resources 2. Visibility	1. Human boundaries 2. Supernatural contact
AN IK 1 Ag. Antonios	metal	1976	3. Liminal location (edge of gorge; village of Aradhena on opposite side)	1. Human boundaries (commune) 3. Specific events and places
AN IK 2 Ag. Eirene Khrysovalantou	metal	later 20th c.	3. Liminal location (old jct of footpaths?)	
AN IK 3 Ag. Eleftherios	stone and whitewash/cement	early 1960s	3. Liminal location (house)	
AN IK 4 Ag. Georgios	whitewashed (can't tell what is underneath; probably stone)	earlier 20th c. if not earlier still; cemented 1972	2. Visibility 3. Liminal location (outside village)	2. Supernatural contact
AN IK 5 Panagia	stone and whitewash	earlier 20th c. if not earlier still	2. Visibility 3. Liminal location (outside village)	
AN IK 6 Ag. Georgios	stone and whitewash	earlier 20th c. if not earlier still	2. Visibility 3. Liminal location (outside	2. Supernatural contact

NUMBER AND SAINT(S)	MATERIAL	DATE	LOCATION	EXPLANATION
AN IK 7 Konstantinos and Eleni	metal	1980s after Greece joined EU in 1981 (hypostega built with EU subsidies)	3. Liminal location (hypostego) village)	
AN IK 8 Ag. Pantes	metal	some time after 1960s	3. Liminal location (old jct of footpaths?)	
AN IK 9 Ag. Panteleimon	stone and whitewash	1948	3. Liminal location (edge of village)	2. Supernatural contact
AN IK 10 Ag. Apostoloi Peter and Paul	metal	later 20th c.	3. Liminal location	3. Specific events and places
AN IK 11 Ag. Georgios	concrete, in shape of church	1997	3. Liminal location (house)	3. Specific events and places
AN IK 12 Ag. Raphail and Nikolaos	metal	older: 1980s; newer: 1998-2000	3. Liminal location (house)	
AN IK 13 Ag. Nikolaos or Panagia	metal	ca 1980	3. Liminal location (crossroads)	2. Supernatural contact?
AN IK 14 Ag. Nikolaos	metal	?1993	3. Liminal location (house)	
AN IK 15 O Khristos	stone and whitewash/ concrete	older: before later1980s; newer: 2000	3. Liminal location (older: crossroads; newer: house)	
AN IK 16 icon too destroyed to tell	stone and whitewash	earlier 20th c. if not earlier still	2. Visibility 3. Liminal location (outside village)	
AN IK 17 Panagia	metal	later 20th c; cf. AN IK 14	1. Resources	4. Vow or promise
AN IK 18 Ag. Theodhoroi	stone and whitewash	1977; moved 1990	2. Liminal location (car crossroad near café)	2. Supernatural contact

at all three levels: the central portion of the Madhares with Mt Pakhnes; Anopoli; Loutro.

4.1.2 Churches in and around Anopoli

From the outset it was clear that the 18 icon stands of Anopoli needed to be considered in relation to the village churches. Five of the ten neighbourhoods have one church each; a sixth, Gyro, has two, for a total of seven neighbourhood churches. All seven seem to have been built by the end of the Venetian period, on stylistic (Gothic arch) and textual grounds. In addition Anopoli has two outlying churches: AN CH 1 Ag. Aikaterini at the east end of the Anopolis Ridge; and AN CH 2 Ag. Nektarios, built in 1971 just outside Kampos. There are also three peripheral churches. Two of them are below Anopoli, AN CH 3 Timios Stavros, just up from the coast, and AN CH 4 the church on the pebble beach at Glyka Nera; while the third, AN CH 5 another church of Timios Stavros, lies between Anopoli and Mouri.

Neighbourhood churches in Anopoli are either 'slope' or 'edge' in location. Mariana is a good example of the slope type, with the church at the top of the rocky ridge, and the houses spread out below it. Other examples are the churches in Limnia and Skala. 'Slope churches' like these can be conspicuously visible by land and by sea. The church in the neighbourhood of Ag. Dhimitrios is a good example of an 'edge' church. Here most houses are built on the sheltering north slope of the Anopolis Ridge, with the homonymous church set on flat ground on the 'unprotected' side away from it. The church lies at the junction of the two main footpaths coming into the neighbourhood from the north. Other examples are the two churches in Gyro, plus those in Kampos and Kampia (see PLATE 7 for the latter).

Thus the neighbourhood churches in Anopoli are split more or less evenly between 'slope' and 'edge' locations. None was visible from the sea; most are not visible from below the village, because of natural barriers like the Anopolis Ridge (see below for discussion of the location of AN IK 16 in relation to the church in Mariana, however).

As for the two outlying churches, the more recent, AN CH 2 Ag. Nektarios in Kampos, built to commemorate local families, did not change the landscape much; it is visible only if one happens to drive past it.[48] But the visual impact of AN CH 1 Ag. Aikaterini was, and is, huge: this small church makes Anopoli visible by implication both by sea, and by land. It is literally visible for miles, and

---

[48] Ag. Nektarios was a 19th c. bishop of Aigina; any church dedicated to him is by definition late. The church of Ag. Nektarios in Anopoli, built in 1971 and dedicated in 1975, is one of only two that I know of in Sphakia to contain an icon of the saint Emmanouil Sphakion; the other is in another later 20th c. church in Askyphou. The inscription in the church in Anopoli says that it was built in memory of local families; oral information added that at least one of the donors built it 'so that he would have somewhere to be buried'.

from every direction: from the north, it can be seen from the road, and presumably from the earlier footpaths, as you come down from the Madhares (north) or from the Mouri area (northeast), and directly from Kavros (northeast); from the west, it is visible from other churches such as Prophitis Ilias (above Ag. Ioannis) and Ag. Vasilios (see PLATE 6 for the location of these last two churches). From the east, Ag. Aikaterini can be seen from the car road where it emerges from the Impros Gorge, and from Frangokastello some 15 km away (it is visible from FK CH 10 Prophitis Ilias). From the south it is visible along much of the coast below, from footpaths and, especially, by sea. Ag. Aikaterini is a perfect example of a 'beacon church'. It is frustrating that we do not know when exactly this church was built, because it was the construction of Ag. Aikaterini which made the village of Anopoli visible from the south; here we can suggest only that it was built some time in the Venetian-Turkish period.

The short pebble beach at Glyka Nera (Sweet Waters) is about halfway between Khora Sphakion and Loutro, bounded at each end by higher, rocky ground. At the west end there is the small Venetian church of Ag. Paraskevi/Santa Veneranda (AN CH 4), which was already ruined at the time of Semitecolo's report in 1639. Later, an icon stand was built on top of it (PLATES 8 and 9). Church and icon stand lie on the coastal route between Loutro and Khora Sphakion, where fresh water can be obtained by a little digging. The chapel and icon stand thus mark the fresh water seep that gave the area its Greek name, and would once have been conspicuous coastal landmarks. Tucked into the western corner of the beach where the ground rises, the two also show where exactly to ascend the low cliff in order to continue to Loutro.

Even more conspicuous is AN CH 3 Timios Stavros, just off the coastal path, slightly closer to Loutro than to Khora Sphakion. The church was built on the rise just west of Glyka Nera, at a sufficient height above the sea to withstand seasonal gales, on or near the commune boundary separating Anopoli and Khora Sphakion. Any structure built at Ponta, the low point to the west, would be destroyed by the waves in winter. A footpath ascending from the coastal path at Ponta continues upwards some 300m. It may be that the church serves as a marker for this path. Timios Stavros is extremely conspicuous by sea, and by land as well, being visible from the terrace of Ag. Aikaterini at the east end of the Anopolis Ridge some 700m above.

The third of the three peripheral churches is another Timios Stavros, northeast of Anopoli (AN CH 5). Timios Stavros lies near the head of the Ilingas Gorge separating Anopoli from Mouri, on the boundary between the old communes of Anopoli and Khora Sphakion. For its role in resolving cases of animal theft, see the discussion on pp. 81–83 below. The church seems to have been built in the Venetian period. Presumably its position on the commune boundary made it suitable for conflict resolution.

4.1.3 Icon Stands in Anopoli

There are four types of location for icon stands in Anopoli: outside the village, between neighbourhoods, on the edge of a neighbourhod; and inside a neighbourhood. Only one, AN IK 11, is truly inside a neighbourhood; the other 17 are all outside, between, or on the edge of Anopoli neighbourhoods; in other words they are all in some kind of liminal position. And again, most of them lie at an intersection.

TABLE 1 and the Catalogue give the relevant information, so I shall not discuss all 18 icon stands in detail. Instead I shall focus on selected examples, starting with the four stone icon stands outside the vilage.

My first example is AN IK 16, technically disused, as its icon is illegible, and no one now remembers which saint it was dedicated to. AN IK 16 lies at the top of the main kaldirimi from Khora Sphakion, itself put out of use when the car road from Khora to Anopoli was built in the 1960s. It was built where the kaldirimi divides into two, one route continuing into Kampia and the southern part of the plain, the other leading to Mariana and the northern part. AN IK 16 is 2m00 tall, and faces downhill; it is still visible from below by day, and would have been even more so when consistently whitewashed; by night it would also have been visible when an oil lamp inside it was lit.

The location of AN IK 16 was very carefully chosen. It was visible to people walking up the kaldirimi long before any part of the village could be seen. Then as you approach the icon stand, you can suddenly see the top of the slope church in Mariana, as well as the newer church of Ag. Aikaterini on the ridge (PLATES 7, 15). My suggestion is therefore that this icon stand showed incomers where the forcefield of Anopoli began, as well as protecting them from the usual crossroads demons. It also showed people in Anopoli where the village ended, as it is clearly visible on the skyline from the modern car road at a point where it lies on the path of the old kaldirimi. (See the discussion of AN IK 17 below for the later history of this junction.)

The placement of AN IK 5 and AN IK 4 confirm this suggestion. AN IK 5 lies below the east end of the Anopolis Ridge, marking a junction in the footpath up from Loutro. It too would mainly have been visible from below; it can also be seen from Ag. Aikaterini.

AN IK 4, dedicated to Ag. Georgios, lies between two junctions. To the southwest, there is a junction between footpaths up from Livaniana and Loutro; to the northeast, there is another between footpaths leading down into Gyro, and towards Riza. AN 4 faces downslope, like AN IK 16 and AN IK 5. Like several other icon stands, it has an associated legend. The name of the area in which AN IK 4 was built is Ta Loumata, and the icon stand lies Tsi Pates tou Agiou Georgiou (at the footprints of St George); the next footprint is on the island of Gavdhos to the south.

I propose that all three icon stands discussed so far, AN IK 16, AN IK 5, and AN IK 4, share a similar function in making the points of entry into Anopoli visible from afar. They show incomers where what I call the forcefield of the village begins, and it is for that reason that they all face downhill. Combined with AN CH 1 Ag. Aikaterini, these icon stands thus make Anopoli visible, and imply protection for it, just as the 'slope' and 'edge' churches do for individual neighbourhoods. I suggest therefore that these three icon stands together mark an outer protective boundary for the village.[49]

AN IK 6 lies on the route leading north from Anopoli through Limnia, near the point where it divides, importantly, between the path leading north to the Madhares, and northeast to the Mouri area. The modern junction in the car road lies some distance to the northeast, a good example of how different the location of car roads and footpaths can be. AN IK 6 faces downslope, and provides an excellent view of the Anopolis Ridge and much of the plain; the neighbourhoods of Riza, Gyro, Ag. Dhimitrios, and Limnia can be seen, as well as the basin of Ts'Asis, the Aradhena Gorge, and Prophitis Ilias to the west. The view would have been even better before pines invaded the now disused agricultural terraces. The local legend is that someone saw a ghost here and built an icon stand, presumably to prevent its return. AN IK 6 marks the spot where people would get their first or their last view of Anopoli, depending on their direction. It thus seems to mark some kind of outer limit for the village – a place which might well seem dangerous. I suggest that this icon stand, too, is 'older', i.e. at least earlier 20th c. in date. All four definitely belong to the time of footpaths and antedate all car roads in Anopoli.

The three remaining stone icon stands are different from the four already discussed: they all lie within the village, either on the edge of a neighbourhod, or between two neighbourhoods. They too lie on or near junctions in routes, and the precise dates of their construction are known. One example is of particular interest. AN IK 9 lies near the west side of Limnia, at the junction of two old footpaths, now partially covered by a paved road. This icon stand was originally free-standing, but a new (concrete) house was built very close to it. AN IK 9 is large (2m00 high) and looks 'old'. But it was built by the husband of my informant in 1948, the year of their wedding. They had both had dreams of dangerous neraïdhes who might have abducted her; he built the icon stand to protect his wife from them, and to prevent any more dreams like that. Neraïdhes are only one kind of peirasmika (πειρασμικά), demons who lurk more or less everywhere, but especially at junctions and crossroads.[50]

The seven stone icon stands thus fall into two distinct categories, defined by location (inside or outside the village), and date (possibly 19th c. or definitely 20th c.). Ten of the remaining 11 icon stands are metal; two are concrete. Six lie at or

---

[49] Cf. Kyriakidhou-Nestoros 1975 on 'sacred perimeters'.
[50] People in Anopoli talked of the dangers lurking at crossroads; one person in Frangokastello spoke of 'dhaimones' at crossroads; cf. Stewart 1991, 84.

near junctions; one is accident-related, and another may also be; and three were built outside or near houses. I will consider several examples.

AN IK 2 is interesting for several reasons. It is a metal icon stand, said to replace an older stone example. It lies near the junction of two old footpaths, one leading west to Ag. Dhimitrios, the other north to Limnia, and to the Madhares and the Mouri area. There is a well or cistern behind it (to the northwest). In terms of cult, it is interesting because it is the only icon stand I know of that contains tamata, the small metal votive plaques commonly found in churches. Dedicated to Ag. Eirini Khrysovalantou, it is beautifully tended, both inside (plastic liner instead of the usual newspaper); and out (large rosemary bush planted nearby). The new (concrete) house to the east has a well-kept garden and I suspect that the same person looks after the icon stand as well.

One icon stand is definitely explained by an accident, in this case an accident that did not happen. AN IK 1 is a rare example of a metal 'accident' icon stand being built on a footpath rather than a car road; it shows the continuity of one reason for dedicating icon stands, despite the change in materials. AN IK 1 is tucked into the first bend at the top of the Aradhena Gorge kaldirimi on the Anopoli side, angled so that it can be lit conveniently by people going up or down. It was built as a thank offering in 1976, by a man who did not have the accident he feared. The bridge over the Aradhena Gorge, which crosses at a different point, was finished only in 1987. AN IK 1, once again, lies at the outer limit of Anopoli, in a place which is obviously dangerous.

The third metal icon stand is AN IK 17, at the top of the footpath up from Khora Sphakion. It lies about 1m00 from AN IK 16, but it faces upslope and in towards Anopoli and the 'slope' church at Mariana (PLATE 15). Its dedicator was a woman from Mariana, the neighbourhood linked by one arm of the footpath; she erected it as a vow (tasimo).

Nowadays it is not unusual to see more than one icon stand along a car road where there are frequent accidents (Khatziphoti 1986, 39 below, 46 below). In the days of footpaths, however, it was rare for there to be two icon stands of any kind in the same location.[51] In this case the differing orientations of AN IK 16 and 17 provides a clue to the need for a second icon stand in the same place. The footpath from Khora Sphakion to Kampia and Mariana was in use when the Greek telecommunications service (OTE) was set up some time in the late 1940s, and the line of telephone poles up to Anopoli still follows the route of the footpath up the slope in this area. As we saw earlier, AN IK 16 faces away from Anopoli and down onto the footpath. But after the car road was built in the 1960s, the footpath was no longer used; pear trees now grow on the path here. In the later 1980s, a new dirt road connecting the main car road to the area of the icon

---

[51] See Plymakis 2001b, 105 top left, for two icon stands in the same place (Papadhiana Temenion Selinou). One is stone and one is metal; both face the same direction. Plymakis states that the metal one replaced the stone one.

stands was constructed. This area used to be cultivated, but is now used for shepherding, and there is a sheepshed nearby. In terms of sequence, I suggest that AN IK 17, which faces in towards Anopoli, was built some time after AN IK 16 fell into disuse. I also suggest that its construction is linked with the resurgence in shepherding made possible by EU subsidies, because the only people now to walk in this area are shepherds. In any case, the dedicator felt that this was a good location in which to fulfil her vow.

Three icon stands seem to have built because of particular houses. AN IK 3 was built by the owner of a nearby house, on her land. This mainly concrete icon stand lies at the end of a makeshift footpath connecting the (old) house with the (new) main car road. AN IK 12 was also built outside a house, in this case a new (concrete) house constructed after the car road.

The most recent icon stand in Anopoli is AN IK 11, built in 1997 just outside a house in Kampos, some distance from the main church of Anopoli in this neighbourhood. It was built of precast concrete in the shape of a church, and was at the time unique in Anopoli. My informants said that there had once been a church on this spot, indeed that a German bomb had fallen nearby. The icon stand commemorates the church (and its preservation from the bomb). There are no other records of this church, material, written, or oral.

To sum up, there is a chronological development in the building material and location of icon stands in Anopoli. I propose here that the four earlier icon stands, that is, pre-20th c., mark crucial crossroads in footpaths outside the village. These icon stands thus make Anopoli and the routes leading into and out of it visible, often in places where the village itself cannot be seen. They also show where the village's forcefield begins and ends. AN IK 4, 5, 6, and 16 are examples of this early type: they are built of stone, and they are clearly part of the world of pedestrians and pack animals, and predate any roads built for vehicles. Two of these icon stands have associated legends (e.g. AN IK 4 and 6) but no one now knows when they were built, and in one case, AN IK 16, no one even knows the identity of the saint.

Four metal icon stands also lie outside the village. AN IK 1 is at the top of the Aradhena Gorge; AN IK 7 and 8 mark junctions on a car road; and AN IK 17 makes it clear that the economic use of that particular area has changed since the construction and disuse of AN IK 16 (see above).

Eight other later icon stands lie between neighbourhoods (AN IK 2, 10, 14, 15), or on their edges (AN IK 3, 9, 13, 17); most are metal, and three are stone. Two of these 'archaizing' stone icon stands were built by couples (AN IK 9 and 17); the wives are sisters and both came from Limnia. The most common location for these icon stands is at the junction of spur roads leading from the main car road to a particular neighbourhood. All ten neighbourhoods have either an 'edge' church or an icon stand.

Last, there are the two icon stands outside houses, AN IK 12 on the main car road, and AN IK 11 in Kampos, built in concrete in the shape of a church, in 1997.

AN IK 11 is the only icon stand to be truly inside a neighbourhood, but it too is liminal, built into the enclosure separating the house from the now paved road.

The placement of icon stands in Anopoli is therefore spatially determined by very localised patterns of land use, and culturally determined by people's views on the dangers of liminal spaces, at various levels and scales. The icon stands complete, on a smaller scale, the marking begun by the churches on a larger scale. In the case of Anopoli, there are (mainly) older churches: three peripheral churches; seven neighbourhood churches; two outlying churches in the plain of Anopoli; and 18 more recent icon stands. The three peripheral churches mark out the southern and eastern boundaries of 'greater Anopoli'. The western boundary is marked by the Aradhena Gorge (with two churches on the western edge of the gorge, and AN IK 1 on the east; see below). The northern boundary is marked initially by AN IK 6 and eventually by a change in terrain, to the mountain desert, still within the commune. All borders with villages are marked with churches: Aradhena, as described; Mouri (AN CH 5 Timios Stavros, inland); and Khora Sphakion (AN CH 3 Timios Stavros on the coast).

The neighbourhood churches mark and protect the slopes and edges of neighbourhoods. The two outlying churches have contrasting visibilities and functions. AN CH 1 Ag. Aikaterini makes the village visible over long distances by land and sea. AN CH 2 Ag. Nektarios, visible only over short distances within the Plain of Anopoli preserves the memory of local families. The icon stands first mark the larger perimeter of the village (the 'forcefield'); then the edges of neighbourhoods, and other potentially dangerous, liminal spaces, such as the edge of the Aradhena Gorge; and finally the interface between individual house plots and public thoroughfares.

4.2 Frangokastello
(PLATES 3 and 4; TABLE 2)

4.2.1 Introduction

The study area here is the core of the Frangokastello Plain, an area of ca 6 km^2, which includes the southern part of the commune of Patsianos, and the extreme southwestern portion of the commune of Skaloti. It is bounded on the west by the low knob marking the main entrance to the area, where FK CH 1 Ag. Theodhoros is built; on the north by FK CH 2 Ag. Ioannis Prodhromos; on the east by FK CH 11 Ag. Georgios outside Skaloti; and on the south by the coastline. The study area includes the two nucleated villages of Patsianos and Kapsodhasos, and the eponymous fort. Patsianos and Kapsodhasos are only just over 600m apart. Similarly, the nearest villages in either direction are very near: Kolokasia/Ag. Georgios, now deserted, is 1.4 km west of Patsianos, while Ag. Nektarios, the new village which replaced it in the 1950s, is 1.6 km to the southwest. Skaloti is 3 km east of Kapsodhasos.

The altitude here is down, with a mixture of the roots of the mountains, where the two villages lie at approx. 200 masl, and the actual coastal plain. Middle in this general area lies in the mountain plain of Kallikrati to the north (ca 700 m), with summer grazing and mitata up high, e.g. in the vicinity of Mt Angathes (peak at 1511 m).

Churches in the two villages of Patsianos and Kapsodhasos reveal a somewhat similar pattern. Each village has two churches: an earlier, Venetian church, constructed where the main footpath reached the edge of the village, and a later, larger, 19th c. church. The more recent churches may suggest a short burst of prosperity in the area just before the middle of the 19th c. (and the major revolt of 1866).[52]

There are also five icon stands in the Frangokastello Plain, all of which are later 20th c.

4.2.2 Location of Outlying Churches in the Frangokastello Plain

TABLE 2 displays relevant information about the 11 outlying churches of the FK study area, plus the chapel of San Marco in the Venetian fort of Frangokastello.

Ten out of the 11 Frangokastello churches are along a route, either a footpath or a car road or both. FK CH 10, Prophitis Ilias seems to be an exception: it has a footpath and now a car road leading to it, but no further; this may be because dead-end routes are common for Prophitis Ilias churches. Churches in this area can be found in all four of the locations listed above: important resources and new activity; visibility; liminal locations; and earlier significant structures.

---

[52] Details of the village churches: Ag. Georgios lies at the original lower, southern edge of Patsianos, now blurred by newer houses built on the car road. The church was on the main footpath which once looped down the western side of the village, along the lower edge, and then up along the eastern side, and on up the gorge. It was recorded in 1637 (Khaireti 1968). Ag. Georgios is relatively large, and has a Gothic arch. Both the architecture and the documentary evidence suggest a Venetian date for its construction. O Khristos, the second church in Patsianos, is a double church with two Gothic arches, with an inscribed date of April 1848. It lies above Ag. Georgios on its own enclosed terrace.

In Kapsodhasos, the older church, Ag. Dhimitrios, is at the upper edge of the old village, on the main footpath leading north to Kallikrati. Ag. Dhimitrios was already a ruin in the 1870s. A dirt road now leads to it, presumably for access to the shepherds' mandra nearby. New icons were pinned up in its ruined apse. Ag. Konstantinos is a double church in Kapsodhasos just above the car road, which here follows the line of the old footpath. It has a datestone of 1836, and in the later 19th c. incorporated Ag. Dhimitrios because by then the older, higher church had fallen into disuse. The ruined church of Ag. Dhimitrios was restored by 2004 (Manouselis 2003–2004).

Local burst of prosperity: Nomikiana (W of Patsianos), mentioned by Pashley in 1837, but not in any earlier document, e.g Tapu Defter ca.1648, was also a product of this brief burst of prosperity. Ag. Zoni may be Venetian but could have predated the village.

TABLE 2: Outlying churches and icon stands in Frangokastello, up to 2000, numbered from west to east.

NAME	MATERIAL	DATE	LOCTION	EXPLANATION
FK CH 1 Ag. Theodhoros 8.24	stone	VT, probably V	3. Liminal location (W entry to plain)	?1. Human boundaries (near commune boundary); 3. Specific events and places
FK CH 2 Ag. Ioannis Prodhromos 8.25	stone	V?	1. Resources 2. Visibility	1. Human boundaries (commune)
FK CH 3 Ag. Pelagia 8.18	stone	VT, possibly V	1. Resources 3. Liminal location (jct in footpaths)	
FK CH 4 Ag. Astratigos (ruin) 8.38	stone	V (and LR)	1. Resources 4. Earlier significant structure (LR basilica, and spolia)	3. Specific events and places
FK CH 5 Ag. Ioannis Vokolos (ruin) 8.48	stone	V?	1. Resources	
FK CH 6 Ag. Athanasios 8.51 (Kapsodhasos)	stone	V (by 1426)	3. Liminal location (between two villages)	1. Human boundaries (commune)
FK CH 7 Ag. Nikitas 8.50	stone	V (and LR)	1. Resources 4. Earlier significant structure (LR basilica, and spolia)	3. Specific events and places
FK CH 8 Ag. Kharalampos 8.50	stone	V	1. Resources 2. Visibility 4. Earlier significant structure (spolia)	

NAME	MATERIAL	DATE	LOCTION	EXPLANATION
FK CH 9 Ag. Ioannis sto Lakko 8.55	stone	V	1. Resources 4. Earlier significant structure (spolia)	
FK CH 10 Prophitis Ilias 8.59	stone	V (14th c.)	1. Resources 3. Liminal location (E edge of plain) 4. Earlier significant structure (spolia)	
FK CH 11 Ag. Georgios 8.71	stone	VT (latest Early T)	1. Visibility 3. Liminal location (outside village) 4. Earlier significant structure (spolia)	
FK CH 12 San Marco in fort (gone) 8.32	stone	by 1631		
FK IK 1 Ag. Ioannis Khrysostomos	metal	1982	3. Liminal location (village, crossroads)	
FK IK 2 icon(s) gone	marble	1990s?	3. Liminal location (house)	
FK IK 3 no icon, only crucifix	marble	between 1995 and 2000	1. Resources	3. Specific events and places
FK IK 4 Panagia 8.33	metal	1980s?	1. Resources 3. Liminal location (crossroads)	
FK IK 5 Khristos o Theologos 8.33	metal	1980s?	1. Resources 3. Liminal location (crossroads)	

Several churches mark the location of water or good land or both. FK CH 3 Ag. Pelagia is a good example of this function. It lies towards the west end of a series of 'wetspots', areas with conspicuously lush vegetation running along the coast towards the fort. Ag. Pelagia is near the westernmost of several wells, at the intersection of the path south from Patsianos and the main coastal path. Local informants have told me (April 1999) that until perhaps 30–40 years ago, people living in Patsianos and Kapsodhasos came to this area to cultivate small gardens; to wash clothes; to get water for themselves and their animals; and to irrigate their crops on the dry plain just inland (i.e. before the large scale irrigation projects funded by the EU, such as the big ditch marked by FK IK 4 and 5).[53]

Another example of a church indicating well-watered land is FK CH 9 Ag. Ioannis sto Lakko. The word 'lakkos' (Λάκκος) we have learnt during the course of our fieldwork in Sphakia, does not in such contexts mean 'pit'; rather, it means a hollow with good soil, in which more water than usual might collect. Such hollows provide better agricultural land than drier areas nearby, and give higher yields. Similarly, FK CH 7 Ag. Nikitas lies at the southern end of the same well-watered area, marked by a line of trees (PLATE 4).[54]

FK CH 5 Ag. Ioannis Vokolos may also mark the location of particularly good land. It lies on the path which leaves Patsianos, runs along a major watercourse at its north end, and ends at FK CH 3 Ag. Pelagia. The area is terraced and is now planted with olives. A local informant told me (April 1999) that threshing was done with oxen in the area of this church, and said that that was why it was dedicated to St John the Cowherd.

As for visibility, FK CH 2 Ag. Ioannis Prodhromos is a beacon church, similiar to AN CH 1 Ag. Aikaterini in Anopoli (see above). It can now be seen from the modern car road where it emerges from the southern end of the Impros Gorge nearly four km away, as well as from local viewpoints. The old kaldirimi was in the Impros Gorge, and FK CH 2 would, similarly, have been visible to people on the footpath coming south from Askyphou as they emerged from the Impros Gorge, approaching the villages of Komitadhes and Vraskas.

At the other end of the visibility spectrum, FK CH 9 Ag. Ioannis sto Lakko is visible only locally, from the villages of Patsianos and Kapsodhasos, and from the two other churches in this locality, FK CH 10 Prophitis Ilias and FK CH 11 Ag. Georgios to the east.

---

[53] Cultivation in the wetspots is mentioned in Fielding 1953, 286. People no longer use these wetspots because the installation of modern water pumps for irrigation means that they can cultivate 'wet' crops anywhere on the plain. Cf. also the catalogue entry for FK CH 3 Ag. Pelagia.

[54] The word 'lakkos' occurs in several village names both in Sphakia (Kaloi Lakkoi, summer village north of Khora Sphakion; Lakkoi, summer village on ridge east of the Sphakiano Gorge), and in other areas, e.g. Lakkoi in the former eparchy of Kydhonia, north of the White Mountains. It also occurs in numerous local toponyms, e.g. stous Lakkous tis Skalotis, mentioned above (p. 31).

The chapel of FK CH 12 San Marco which was added to the fort at Frangokastello is in a different category from the 11 outlying churches already discussed, first because it was built into the fort rather than being separate from it. Second, as a Venetian, Catholic church, rather than a Greek, Orthodox one, it was part of the domination of Sphakia and the rest of Crete by an external empire. But in terms of visibility, the fort and its later chapel immediately became an important part of the landscape, and together constituted a conspicuous landmark, built by an occupying power, visible over long distances by land and by sea.

Two churches were built over Late Roman basilicas. FK CH 4 Ag. Astratigos lies over a Late Roman basilica on the western edge of a large Late Roman settlement; both churches are on the north-south path leading from Patsianos to the coast at FK CH 3 Ag. Pelagia (PLATE 18). FK CH 7 Ag. Nikitas was constructed over a basilica with a pebble mosaic which lay near the coast, again in an area with significant Late Roman occupation (PLATE 19). As usual in such cases, the later, smaller church overlies an earlier, larger basilica. Both Ag. Astratigos and Ag. Nikitas incorporate Proconnesian marble columns from their predecessor. Being built over an earlier Christian structure does not ensure a later church's survival: Ag. Astratigos was already a ruin when Hood saw it in the 1950s. Four other churches incorporate Late Roman spolia: FK CH 8 Ag. Kharalampos; FK CH 9 Ag. Ioannis sto Lakko; FK CH 10 Prophitis Ilias; and FK CH 11 Ag. Georgios. There are no other signs of a Late Roman basilica in their immediate vicinity, however.[55]

It would be a mistake to think that all Late Roman basilicas somehow required a later church, as not all early Christian basilicas in Sphakia (or elsewhere) are treated in this way. Loutro had several Late Roman basilicas, only one of which has a later church (with, as we saw above, another now marked by an icon stand). Byzantine–Venetian–Turkish churches built over Late Roman basilicas are therefore the result of some kind of selection, not just a knee-jerk reaction (Cf. pp. 70–73 below).

Several Frangokastello churches seem to mark boundaries between villages or communes or both. The beacon church FK CH 2 Ag. Ioannis Prodhromos has already been mentioned; it lies between the old village of Kolokasia/Ag. Georgios and Patsianos, just west of the official commune boundary, below a spring. (Ag. Nektarios is the new settlement built along the car road, which bypassed the old village.) Similarly, FK CH 6 Ag. Athanasios lies between Patsianos and Kapsodhasos, on the commune boundary separating Patsianos from Skaloti. Two churches lie between Kapsodhasos and Skaloti, FK CH 10 P. Ilias and FK CH 11 Ag. Georgios, presumably marking the boundary between their territories; interestingly, neither village can be seen from the latter.

---

[55] Hood 1967. Cf. Williams 1984 on how far people are generally willing to carry spolia.

4.2.3 Dating of Outlying Churches in Frangokastello

As the catalogue shows, the only precise dates for Frangokastello churches derive from documents or graffiti; the other, vaguer dates are based on architectural features such as pointed 'Gothic' arches and the presence of wall-paintings. Only one church in the study area, FK CH 7 Ag. Nikitas, has a legend associated with its construction; other legends are associated with subsequent events.[56]

It is appropriate now to see how the landscape of the Frangokastello study area developed over time. We know that the basic Byzantine–Venetian–Turkish settlement pattern was established no earlier than the turn of the first-second millennium A.D. As stated at the beginning of this section, the two villages here lie at the roots of the mountains. It is therefore interesting that the earliest exokklisi in the Frangokastello area is near the coast.

FK CH 7 Ag. Nikitas was certainly built before the nearby fort at Frangokastello: it gave its name to this area, which was still known as Santo Nicheta when the fort was constructed ca 1371–74; its frescoes are dated to the second half of the 13th c.[57] One distinct possibility is that this church was built while the local settlement pattern was still fluid, that is, while the villages of Patsianos and Kapsodhasos were still coming into being. The church was constructed over a Late Roman basilica near a water source and on good agricultural land. Ag. Nikitas could thus have served as a way of laying claim to this land, and as a visible marker of new and continuing activity here.

That FK CH 7 Ag. Nikitas may coincide with the formation of the village system is an important point. It suggests strongly that exokklisia could be used to mark out territory before the pattern of settlement was fully developed, or while it was developing.

FK CH 8 Ag. Kharalampos may also have had an earlier Venetian phase, because of the tiles in the southwestern corner (M. Hahn, pers. comm.). Ag. Kharalampos certainly lies on the coastal path, and it has a monastery. It is one of five Frangokastello exokklisia with a cemetery. It includes Late Roman spolia, as already mentioned. I suggest that Ag. Kharalampos was built to show that the immediate area was one which was coming into use as a new (that is, early Venetian) focus of activity.

The next securely dated church is FK CH 10 Prophitis Ilias, whose wall-paintings are dated to the 14th c. (see Catalogue for references). As churches to Prophitis Ilias need not have a direct relationship with specific villages, the Frangokastello example does not help us with the date of Patsianos and Kapsodhasos (or Skaloti to the east). But the date of FK CH 6 Ag. Athanasios is

---

[56] Various legends are told about Ag. Nikitas (the church and/or the saint) – Christian girl abducted by 'ruffians' or by Barbary pirates; these are summarised in Llewellyn Smith 1965, 153–155 and Khrysoulaki-Paterou 1986, 56–60, 73–74; cf. also the catalogue entry for FK CH 7.

[57] The complexities of the dating of FK CH 7 Ag. Nikitas are summarised in the catalogue entry; see also Andrianakis 1998, 12, and cf. the version of the 17th c. Venetian map of the area on p. 7.

important, because this church marks the boundary between two village territories. It was certainly built by 1426, because of a graffito (Gerola 1961). I suggest that FK CH 6 Ag. Athanasios is a definite terminus ante quem for the villages, and that therefore Patsianos and Kapsodhasos were established some time between the 13th (FK CH 6 Ag. Nikitas) and 15th centuries.

All except one of the other churches studied here seem to be no later than Venetian, because of their Gothic arches or the presence of wall-paintings, or both. FK CH 4 Ag. Astratigos is Venetian, and FK CH 3 Ag. Pelagia probably is too. Only FK CH 9 Ag. Ioannis sto Lakko has bacini holes, which are a Venetian-Turkish feature. FK CH 3 Ag. Pelagia may be later Venetian.

Thus the outlying churches in this area all seem to belong to the Venetian period, with FK CH 7 Ag. Nikitas one of the earliest. The date of the chapel of San Marco is not known, but it can be seen inside the fort on Monanni's drawing of 1631. Its date must therefore remain a rather vague Venetian, late 14th to 17th.

As for the village churches, we saw above that Ag. Dhimitrios at the top of Kapsodhasos was definitely Venetian, and that O Khristos in Patsianos probably was (p. 43 n. 52). A document of 1637 mentions Ag. Georgios (Khaireti 1968), confirming its Venetian date. Both villages are mentioned in a Turkish census record of 1649–50 (Tapu Defter ca. 1648). Then come the two 19th c. churches, one in each village.

The most recent additions to the sacred landcape of the Frangokastello study area are the five icon stands. Two metal icon stands were built at a crossroads near the fort, some time in the last 30 years (FK IK 4 and 5). A third icon stand, at the crossroads on the west side of the plain, is dated to 1982, well after the coming of the car road (FK IK 1). Two marble icon stands were built more recently, one outside a house and the other by the road where a fatal accident took place (FK IK 2 and 3).

A general question arises from this summary: is the sacred landscape in the study area different from the rest of the surrounding area (from Komitadhes to Argoule), in terms of the date, number, and function of outlying churches?

The oldest church in the surrounding area is Ag. Georgios 330 m south of Komitadhes, though still some distance from the coast (8.01). The three bacini built into its façade suggest a very early Venetian date, possibly 13th c.; wall-paintings were added in the 14th c. It was said to have been built after a victory over corsairs.[58]

Komitadhes itself is said to be a Venetian foundation, its name possibly derived from 'noble lords' (komites). The earliest mention of the village name

---

[58] Gerola 1905–32, II 308, 334, IV 472; Gerola 1961, 48 no. 218, Lassithiotakis 1971, 111–114 and figs 426–444; Andourakis 1978, 19–22). Ag. Georgios is one of five exokklisia near the village of Komitadhes. The others are Ag. Dhimitrios, east of Komitadhes, with 4 bacini, 12th –14th c; Panagia I Thymiani with monastery, n.d.; Ag. Pavlos on shore traditionally founded ca 1500; Ag. Antonios in ravine below village.

occurs in 1390 (Manoussakas 1958, 396, from Duca di Candia 11, Atti Antichi 15, 29r). It may be that Ag. Georgios was built before Komitadhes, in a situation similar to that of Ag. Nikitas and the villages above it.

As for the number of exokklisia, only Komitadhes has anything like as many as the Frangokastello study area does. My analysis suggests that two of the exokklisia near Komitadhes were built for a reason familiar from the area of Patsianos and Kapsodhasos: to mark important resources, in this case farm land (8.03 Ag. Georgios, to the south-southeast of Komitadhes) and to make an important transition visible (8.01 Panagia i Thymiani, at the entrance/exit of the Impros Gorge).

Returning to the smaller Frangokastello area studied here, we can analyse the number of exokklisia here as well. If we discount FK CH 12 San Marco, built for external rather than internal reasons, we are left with 11 churches. Four of these are boundary churches, some with joint links with Kolokasia to the west and Skaloti to the east, and one is a Prophitis Ilias, which as usual is on a hill. But all of the remaining seven, and indeed one of the boundary churches as well (FK CH 2 Ag. Ioannis Prodhromos), mark the location of water or good land or both. Thus there may be a direct relationship between the available amount of good land and water, and the number of churches in a given area (see discussion in section 4.3 below).

Population might also be a factor but this is difficult to reconstruct for all the periods involved. Patsianos alone had more families than any other village in 1649–50; Patsianos and Kapsodhasos together had nearly double the recorded population of Komitadhes in those two years. But the single most useful factor for predicting rough numbers of outlying churches is the set of resources in a given area, and vice versa.[59]

4.2.4 Icon Stands in the Frangokastello Plain

As we saw earlier, all five icon stands in the Frangokastello area studied here were built in the 20th c., long after the outlying churches. Only one is near a village (FK IK 1, near Patsianos). The rest are on or near the main road running more or less east-west along the coast. There are no old-fashioned stone icon stands in the study area (though see below). The three metal icon stands all mark crossroads: FK IK 1, set up in 1982, sits on the southeast side of the crossroads where the car road coming in from the west divides, one road continuing to

---

[59] For details of the Ottoman and Greek sources for population figures in Sphakia, see the forthcoming vol. I of the final Sphakia Survey publication. For the relationship between prosperity and resources (rather than population), see Nixon and Price (1990) who analysed information for 5th c. B.C. Greek cities and found that classical poleis making large contributions in the Athenian Tribute Lists were prosperous because of large resources, not because of large populations (difficult in any case to quantify), nor because of large territory; cf. n. 64 below.

Patsianos and the other going south to the coast. FK IK 4 and 5 are at a crossroads near the fort, where two parallel dirt roads (W and E), with a major irrigation and drainage ditch between them, lead northeast of the main car road. The two marble icon stands mark more personal locations: FK IK 2 was set up outside a house; and FK IK 3, which shows where a fatal car accident took place, is remarkable for not actually having an icon, though it does have a crucifix.

There is only one other icon stand in the whole of the surrounding area, on the shore in a locality called stous Lakkous tis Skalotis, south of Skaloti (mentioned above on p. 31). Built of small stones and white-washed, it commemorates the recent, accidental death by drowning of a wife helping her husband to pull in their fishing nets. The scarcity of icon stands is thus consistent throughout this whole area, and so is their recent date. None of these icon stands is part of Byzantine–Venetian–Turkish Frangokastello. There are thus some sharp contrasts between Frangokastello and Anopoli, in terms of the number, date, and construction materials of their icon stands.

4.3 Brief Comparison of Anopoli and Frangokastello
(TABLES 1–6, and cf. TABLE 10, Appendix 2)

Both outlying churches and icon stands in Anopoli and Frangokastello have similar locations. Outlying churches in both areas mark important resources, and the link between exokklisia and resources is a topic to which we shall return. Both areas have at least one beacon church which is visible over long distances outside the two plains, as well as several churches which are clearly visible within them. They can also indicate liminal points, such as entry points to their respective plains. In both areas, a church or an icon stand can mark the location of an earlier church, real or otherwise (Anopoli: AN IK 11 said to mark location of church; AN CH 4 church at Glyka Nera has a later icon stand on top of it; Frangokastello: FK CH 4 and 7 are churches built over Late Roman basilicas).

Comparing Anopoli and Frangokastello in terms of explanation is more complicated, because the churches of Frangokastello are older, and it is seldom that we have direct information about the reasons for their construction. Nonetheless, I have suggested that outlying churches in both areas were built to mark resources in places of then new activity, and that they serve as markers for human boundaries such as lines between communes. People in both areas are certainly aware of supernatural dangers (e.g. dhaimones at crossroads), and the effectiveness of sacred structures such as icon stands to dispel them; and they are also familiar with the idea of using outlying churches and icon stands to commemorate specific events and places, and to fulfill vows.

There are, however, some significant differences between the sacred landscapes of the two areas, notably in terms of the relative proportions, chronology, and location of icon stands and outlying churches, as seen in TABLE 3.

TABLE 3: Comparison of outlying churches, village churches, and icon stands in Anopoli and Frangokastello.

	ANOPOLI	FRANGOKASTELLO
area studied here	12 km²	8.5 km²
no of exokklisia in area studied	2	12
exokklisia per km²	1/6.0 km²	1/0.71 km²
no of villages	1	2
ratio of villages to exokklisia	1:2 = 1:2	2:12 = 1:6
no of village churches	8	5
total no of churches (exokkolisia plus village)	2 + 8 = 10	12 + 5 = 17
no of icon stands	18	5
total churches per km² (ex plus village)	10/12 km² = 1/1.2 km²	17/8.5 km² = 1/0.5 km²
icon stands per km sq	1/0.66 km²	1/1.7 km²
exokklisia and icon stands per km²	20/12 km² = 1/0.60 km²	17/8.5 km² = 1/0.5 km²
date range of exokklisia	VT, 20th c.	B,V,T
date range of village churches	V, VT	V, VT, T
date range of icon stands	?late 19th c. – 20th c.	later 20th c.
materials used for icon stands	stone, metal, concrete	metal, marble

Anopoli has 18 icon stands and five outlying churches, with only two in the plain itself, while the Frangokastello area has 11 outlying churches and five icon stands.

There is also a clear chronological difference in the deployment of outlying churches and icon stands. Anopoli has several 'older' icon stands, possibly 19th c., while all of the icon stands in Frangokastello are later 20th c.; one of them is made of marble, a 'richer' material not represented in Anopolitan icon stands. The village churches in Anopoli are as early as many village churches in Frangokastello, but the outlying churches in Frangokastello (at least 14th c. onwards) are earlier than those in Anopoli (one later 19th c. and one 20th c.).

In terms of location, icon stands in Anopoli mark a wider variety and scale of liminal points, from the forcefield of the village, to neighbourhoods, to accidents (on a footpath), to individual houses. In Frangokastello, the icon stands are more recent, as we have seen, and mark a narrower range of points (junctions of car roads, accident on a car road, individual house).

As for outlying churches, in the Frangokastello area they do mark boundaries, in this case between the two villages and their immediate neighbours to the east and west, but most exokklisia indicate important resources, such as water and good land, in the plain below them. Good land in the Anopolis plain, by contrast, is not marked in the same way. The non-nucleated structure of Anopoli means that there are more village churches (eight in seven of the ten neighbourhoods) than a nucleated village would normally have. A comparison of the outlying churches per km^2 in the two areas shows that Anopoli has a ratio of 1:6km^2, while Frangokastello has a ratio of 1:0.55 km^2. If the village churches are included, then the figures are 1:1.2 km^2 for Anopoli and 1:0.38 km^2 for Frangokastello. Thus the two places do use the same kinds of sacred markers, but in different proportions and with different priorities for marking.

It is useful at this point to provide a wider context for the two study areas, both inside and outside Sphakia. TABLE 4 shows that the eight regions in Sphakia as defined by us are very variable in size. Similarly, the numbers of exokklisia per region, and the numbers of exokklisia per square kilometer in each region are also highly variable. It is the number of Byzantine–Venetian–Turkish settlements, occupied and deserted, which gives a crude index of the relative prosperity of each region; settlements are likely to be established near good agricultural resources, as Bevan et al. (2003, 230) have suggested for second millennium A.D. settlements on Kythira. So far, not perhaps so surprising.

But what is surprising is that the ratio of all settlements (those occupied in 2000 plus those deserted by that date) to the total number of exokklisia is remarkably consistent: it is usually around 1:2, that is, one settlement to two exokklisia. In Sphakia, this consistency among regions – for example, Regions 4 (1:2) and 8 (1:2.25), the two studied here in whole or in part – suggests that there might be a predictable relationship between the number of settlements, the number of exokklisia, and the amount of resources, in particular arable land, even when the actual terrain is very different. Much of Region 8 (Frangokastello, partly studied here) consists of a relatively flat coastal plain; Region 4 (Anopoli), includes an alluvial mountain basin punctuated by rocky outcrops.[60]

While the number of settlements and of exokklisia may be predictable, the precise location of exokklisia may not be, in terms of proximity to settlements. A settlement will usually be established near the largest single package of resources; the location of more distant resources will be marked by remoter exokklisia. For example, 3.08 the village of Ag. Ioannis has two churches just outside it (3.03, Ag. Ioannis and Panagia, 600m more or less due south of the village), but it also has 3.14 Prophitis Ilias and 3.01 Ag. Pavlos (2.43 km and 3.15 km respectively; cf.

---

[60] Rackham and Moody (1996, 181, 183 with Fig. 16.2 map) give an estimate of five mediaeval churches per commune, plus as many more post-mediaeval, for a total of ten churches per commune. It is not clear from their map whether 'churches' in this case means outlying or village churches or both. If they mean exokklisia, then their estimate seems high for communes with relatively scarce resources, such as Ag. Ioannis west of Anopoli (Region 3 in Sphakia Survey terms), which has only six. And Sphakia overall has nine communes, but only 66 exokklisia altogether, instead of the 90 that Rackham and Moody's figure of ten per commune would suggest (see TABLES 4 and 10 for figures). For this reason I think that the two exokklisia per *village* ratio discussed in the text is more reliable as a predictor, but as stated, I have tested this ratio only for Sphakia and Kythira.

TABLE 4: Outlying churches and icon stands in Sphakia by region.

REGION NUMBER AND NAME	AREA IN KM SQ	SETT OCC. IN 2000	DES. SETT	EX	TOTAL SETT:EX	EX/AREA IN KM SQ	REMOTE EX?	EX ONCE PART OF SETT?	ICON STANDS IN REGION?	'OLD' ICON STANDS ?
1. Trypiti-Samaria	94	1	3	13	4/13 =1:3.25	1/7.23	yes	no	yes	at least 1
2. Madhares	90	0	0	1	0:1	1/90	n/a	n/a	yes (1)	no
3. Ag. Ioannis-Aradhena	44	2	3	6	5/6 =1:1.2	1/7.3	yes	yes (1)	no	no
4. Anopoli (region)	36	1*	0	2	1:2	1/18	no	no	yes	several
5. Livaniana-Louttro	6	2	1	7	3/7 =1:2.33	1/0.88	yes	yes (1)	yes	at least 1
6. Mouri-Khora Sphakion	39	1	6**	6	7/6 =1:0.85	1/6.5	yes	yes (2)	yes	at least 1
7. Askyphou	73	2*	0*	4	2/4 = 1:2	1/18.25	yes	no	yes	several
8. Frangokastello (region)	90	10*	2	27	12/27 = 1:2.25	1/3.3	yes	no	yes	not in study area
TOTAL	472	29	15	66	44/66 =1:1.5	1/7.15	variable	variable	variable	variable
Regions 3-4-5	86	5	4	19	9/19 =1:2.11	1/4.52	yes	yes (2)	yes	yes

ex = exokklisia (outlying churches)

des = deserted

occ. = occupied

sett = settlement(s)

* village(s) with multiple neighbourhoods, some of which are now deserted non-nucleated: 4. Anopoli; 7. Askyphou, Impros; 8. Asphendou; Kallikrati nucleated: 6. Khora Sphakion

** 6.02 Mouri, 6.03 Koutsoura, 6.01 Kavros counted as deserted, plus 6.26 Lakkoi, 6.10 Kaloi Lakkoi, and 6.09 Ta Dhikhalomata

PLATE 6). It may be that the nearer exokklisia will tend to mark resources directly linked with agriculture, while the more distant ones will mark a wider variety of 'useful' places, including among others those connected with pastoralism, but this is a hypothesis which will require further testing. But it is already clear that knowing where a particular settlement is will tell you where some of its resources are. Only adding the location of the relevant exokklisia will give a complete picture of local resources.[61]

A brief examination of the Byzantine–Venetian–Turkish settlements and exokklisia in Regions 3, 4, and 5 will further contextualise some of the statements made so far; see the joining maps in PLATES 1 and 6, plus TABLE 5, with TABLE 13 for further detail on Regions 3 and 5. This larger area – at 86 km², nearly as large as Region 8 (90 km²) – includes settlements, occupied and deserted, in all three regions, plus the oldest exokklisi in Sphakia, 3.01 Ag. Pavlos, as well as one of the newest, the church at Ta Marmara discussed above (p. 24). The map provides a useful contrast between nucleated settlements (3.08 Ag. Ioannis, 3.20 Aradhena) and non-nucleated settlements like Anopoli. It also makes clear how incomplete our picture of this area would be without the exokklisia. The combination of settlements (with and without churches) and exokklisia shows how the proportion of resources changes from west to east: Anopoli is better resourced than, say, Aradhena.

This is not to say that the distance between villages or major packages of resources is not important: it is. As we saw above, the settlement: exokklisi ratio for Regions 3–4–5 and 8 is rather similar, 1:2 and 1:2.25. But TABLE 5 shows that the overall distance between settlements in the two areas is very different. The figures given here are 'as the crow flies' distances, ruled off maps; timed walks would be better, but these figures nonetheless provide some rough comparisons.

---

[61] The number of churches <u>inside</u> settlements is less predictable, but also seems to correlate with prosperity. For example, we know the Sphakiote settlement with the largest number of 'inlying' churches – Khora Sphakion, with four neighbourhoods, and more than 60 churches – had a thriving ship-building industry in the 18th c. and well-developed trading links, i.e. resources based on non-agricultural activities. The churches, ships, and 'palaces' of Khora are mentioned generically in the *Song of Dhaskalogianni* (Barmpa-Pantzelios n.d., ll. 951–952):

Πού 'ναι ή Χώρα τῶ Σφακιῶ, με τὰ πολλὰ καράβια,
Με τσ' ἑκατὸν τσοι ἐκκλησὲς, τὰ πλούσα τὰ σεράγια;

Pou 'nai i Khora to Sphakio, me ta polla karavia,
Me ts'ekaton tsoi ekklises, ta plousa ta seragia?

Where is Khora Sphakion, with its many ships,
With its one hundred churches, and its rich palaces?

Furthermore, it is worth noting that Region 6, which includes Khora Shakion, also has the lowest ratio of settlements to exokklisia (1:0.85). On the island of Anaphi, field chapels provide another material correlate of resources in use: Kenna (1991, 107 states that ossuaries like miniature churches 'were built out in the field and [in the 1960s] could be seen on almost every hillside all over the island'.

TABLE 5: Nearest settlements in Regions 3-4-5, 8.

FROM	TO	FIGURE IN KM
Ag. Ioannis	Aradhena	4.03
Ag. Ioannis	Livaniana	4.37
Aradhena	Livaniana	2
Aradhena	Loutro	3.18
Aradhena	Anopoli/ Ag. Dhimitrios	1.08
Loutro	Anopoli/ Kampia	1.85
Komitades	Vraskas	1
Vraskas	Vouvas	1
Vouvas	Nomikiana	0.5
Nomikiana	Ag. Nektarios	2
Ag. Nektarios	Patsianos	2
Patsianos	Kapsodhasos	0.55
Kapsodhasos	Skaloti	3
Skaloti	Argoule	1

For example, the average distance between Anopoli (Region 4) and the nearest villages at Aradhena (Region 3) and Loutro (Region 5) is 1.46 km, while the distance between Patsianos and Kapsodhasos (Region 8). On average, villages in Regions 3–4–5 are 2.75 km apart, while those in Region 8 are only 1.38 km apart. The overall ratio for the distance between settlements in the two regions is therefore 2.75 (in Regions 3–4–5) to 1.38 (in Region 8), or 1.99 to 1. In other words, villages in Regions 3–4–5 are very nearly twice as far apart as those in Region 8. But these are only the villages occupied in 2000, and the deserted settlements in Regions 3 and 5 reveal that more land in these regions was more intensively exploited, in agricultural terms, when these settlements were occupied.[62]

A final comparison between Sphakia and the island of Kythira (TABLE 6) shows very clearly that Sphakia is a larger area with fewer resources. Kythira, though only two thirds the total size of Sphakia, has twice the number of exokklisia, and more than twice the number of villages. If Sphakia were like Kythira it would have 119 villages and nearly 230 exokklisia! Kythira has a familiar ratio of settlements: exokklisia of 1:1.9 (or roughly 1:2 again; see pp. 52–53 above); while the overall Sphakia ratio of settlements:exokklisia is somewhat lower at 1:1.5. It comes as no surprise that the number of settlements and

---

[62] These regional figures blur the difference between the study areas of Anopoli and Frangokastello. The Frangokastello settlement: exokklisi ratio is 1: 5.5, compared to 1:2 for Anopoli. Similarly the distance between Patsianos and Kapsodhasos is 0.55 km, while the average distance between Anopoli and Loutro and Aradhena is 1.46 km. See PLATE 3 and TABLE 3.

exokklisia per unit of area is much larger on Kythira than it is in Sphakia, and that the average distance between settlements is much smaller.[63]

In short, the exokklisia correlate positively with the presence and use of resources in the locality. The dates of the churches – when these are known – can help to determine which resources were exploited and when, and therefore in what order. The earliest churches will suggest which resources were first seen as significant. For example, the Byzantine or early Venetian church of Prophitis Ilias (1.04) overlooking the Trypiti Gorge divides the resources of the commune of Ag. Roumeli from those of the commune of Sougia. Later in a local sequence, the maintenance of churches in an area where a settlement has been abandoned can indicate that the area is still 'resourceful', as in the case of Prophitis Ilias, and also Ag. Nikolaos (1.01), actually in the Trypiti Gorge. No one has lived in the nearby village of Peradhoro (1.06) for 200 years, but members of the Tzatzimakis family of new Ag. Roumeli to the east still have beehives in the gorge, and use it as winter pasture for goats, so there are economic reasons to return to it.

Thus for a variety of reasons, 'farther' exokklisia need to be included in the resource package for a given village, as well as 'nearer' ones. The presence of archaeological material in a particular area is always of interest, but in the Byzantine–Venetian–Turkish period, it is the presence of a more diagnostic feature such as a church which can confirm that the economic activity there was significant. This information may give a partial explanation for the restricted altitudinal range for exokklisia. As we saw earlier, churches occur mainly at the down and middle altitudes and almost never at the up altitude. Thus there is Byzantine–Venetian–Turkish (and earlier) archaeological material up in the Madhares, but only one church. It may be that although economic activity at this altitude is possible, the Madhares were perceived as an area with insufficient resources for year-round occupation. As a result, the package of resources here was not thought significant enough to be marked by churches.[64]

---

[63] For Kythira, see Bevan et al. 2003, esp. 232–233; two distance ranges between villages were more frequent than expected, 300–400m and 500–700m. Again, it is important to realize how variable these ratios are within Sphakia. Frangokastello overall, with 27 churches in 72 km^2 (ratio of 1/2.66 km^2), comes closest to the exokklisia/area figure for Kythira. The figures for the Frangokastello study area are 12 exokklisia in 8.5 km^2 (1/0.5 km^2), i.e. much denser than Kythira. By contrast, Anopoli has two exokklisia in 12 km^2 (1/6 km^2), a far sparser distribution than that found on Kythira.

[64] It is important to note that altitude is relative; there are many year-round villages at much higher altitudes in Turkey (Coulton, pers. comm.).

As for the relationship between economic activity and population, there may well be one, but it is dangerous to assume that it is direct. For example, people used to assume that you could work directly from the amount of money assessed in the Athenian Tribute Lists of the 5th c. B.C. to the populations of contributing cities; other work has suggested that this is not possible and that in fact the assessments are directly linked to the resources (and economic activity connected with them) of contributors. In the case of Byzantine–Venetian–Turkish Sphakia and 20th c. Sphakia, the churches give direct information about the use of resources; in other cases, the diagnostic features may be

As for icon stands, TABLE 4 gives a sketchy idea of where they occur. They do not usually mark the presence of resources or economic activity in a direct way. The 'older' icon stand in Region 1 mentioned above (p. 24) which marks a spring is exceptional.

The presence and number of icon stands seem to co-vary with non-nucleated settlement. The mountain plain of Askyphou has several neighbourhoods, like that of Anopoli, and there are several 'older' stone icon stands in Askyphou, as well as newer metal ones. Many of these were originally placed at the intersection of footpaths, some of which have now been replaced by car roads.[65]

And finally, it is significant that both icon stands and churches can go out of use. In the case of Glyka Nera, the outlying church was literally superseded by an icon stand built on top of it; eventually the icon stand also went out of use, and was no longer maintained. Similarly, when the footpath marked originally by AN IK 16 went out of use, so did the icon stand. AN IK 17 re-marks the same area in a different way, reflecting changes in local land use. It is important to note that it is not necessarily the most remote exokklisia or icon stands that go out of use. FK CH 5 Ag. Ioannis Vokolos is only a few minutes' walk from Patsianos but it is now in ruins; Ag. Pavlos 6.5 km north of Khora Sphakion (6.23) is still in use even though the summer village at Kaloi Lakkoi to the north is not. What counts is the strength of the continuing ties between people and specific places in the landscape. It is therefore highly significant when people decide to restore exokklisia which have fallen into disrepair, or even ruin; this issue is discussed in greater detail in section 5.5 below.

Areas do not stay 'holy' or require the kind of continuing protection afforded by icons just because they have already had churches or icon stands built on them. If areas go out of use, then, after an interval difficult to calculate, sacred markers are no longer maintained.

The analysis so far has shown the importance of time depth in the development of these sacred landscapes. Outlying churches are an older form than icon stands, and can be as early as established settlements. They are visible over longer distances and mark the boundaries of larger units such as communes and villages. Icon stands are smaller and more recent, perhaps only as old as the 19th c.; in the two study areas, they seem almost always to be associated with some form of settlement.

During the 19th and 20th cc., I suggest that there was a change in the marking function of icon stands in Anopoli, from marking and separating areas, such as major intersections in footpaths outside villages, to protecting ever smaller units

---

indirect, as in the case of the mints for 5th c. B.C. cities; see Nixon and Price 1990, cited in note 59 above, for a fuller discussion of the 5th c. B.C. example.

[65] But cf. Machin 1983, 114, cited above in note 33 on Asi Gonia. This village is nucleated, yet has a number of icon stands, including at least one of the 'older' type; see Plymakis 2001b, 55, lower left (Gorge of Asi Gonia). For a more detailed discussion, see pp. 77–78 below.

within them, first at junctions between neighbourhoods, then possibly on their edges, and finally, standing guard outside individual houses. Like the churches, icon stands are still to be seen as part of a dynamic system, but a system which itself is changing. In Frangokastello, icon stands are a very late addition to the local sacred landscape, possibly beginning as late as the 1980s.

In the sections below I shall take an even longer view of these two areas, discuss their sacred landscapes from the Late Roman period until the end of the 20th c. A.D. These broad diachronic comparisons, made possible by the consistent collection of survey data, may further sharpen our pictures of these two areas. I will be discussing evidence for the sacred landscape in these periods, with additional remarks on the settlement patterns where relevant. This section and the two that follow depend heavily on the analysis of individual site trajectories, as discussed in Appendix 2 below.

TABLE 6: Outlying churches in Sphakia and Kythira.

	SPHAKIA	KYTHIRA
area	472 km²	278 km²
villages occ. in 2000	29	70
villages/km²	1/16.27	1/3.97
sett +des	29 + 15 = 44	?
exokklisia	66	134
ex/km²	1/7.27 km²	1/2.07 km²
sett:ex	44:66 = 1:1.5	70:134 = 1:1.9
settlem'ts plus ex	95	204
sett+des+ex/total area	110*/472 km² = 1:4.3 *110= (29+15)+66	204/278 km² = 1:1.36
sett+des+ex/ relevant area	110/382 (472-90*) km² = 1:3.47 *area of Region 2	204 + ?/278 km² 1:1.36
predicted vill /total area	119 (472 div. by 3.97)	17 (278 div. by 16.27)
predicted ex/total area	228 (472 div. by 2.07)	38 (278 div. by 7.27)

Sources: Number of villages on Kythira, area of island: Bevan et al. 2003: 231 (figure given is 60–80; figure used here is 70); number of exokklisia on Kythira: Conolly pers. comm. 2004

5

CHRONOLOGICAL EVOLUTION OF THE SACRED LANDSCAPE OF SPHAKIA

5.1 The Late Roman Period and the Predisposition of the Landscape

In this section I will look at the sacred geography of the Late Roman period in the Anopolis and Frangokastello Plains, in order to see how the landscape was predisposed before A.D. 1000.

In the Late Roman period, Crete was part of the Roman province of Crete and Cyrene, with its capital at Gortyn in the Mesara Plain near the south coast of the island. This period was the last time that there was ever a major centre in the Mesara. It was also the last urban period for Sphakia, and the last time that there was a bishopric here, based at the Theotokos basilica at Phoinix/Loutro (see section 5.3 below on the Venetian period).

Under the Romans, piracy diminished, which meant that living down on the coast was no longer dangerous as it had been in the Hellenistic period.[66] The Roman and Late Roman periods were also the time when the grain route from Egypt to Rome gave a boost of prosperity to settlement on the south coast of Crete, including those in the southwest such as Tarrha and Phoinix. Until the 4th c. A.D., Greek and Roman religion had been the official religion of the Roman empire; when Christianity became the new official imperial religion at the end of the 4th c. A.D, it then compulsorily replaced Greek and Roman religion in Crete, as in all other parts of the Empire. On Crete this change became materially obvious with the construction of basilicas in the 5th and 6th c. A.D. Some basilicas were built over existing temples, while others were built on newly sanctified ground. There were concomitant changes in settlement pattern as well as in religion, and the basilicas provide a good dating index for both. In addition the

---

[66] Nixon and Moody et al. 1989; cf. Sanders 1982, 31.

basilicas are not evenly distributed over the island and reveal interesting pockets of prosperity.

In Sphakia, both Anopoli and Frangokastello reveal major changes in the settlement pattern and sacred landscape in the Late Roman period. In the earlier Archaic-Classical-Hellenistic period, there is a large, nucleated settlement away from the coast in both areas; later this is no longer the case. In Anopolis, the polis on the ridge, where a possible cult area has tentatively been identified, was effectively deserted. Late Roman settlement at this altitude (middle) consists of small establishments on the plain. The major Roman and Late Roman settlement was down at Loutro (ancient Phoinix). Loutro had certainly been used in earlier periods, and in the Hellenistic-Early Roman periods we suspect that one small area of the peninsula was used for some cult purpose. In the Late Roman period, no fewer than five basilicas were built at Loutro on the east side of the peninsula within an area of roughly 250m x 250m, or about one eighth of a square kilometer, all of which would have been visible to vessels approaching the main harbour on the eastern side of the peninsula.[67]

In earlier Archaic-Classical-Hellenistic Frangokastello, there was a major settlement at Patsianos Kephala (8.30) at 200 masl, about 2 km from the coast. But by the Late Roman period, Patsianos Kephala was more or less deserted, and instead there were two substantial, but smaller, settlements near the coast at Trochali (8.23) and Ag. Astratigos (8.38), with a possible third at Ag. Nikitas (8.50). There are also many smaller Late Roman loci, (presumably individual houses) just to the north, still on the coastal plain, and the terrace walls constructed by the end of the Late Roman period in this area can still be seen.[68] Agiasmatsi (8.61), the sacred cave which had flourished in the Hellenistic-Early Roman period, located somewhat higher than Patsianos Kephala at 296 masl, lost its sacred function in the Late Roman period.[69] Two Late Roman basilicas were built in the area near the coast, at the sites later occupied by FK CH 4 Ag. Astratigos and one at FK CH 7 Ag. Nikitas.

Thus at the end of the Late Roman period there are important differences between Anopoli and Frangokastello, in terms of the predisposition of the two landscapes. Both areas saw their largest settlements (Anopolis and Patsianos Kephala) disintegrate, but there were significant differences in what happened next. Activity on the Anopolis Ridge decreased dramatically, with few durable

---

[67] I am grateful to Jennifer Moody for pointing out the visibility of the five basilicas. It is tempting to see these Loutro basilicas as the result of competitive display. Cf. Itanos, where at least two basilicas were built side by side in a small area ('Basilica B'), in an area away from the main settlement, but near the sea, from which they could have been seen; Greco et al. 1998, plan p. 587; Greco et al. 2000, plan p. 548, showing the newly excavated houses around Basilica A. On a site visit to Itanos in 2002, I saw what looked like a third ecclesiastical building to the north of the two basilicas.

[68] Nixon and Moody et al. 1994, 260 and fig. 6; cf. Price and Nixon 2005.

[69] Francis et al. 2000; and cf. also Alcock 2002, 113–115 and fig. 3.7, who is wrong to imply that use of the Agiasmatsi cave as a cult place continues after the Early Roman period.

remains of the Roman or Late Roman period; indeed major Late Roman activity in this general area took place away from the ridge and the mountain plain, at Loutro. Frangokastello saw a smaller spatial shift within the area studied here, and was left with durable Late Roman remains in the form of basilicas and terraces. But it was the basilicas in Loutro and Frangokastello that showed most clearly where Late Roman activity had been.

5.2 The Contribution of the 7th–12th Century: Icons and Borders

Ag. Pavlos (3.01), built some time in the 10th or 11th c. A.D., is the earliest post-Roman church in Sphakia, and the only securely dated structure of any kind in this period. It is immediately recognisable as a church because of its orientation and its cruciform plan, but it is not a basilica. It is much smaller, and far too small to be a truly congregational building; it has no mosaics; it is built of small cut stones, not Roman bricks. It was, and is, outside a settlement. Ag. Pavlos thus represents something different, a new tradition in church architecture. We have already (in section 3.4.1, on location) gained some understanding of the reasons for its location – fresh water, coastal route, near path up to fertile land, where eventually the village of Ag. Ioannis would be – but what changes and developments lead to this new architectural form?[70]

In the 7th c. there had been an important post-Roman development: the emergence of icons as a powerful kind of sacred picture, powerful enough to

---

[70] Ag. Pavlos (3.01): Small cruciform chapel on coast east of Ag. Roumeli, at 20 masl. A good hour's walk (ca 3.5km) from Ag. Roumeli on the coastal footpath that continues to Loutro and beyond, west of the junction with the path down from Ag. Ioannis. Dated to 10th–11th c., and founded by Ioannis Xenos (according to *Life* in Tomadhakis 1983–84, 7; the *Life* at 11 is an inferior version of the 18th–19th century). The chapel is small, ca 6.50m x 8.30m; no exterior plaster, no bacini; with frescoes, c. 1300; Gerola 1961, 47 no. 210; Lassithiotakis 1971, 101–5, with plan and elevation; Gallas et al. 1983, 256–257, with plan and elevation; Tsougarakis 1988, 119–20; Bissinger 1995, 84. Cyriacus of Ancona, writing after a trip from Khania to the northern foothills of the White Mountains in AD 1445, reports that 'There until our own day the Cretans keep a chapel sacred to him, and we heard that sailors often refer to these mountains as "St. Paul's".' (1445/2003, 186–7).

There is water fresh enough to drink in the beach gravel below chapel (though it can apparently can dry up in late summer); emphasised by Buondelmonti 1897, 110 (long version), 143 (short version); and by a listing of naval coastal resources (Semitecolo 1639/1999, 19).

As well as information on the location of Ag. Pavlos, we have some explanations for the construction of the church. According to local legend, St Paul baptised the first Christians on Crete here, because of the fresh water, which had curative properties (Pashley 1837, 2. 259 and Löher 1877, 206–7 (Politis 1904, no. 197)); cf. Fielding 1953, 265, who gives another local legend that St Paul also liberated Crete from 'wild beasts and noxious animals'). Pappa Georgios Saviolis (Anopoli), interviewed by me in 1992, said that the church was built on this spot to commemorate St Paul's actions here. The baptismal legend in particular may explain why Ioannis Xenos went here, and founded a church which, uniquely among his eight foundations, lacked a monastery.

provoke a move to banish them from the Greek Orthodox Church in the form of iconoclasm, 726/30 - 787.[71] Within a century iconoclasm was condemned as heresy (846), and to this day icons remain a defining aspect of Hellenic Christianity. One of the major functions of churches is to act as a container for icons; indeed the growing importance of icons as an almost architectural element in Byzantine churches can be seen clearly in the development of the screen, which was transformed from an optional barrier between nave and chancel before iconoclasm, to a templon on which icons could be hung from the 9th c. onwards, to the essential wooden wall or iconostasis, with a full set of icons in several registers marking the complete separation between priestly sanctuary and congregational space for lay-people. The earliest iconostases emerged in the 11th or 12th c., and were certainly the norm by the 14th c.[72]

Another product of this liminal period in Greek history is the 11th –12th c. epic Dhigenis Akritis, the frontiersman of double descent. Vasilis, the hero, is the son of an Arab emir who abducted a Rhomeic (Greek Christian) general's daughter, and was later converted to Christianity because of her (ll. 43–53). The story is set in Syria and Turkey on the Byzantine version of the Roman limes (again, an example of the Late Roman predisposition of the Byzantine landscape). The poem is, understandably, preoccupied with borders and edges and frontiers, or rather with the border/edge/frontier (that is, the eastern border) between the Christian and Muslim worlds. When Vasilis and his wife die together, people from both sides of the frontier come to their funeral; later a tomb was set up. It is surely significant that this commemorative structure was given a visible place in the landscape, indeed that it was set up in a pass (Greek kleisoura), where people could see it from a distance:

> When the hymns at the burial had duly been performed
> and everything in the house given to the poor,
> they buried the remains fittingly in a monument, [en mnemati]
> and built a tomb for them up in the pass
> near a place called Trosis.
> Akritis the Frontiersman's tomb was set up on an arch,
> it was constructed wondrously from purple marble
> and it could be seen from a distance on the mountain ridge
> so that strangers who saw it uttered blessings on the young people;
> for what is raised high can be seen from far and wide.
> Then they all climbed up, those who had gathered on that occasion,
> the magnates, the leaders and all who at that time
> had laid wreaths on the tomb; as they walked around it,
> weeping uncontrollably, they began to speak...[73]

---

[71] Cormack 1997, 12.
[72] Cormack 2000, 150–151.
[73] *Digenis Akritis*, Grottaferrata 8.235–244, text and translation in Jeffreys 1998, 230–231.

The poem was immediately and widely popular, particularly on Crete where both the original and other 'akritika' were widely known at an early date. Indeed, one of the two earliest MSS, Escorial (late 15th/early 16th, to Grottaferrata's 14th) may be from Crete, and West Crete at that (G. Morgan 1960, 44–48). In any case, the Christian – Muslim frontier, far from being a remote concern of distant emperors, was a subject of burning actuality in Crete, where, in the 11th c., the Arabs had been gone for less than a century.

The Arabs had come to Crete from Spain in the west, not from the Rhomeic east, and they were more or less tolerant of Christians. The Arabs did not force people to convert to Islam; they did not destroy existing churches; they may even have permitted the construction of new ones. Nonetheless the popularity of the story of Dhigenis Akritis, the twice-born frontiersman – is immediately understandable.[74] Equally, the description of Dhigenis' tomb, literally a beacon of Greek Christian faith, set in a highly visible place in the landscape, must have had a special resonance for people living in a place whose island had so recently been invaded. Within Sphakia there is at least one place called Dhigenis, in the commune of Asphendou, towards the lower end of the Asphendou Gorge, not far from the village of Kolokasia/Ag. Georgios.[75]

Thus the church of Ag. Pavlos, discussed at the beginning of this section, was the shape of things to come in the post-Roman world, because it was different from Roman Christian buildings. Earlier I suggested that the continuity of location seen at Byzantine–Venetian–Turkish churches built over Late Roman basilicas distracts us from the discontinuities of church form, location, and function. Late Roman basilicas are precisely that, a Roman building type. Byzantine–Venetian–Turkish churches have a different form, and they are smaller; this difference in size is important because it suggests that congregational space was essential in the earlier period but not in the later one. The essential function of these new, Greek churches was to be containers of icons. The 8th–10th

---

[74] Christides (1984, 108–114) gives a careful account of what the Arabs did and did not do on Crete, rightly emphasising the gap between popular views of the Arabs as destructive of Christianity, and the reality of their rule on Crete. Theodosios the Deacon's poem 'The Taking of Crete', i.e. by Nikiphoros Phokas in 961, provides a clear and early example of Greek hostility to Arabs; see Panagiotakis 1960. The poem, dated to late 963, chronicles and exalts the Greek victory, but it gives almost no details about Crete or Cretans. There are no references to Herakleion (whatever it might have been called at the time), to specific Cretans, to saints, or to churches or icons. Cretan memory of the Arab defeat persisted after 961 – the first International Cretological Congress was held in 1961 explicitly to commemorate the 1000th anniversary – but it was the far more vivid and precisely located 'Dhigenis' which would provide the memorably poetic encapsulation of the relationship between Rhomeic Greeks and Arabs.

[75] Geronymakis 1996, 13, no. 290 and map. Geronymakis, when interviewed in September 2004 about this toponym, said that Dhigenis' horse went to this spot in the Asphendou Gorge during a hunt. The story is a bit vague, but Geronymakis' association of the toponym with Dhigenis Akritis was not. Cf. Kondylakis' novel *Patouchas* (1987 [1891], 84) where Manolis' strength elicits the comment, 'He's a regular Digenis!', i.e. the poem was commonly known in Cretan villages in the 19th c.

cc. follow more or less immediately on the creation of icons and their near destruction, in iconoclasm. A church with an icon opens the all-important window between this world and the next. Thus even a small church 'in the middle of nowhere' can make this crucial link, and in so doing, act as a visible, Greek statement of faith and allegiance (Cormack, 1985, 1997). The quality of the icon and its containing architecture – quality in art historical terms – are completely irrelevant. It is their combined presence that is powerful.

In terms of changing church function, Ag. Pavlos shows that using sacred structures to mark and delimit features of the landscape in a particular way is a defining characteristic of 2nd millennium A.D. Sphakia from the beginning of the period. Sphakia had already been christianised under the Romans. But churches like Ag. Pavlos, built from the 10th–11th c. onwards, combined new architectural forms with new functions: they were containers of icons; outside settlements, they marked economically important features such as water sources; and in addition, they were also a way of responding to external threats, in this case, Islam, encountered directly through the Arab invasions, and indirectly through Dhigenis Akritis and other poems. The churches could make the presence of Hellenic Christianity visible in the landscape, and they could also declare the boundary between it and other cultures.[76]

We have seen that Ag. Pavlos marked signs of new activity in one part of Sphakia. Indeed it constitutes almost the only definite signs of any new activity in the area.[77] Here it is important to note that the churches are at least as old as any settlement that may have existed in this period. Some aspects of the relationship between sacred landscapes and settlement patterns were considered above (pp. 60–62), and we will return to this question in the next section.

5.3 Perambulation and Pasturage: Setting Boundaries and Defending Orthodoxy in Venetian Crete

In this period there was tension between two basic processes: 1. the continuing formation and crystallisation of all features of the 'traditional'/modern landscape, including the settlement pattern which remained more or less the same until the

---

[76] There was a similar phenomenon in Spain when Christians reconquered territory held by the Arabs. The 12th c. church of Nuestra Señora de Chilla near the village of Candeleda is an example. Finardo, a shepherd, who was looking after his flock in the ruins of an earlier church dedicated to Mary, had a vision of the Virgin not long after the reconquest of the Tagus valley. She asked him to rebuild her church on the spot, some 7 km from Candeleda (López and Ángel 1995, 60f.).

[77] The Sphakia Survey has recovered fragments of 11th–12th c. amphorae from a few sites, including 3.02 Ano Periana, in the same area as the village of Ag. Ioannis above 3.01 Ag. Pavlos. No pottery of this date was found in either of the two areas studied here (Anopoli and Frangokastello). Evidence from the pollen core taken at Kallikrati northeast of Frangokastello may indicate tree-felling in order to clear land for farming at around the turn of the millennium; see Atherden and Hall 1999.

mid 20th c.; and 2. the necessary development, at the same time, of an accommodation to the external reality of Venetian rule. Throughout the period the churches, inside and outside settlements, provide crucial information about both these processes. While their architecture and decoration reveal Venetian influence, the new grammar of their location reflects and proclaims a concern for, and a continuing defence of, Hellenic Orthodoxy.

There is, fortunately, more archaeological and architectural evidence on the ground for the 12th–15th c. than for the preceding Byzantine period, certainly enough to see that whatever happened in between, the landscape emerging in the Venetian period in Sphakia is very different from that of the Late Roman period in two ways.

First, life is lived on a smaller scale. The Venetian settlement hierarchy in Sphakia is flatter than that of the Late Roman period, consisting mainly of larger and smaller villages. For cities and cathedrals alike, one must look outside Sphakia, which from this period on has only the lower end of the secular and sacred hierarchy. Thus most Sphakiote churches in this period are small. Not only are there no longer any cathedrals in Sphakia, there are few truly congregational churches even in villages. Similarly, monastery churches in Sphakia are very small establishments with accommodation for at most 10 resident monks. In dissected terrain, however, a structure need not be large to be seen from a distance. The small scale of church-building was accompanied by high visibility.

Second, there is a general preference for inland and upland locations for villages, so that most of them were established away from the coast and, wherever possible, were actually invisible from the sea. Naturally the coast was used, but people tended not to live there if they could avoid it. Thus the Late Roman city on the coast at Tarrha dwindled into the anchorage for the inland village of Ag. Roumeli, hidden inside the cliffs at the bottom of the Samaria Gorge. Even more dramatically, the thriving port town (and the associated bishopric) at Loutro/Phoinix effectively disappeared, the main settlement of this area transferring to the new village in the Anopolis Plain. Even in Frangokastello the two villages of Patsianos and Kapsodhasos, though visible from the sea, are nonetheless right at the roots of the mountains.[78]

It is beyond the scope of this book to go into great detail on the new settlement pattern, but a few general statements will help to make some of the most important points, For example, it seems to have taken a surprisingly long time for the new settlement pattern to jell. The earliest datable pottery in Sphakia for this period, which takes the form of imported fine wares, is 13th c., in other words later than the 10th–11th c. construction of Ag. Pavlos (though contemporary with its frescoes). Thus there was definite settlement activity in Sphakia, but much of it may have been on a very small scale indeed; and aspects of the new sacred

---

[78] And the summer villages in the mountain plains above (Asphendou, Kallikrati, etc) are completely invisible from the sea.

landscape seem to have come first in some cases. This view coincides with that of Bevan et al., who point out that '"becoming" a village is a dynamic process', and that part of that process involves establishing clear individual catchments (2003, 231). It is therefore logical that churches would play an important role as boundary markers from the earliest stages of this dynamic process.

Given their different altitudes and settings, it is prehaps not surprising that the new landscape takes different forms in Anopoli and Frangokastello. The new settlement pattern in Anopoli was very different from that of earlier periods. There was no new settlement on the ridge; instead neighbourhoods were established on the individual rocky outcrops around the plain. But the earliest pottery found in Anopoli comes from two locations outside the neighbourhoods, and not later inhabited; it dates to the 13th c. The earliest textual mention of the agglomerated village of Anopoli is 14th c., and six of the seven neighbourhoods with churches are mentioned by name in a 17th c. document. None of the churches in Anopoli has a precise date of its own, so we are dependent on textual references. The earliest of these is a 17th c. official register of all churches in the province of Khania, which mentions only three.[79]

In Anopoli it seems as though the neighbourhood system was beginning to be established by the 14th c., possibly after a period of experimentation in the 13th. Some of the neighbourhood churches could have been built this early, with other being constructed later in the Venetian period after the period of depopulation (the short century between 1367 and 1453, following the Kallergi Revolt). Once again, it is particularly frustrating not to be able to date AN CH 1 Ag. Aikaterini. It is nonetheless possible to suggest that the neighbourhoods and their 'inlying' churches developed more or less in tandem.[80]

---

[79] Locations with 13th c. pottery (outside village and not later inhabited): 4.01 Ts'Assis; 4.53 Obsidian Site. Earliest mention of the village of Anopoli is 14th c.; Noiret (1892, 36, 488) mentions an actual ban on settlement in 1364, after the revolt of the Kallergi which began in Rethymnon but spread to the whole island. When the Kallergi fled to Anopoli, the Venetians banned settlement in Anopoli, Lasithi, and Eleftherna; Xanthoudides 1939, 99–110. The traveller Buondelmonti, who visited Anopoli in 1417, noted that the plain was used only for pastoralism, and that the locals would suffer severe punishment if they did any cultivation. Only in 1453 was the ban on settlement lifted, and Anopoli again repopulated and replanted. Six of the seven neighbourhoods of Anopoli with churches are mentioned by name in a 17th c. document (Trivan 1644).
Ag. Georgios (neighbourhood of Kampos), Ag. Dhimitrios (in the homonymous neighbourhood), and Theotokos (most probably the Panagia in Mariana); Khaireti 1968, but note that the neighbourhood of Mariana is not mentioned in any documents.
[80] What we can say is that other parts of Sphakia, such as the village of Ag. Ioannis and the Frangokastello area, do have churches definitely dated to the 13th and 14th centuries, but that Anopoli does not. This situation is different from that of the areas east and west of Anopoli.
The frescoes still visible in 3.01 Ag. Pavlos below the village of Ag. Ioannis (west of Anopoli) are 13th c., but all the other datable churches here are 14th c.: 3.03 Panagia and 3.04 Ag. Ioannis, both outside the village of Ag. Ioannis; 3.20 Mikhail Arkhangelos at the edge of the village and gorge of Aradhena. 6.18 Ag. Apostoloi at the top of Mesokhori in Khora Sphakion (east of Anopoli). As for

In Frangokastello, we have a a slightly different situation after the Late Roman period. As in Anopoli, the main settlement area moved, but in this case not so far: two new villages, Patsianos and Kapsodhasos, were eventually established at the roots of the mountains, while the local resource base, the Frangokastello Plain, remained the same.

Of the 11 Orthodox churches in Frangokastello, eight are definitely Venetian, and the other two (FK CH 2 and 3) probably are. The two earliest churches with secure dates are both 14th c.: FK CH 7 Ag. Nikitas, built before 1340, when the decision to build the fort at Frangokastello was taken; and FK CH 10 Prophitis Ilias with its 14th c. frescoes. Functionally, the churches datable to the 14th–15th c. fall into two overlapping categories: they mark new activity around particular resources (water, arable land) in the Frangokastello Plain, and they mark the location of various boundaries; by this time, both the new activity and the boundaries are presumably linked with the two villages.[81] Thus the churches and villages constituted part of the same system.

In both areas, the new landscape, both sacred and secular, seems to have jelled only in the 13th–14th c. In Anopoli, the territory immediately associated with the new settlement pattern was encircled by neighbourhoods and 'inlying' churches, in the edge or slope locations already discussed. It was made perfectly clear who would be using the fertile land of the plain so protectively enclosed.

In Frangokastello, the local territory was outside the two villages. The inlying churches of Patsianos and Kapsodhasos were not sufficient to mark the boundaries of local activity in the well-watered plain; the outlying churches made it clear the that landscape was in use, and what some of its boundaries were.

Two Greek documents confirm the suggestion made here, first that the landscape of Venetian Sphakia was still fluid in the 12th c., but had taken on its more or less final form by the early 15th c.; and second, that churches (inlying and outlying) and boundaries were inextricably linked from the beginning of the period. The first document is a perambulation of Sphakia allegedly dated to 1184, and the second is a 1435 treaty resolving disputes over pasturage.

The perambulation, one of 12 charters allegedly granted by the Byzantine emperor Isaac II Angelos, restores or grants the governance and revenues of a territory which may have been dependent on Anopoli to the Skordhylis family. The charter uses 41 place names to outline the boundary of the territory, starting

---

the Madhares, whose use is in some periods directly linked with Anopoli, we know that they were certainly in use in the early Turkish period (Randolph 1687, 85), but we have no definite date for 2.37 Ag. Pnevma. Pottery from the area of this church includes Late Venetian fine wares, presumably linked to use of the church, and giving a terminus ante quem for it, as well as Turkish material. For the dates of churches in Frangokastello, see pp. 43–47 above.

[81] New activity: FK CH 4 Ag. Astratigos, FK CH 5 Ag. Ioannis Vokolos, FK CH 7 Ag. Nikitas, FK CH 8 Ag. Kharalampos, FK CH 9 Ag. Ioannis sto Lakko. Boundaries: FK CH 1 Ag. Theodhoros at west, FK CH 6 Ag. Athanasios between Patsianos and Kapsodhasos, FK CH 10 P. Ilias between Kapsodhasos and Skaloti, FK CH 11 Ag. Georgios at the eastern end of the area.

near the future Frangokastello, running along the north side of the White Mountains, and continuing down to Agia Roumeli and the coast below it. This area was therefore much the same as the modern eparchy of Sphakia, but somewhat shorter at the east and west ends. The name 'Sphakia' does not appear in the charter, and is first attested in the early 15th c. Venetian traveller Buondelmonti (1422).

The vast majority of the 41 place names are not those of settlements, but natural features (e.g. Three Olive Trees); many of these names can still be located with some precision. It is important to note that these toponyms are real, even if the document is more recent than claimed. It is of great interest that so few villages or churches are mentioned in this document, even in cases where they almost certainly lay on or near the boundary. The village in Samaria is not mentioned, though the line runs down the Samaria Gorge. But already it is the church in the inland village of Ag. Roumeli, or more precisely its bema, which marks point 40. The charter makes it clear that this is a territory worth controlling and exploiting, but leaves the impression that it is in the process of development.[82]

The pasturage treaty of 1435, some 250 years later, provides a major contrast.[83] It records how a dispute over pasturage between two families was resolved by a marriage, and it give the new boundary of the land owned by Geronimos Skordylis, which ran along the westside of the Sphakiano Gorge from Kaloi Lakkoi ('middle' altitude) to Khora Sphakion ('down'). Nearly all of the toponyms used to trace the boundary toponyms refer to settlements (villages or neighbourhoods) and to churches. Crucially, the boundary line – precise enough resolve a dispute which had already caused several deaths – would have been hard to draw without the churches, both outlying (6.23 Ag. Pavlos, where the Sphakiano splits into two), and slope/edge (Ag. Apostoloi, a very conspicuous church at the top of 6.18 Mesokhori, a neighbourhood of Khora Sphakion).

The perambulation reveals, if not a 'before' stage in the development of BV Sphakia, then certainly an early 'during'. As early as the 12th c., churches (but not villages) are already used and accepted as indisputable boundary markers. By 1435, on the other hand, both churches and villages seem to be more or less in place, with outlying churches clearly used as precise landmarks in this part of Sphakia. Thus much of the familiar Byzantine–Venetian–Turkish landscape of Sphakia, churches and settlements, came into being during this crucial period, from the 12th to the 15th c. Once again, it is important to stress that the earliest Byzantine–Venetian–Turkish landscape of Sphakia includes outlying churches, notably 3.01 Ag. Pavlos on the coast below Ag. Ioannis. Outlying churches are not an addition to traditional-modern Sphakia, but an integral part of it.

---

[82] Gerland 1903–08; Xanthoudides 1939b.
[83] Vourdoumpakis 1939b.

Taken together, the two documents and the archaeological and architectural evidence suggest that larger boundaries, for example the region defined by the charter, were marked out first, and that smaller boundaries, such as village territories, may have been marked out later, during what is after all a relatively long sequence of development. In this case, the marking is at least partly done by sacred structures in the form of outlying churches.

One of the frustrations of the Venetian period in Sphakia is the lack of the very detailed records kept for other parts of Crete. We cannot therefore be certain that the commune boundaries so well-known in later periods were established by the early 15th c. But the positioning of churches such as FK CH 6 Ag. Athanasios (definitely built by the 15th c.) on the line later known as the commune boundaries between Patsianos and Skaloti is highly suggestive.[84]

We turn now to the second theme of this section, the accommodation to Venetian rule. The Venetians were efficient imperialists on Crete; they were also fiercely hostile to Orthodox Christianity. They drove out Orthodox bishops, they forbade the ordination of new Orthodox clergy, and they sent Venetian (Catholic) families as colonists.[85]

Under these circumstances, it is astonishing to see clear evidence of Venetian influence on Orthodox churches, both outside, in the application of bacini from Italy, often over church doorways and apses; and inside in the adoption of the Gothic arch.[86] How could the Orthodox inhabitants of Crete so readily absorb and display elements brought by their Catholic conquerors? One could say that simply building an Orthodox church in the Venetian period could be considered an act of defiance or resistance: we have seen how visible even small churches can be in dissected terrain. We have also noted the increasing importance of icons as quasi-architectural features inside churches, in noting the development from screen to templon to iconostasis, which had become the norm by the 14th c. It is of course important to realise that different levels of Cretan society had different responses to Venetian rule at different times; for example, the Skordhylis family of Sphakia, after an initial period, actually regained their land under the aegis of the Venetians.

But there is another important aspect of churches in Crete (and possibly elsewhere), and that is the incorporation of earlier Christian architecture, both basilicas and spolia. Many mediaeval churches in Crete are built on the ruins of Late Roman basilicas. In Sphakia there were 10 Late Roman basilicas (one in Poikilasion; one in Tarrha; one in Aradhena; five in Loutro; two in Frangokastello). The Sphakiote basilicas without later churches are all in areas not

---

[84] For the role of churches on commune boundaries in resolving cases of animal theft (xekatharisma) see p. 37 above, and pp. 81–83 below. Basilicata shows a 'linea' down the middle of the Frangokastello Plain. The 18th c. British traveller Pococke also saw a wall here; Pococke 1743–45, II. 241.

[85] Cormack 1997, 180, 181, 203, 204, 208, 210, 213.

[86] The Gothic arch was adopted in the Venetian period, but also used in the Turkish period.

as extensively used in the Venetian period. For example, the coastal basilica in Loutro did have a church built over it, but the other four, which lay in an area no longer inhabited, did not.

Altogether there are five basilicas with later churches in Sphakia: the one at Loutro mentioned above, plus one each at Tarrha and Aradhena, and two at Frangokastello. In every case, the smaller, later churches are, as elsewhere in Crete, very carefully positioned over the larger, earlier basilicas: the new structure usually sits exactly on the bema or sanctuary of the old one. The two examples in Frangokastello, FK CH 4 Ag. Astratigos and FK CH 7 Ag. Nikitas (PLATES 18 and 19), are good examples of this phenomenon.[87] The placement of all five later churches therefore shows not simple religious continuity, but deliberate choice.

Similarly, the inclusion of earlier Christian spolia in later churches is also the result of a deliberate choice. In Frangokastello, there are four churches with spolia (FK CH 8 Ag. Kharalampos new activity, FK CH 9 Ag. Ioannis sto Lakko new activity, FK CH 10 Prophitis Ilias boundary, FK CH 11 Ag. Georgios boundary). All except one (FK CH 10) have a spolium with a cross on it, sculpted as part of the original block. The reuse of these spolia means the explicit, visible parading of authentic palaeo-Christian elements in the new churches of the Venetian occupation.

In trying to find an interpretation for these phenomena, it is crucial for the researcher to note that all of these churches, both basilica-churches and spolia-churches, are part of a new landcape with its own grammar of location. It is not enough to say that this incorporation is simply 'cult continuity'. Nor will an explanation based only on legitimation of a new order, as proposed for early Iron Age Greek mainland hero cults, suffice in this case.[88]

There is now some excellent work on spoliated buildings and how to interpret them, focussing on the re-use of ancient, i.e. pagan, spolia in Christian buildings. Hansen (2003, 245) comments that the inclusion of spolia in churches both 'marked a departure from the classical tradition', and made use of their power 'to promote the recollection of a past renewed and fulfilled through Christianity'. And Papalexandrou (2003, 63–77) has shown that fragments were positively rather than negatively seen by the architects of spoliated buildings, and that the selection and placement of these fragments are, again, the result of deliberate choices, as in the 9th c. Church of the Panagia at Skripou (ancient Orkhomenos).

If the use of ancient, non-Christian, spolia has something to do with transformation after a break with the past, what then is the significance of palaeo-Christian spolia in churches, which must represent some kind of claim to continuity, rather than a mark of discontinuity? Is there a single mode of interpretation which can accommodate these spolia as well?

---

[87] See Sanders 1982, ch. 7 Basilicas, for the location and position(s) of other Roman basilicas and churches in Crete.
[88] Murray and Kardulias 2000, 153; Coldstream 1976. Cf. Snodgrass 1980, 38–40, Nixon 1991.

It is the work of Carruthers, who focusses on memory in general, which offers the most useful way of understanding the use of palaeo-Christian spolia. In discussing the construction of public remembering and forgetting, again with reference to the transition from ancient Greek and Roman religion to Christianity, Carruthers says that

> ...when we speak of 'place' in memory, we refer not to a literal spot or space, but to location within a network, 'memory' distributed through a web of associations, some of which may involve physical space..., many of which are socially constructed and maintained conventions..., and all of which only become active in the minds of people making such webs of association (1998, 54; author's emphases).

Including pagan spolia in Christian churches, according to Carruthers, involves remembering, but differently, with a new set of associations. Each new structure – Carruthers is speaking of basilicas in the eastern Roman Empire – was a node of a new public memory network, 'a site for memory-making', constructed through processions and other ritual practices.[89]

To return to Sphakia, the reuse of palaeo-Christian basilicas and spolia can also represent remembering differently, with a new set of associations. It is true that these palaeo-Christian elements represent a religious tradition which is not being repudiated (although it was interrupted), but basilica- and spolia- churches do have new associations because they have been selected for newer churches; at the same time, and this is crucial, other important elements of the same period have *not* been selected. A new landscape is being created through these selections of older Christian buildings and architectural elements.

I suggest that what we have in Venetian Sphakia is the expression of a particular chronology of desire, made material and visible through the incorporation of earlier Christian elements, especially in the case of the churches built over basilicas, but also in the churches which include palaeo-Christian spolia. The desired chronology is one that links local Orthodox Christianity with an earlier authentic and original Christian presence, ruined but not destroyed (according to local tradition) by the Arabs. The placement of new churches over basilica sanctuaries shows a precise awareness of the older structures, and a desire to bind two points in time into one authoritative chronology.

Churches on basilicas and churches with palaeo-Christian spolia are a visible way of recalling that the people in that area had been properly, 'authentically', Christian for centuries before the Venetians took over. As we have already seen, outlying churches like Ag. Pavlos (3.01) are a fundamental part of a new, Hellenic (not Roman) form of Christianity which becomes visible around the turn of the

---

[89] Carruthers 1998, 46–57; the phrase 'a site for memory-making' is on p. 56. Carruthers' work is also important for memory and the performance of landscape; see the section below on pp. 101–102 and n. 129 where the passage is quoted in full.

second millennium A.D. Linking this new form of Christianity with an older one was a way of strengthening it – remembering differently, with a new set of associations. Some palaeo-Christian elements are chosen for incorporation in the new public memory network of the Venetian period, while others are not. The incorporation of earlier basilicas and spolia is thus a way of creating memory theatres dedicated to defensive autochthony, by insisting that Christianity had already existed in the area – threatened, endangered, but ultimately strengthened and fortified by icons.[90]

The use of churches built in the Venetian period to mark out new boundaries is also significant. The largest scale of the boundaries marked is at the commmune level, with some churches also 'accidentally' marking eparchy boundaries (Prophitis Ilias 1.04, boundary with Selino, and Ag. Pnevma, 2.37, boundary with Apokoronas), but then there were no longer any urban centres in Sphakia in this period. Venetian documentary evidence from the Peloponnese, where there were cities, suggests that the communes there 'certainly appeared to exert a considerable role in local administration'.[91] It may be that there is a strong link between the establishment of commune boundaries and the construction of exokklisia as a means of marking them. We saw that establishing boundaries through sacred structures is often an early concern in the establishment of new settlement patterns. In this case, there is an important difference: people in post-antique Crete were conscious that other powerful religious systems had existed in the past. Any boundaries that were established in this period were both territorial and conceptual, including Orthodoxy and excluding all 'foreign' cults such as Islam (remember the continuing popularity of Dhigenis Akritis) and Venetian Catholicism.[92]

---

[90] Alcock 2001, 2002; Nixon 2004. Cf. the chronology of desire espoused by a character in Kondylakis' novel *Patouchas* (1987 [1891], 63–64):

> 'What Saïtonicolis knew for certain was that Crete, before it was taken by the Franks and then from the Franks by the Turks, belonged to the Christians and the Christians would take it again.'

[91] Davies 2004, 109. The Venetian occupation of the Peloponnese (1688–1715) comes after a period of Ottoman rule, rather than before it as on Crete.

[92] Faure (1979, 80) suggests that there are three major periods of construction for the 'overhang' or 'rock shelter' churches mentioned above (p. 20 and n. 20): the 13th–14th cc; the 17th–18th cc.; and the 19th c. He describes these periods as times when the Cretans were the most unhappy and the most enslaved. The analysis here suggests that, at least in the Venetian period, there are other reasons for general church construction (claiming areas where there was new activity connected to a specific set of resources, marking boundaries) which might also affect the construction of 'overhang'/'rock shelter' churches.

5.4 Sphakia under the Turks

The Turkish capture of Crete initially had little destructive effect on the landscape of Sphakia, sacred or otherwise: the major change was that the power of taxation had moved from Venetians to Ottoman hands. The Turks had no wish to convert infidels anywhere; they wanted only to tax them.[93] Indeed, we believe that the (17th –) 18th c. was the time of Sphakia's largest population.[94]

Outside Khania and Rethymnon, there were few mosques in West Crete; the mosque nearest to Sphakia was set up in the central church in Kantanos Selinou. As for Turkish presence in Sphakia, few Turks lived there; some worked in Khora Sphakion, the then administrative centre of Sphakia.[95] Nonetheless the Revolt of Dhaskalogianni began in Anopoli in 1770, and the consequences were severe: Anopoli and other villages in Sphakia were burnt. The memory of this revolt has remained hugely important until today, both inside Sphakia, and outside it. [96]

---

[93] Turkish census and taxation records for Sphakia are preserved in the archives in Istanbul; they reveal, among other things, that the Turks started taxing Sphakia before they had conquered the rest of the island. Dr Machiel Kiel discovered these records and did a preliminary assessment of them for us; they will be studied in an article written jointly by M. Greene, S. Price, L. Nixon, and O. Rackham. On the issue of Turkish taxation of Sphakia see Parlamas 1953, 235–8.

[94] In Anopoli there are three neighbourhoods which may have been established in the (17th–)18th c.; footnote 79 above. There are four neighbourhoods which are not mentioned in the 17th c. documents: Riza, Pavliana, Mariana, and Vadhiana. Mariana has a church with bacini, which date to the Venetian or Turkish period, so the church at least is old. But the other three neighbourhoods do not have churches (though Ag. Aikaterini is said to belong to Riza). Riza spreads east of Gyro and is hard to separate from it. Neither Pavliana, near Limnia, nor Vadhiana was mentioned by Pashley who lists the other eight neighbourhoods of Anopoli (1837, II. 191). Pavliana was abandoned in the 19th c., Vadhiana in the later 20th c. I would like to suggest that Riza, Pavliana, and Vadhiana were perhaps post-Venetian neighbourhoods, founded in the 17th or 18th c.

[95] One possible sign of their presence is the piece of marble inscribed in Ottoman Turkish, reused as a step up to the altar in the church Ag. Apostoloi above Khora.

[96] The historical information in this and the next two footnotes was compiled by Simon Price for his chapter on the Byzantine–Venetian–Turkish epoch, to be published in vol. I of the final publication of the Sphakia Survey. I am most grateful to him for making it available for me to use here.
1770: Dhaskalogianni, who was from Anopoli, led the revolt of 1770, as a result of which the village was burnt. Destruction of Ag. Roumeli in 1770 still evident in 1834 and 1845 (Pashley 1837, II.263; Raulin 1869, 88). Destruction of Vronda, Vraskas and Komitadhes; then Mesokhori, Georgitsi and Tholos, ruins still (Mourellos 1950, I.159). Sphakia lost its flocks (Olivier 1801, II.202–213; Howe 1825/1907, I.123; Mourellos 1950, I.203–4). See also Triantaphyllidhou-Baladié 1988, 278 n.49, 288 n.78 (French consul reported that the Turks burnt all the villages of Sphakia).
Memory of Dhaskalogianni and his revolt: the *Song of Dhaskalogianni* was known to everyone in Sphakia. According to Marina Pyrovolaki, whose family is from Anopoli, even 20 years ago people in the village used to recite the *Song* together for entertainment. The first time I visited Sphakia in 1982, one of the people working on the boat from Khora Sphakion to Gavdhos spontaneously recited the two lines quoted above in n. 61. The statue in the square in Kampos in Anopoli commemorates Dhaskalogianni. One of the boats plying the coast of Sphakia is called the *Dhaskalogianni*. The new Khania International Airport, opened in the later 1990s, is named Dhaskalogianni Airport; there is a

The 19th c. saw several revolts affecting Sphakia. In 1821 houses were burnt all over Sphakia; flocks and ships belonging to people in Anopoli were destroyed. In 1824, more than 2000 olive trees in Anopoli were burnt. In the 1828 uprising in the Frangokastello Plain, FK CH 8 Ag. Kharalampos was equipped with gunslits.[97]

Spratt, visiting eastern Crete in 1853, describes the effect of a then newly refurbished church near Ierapetra:

> Upon [a] summit, at more than 3000 feet [1800 masl] above the sea, there is a Greek chapel dedicated to the Holy Cross (Hagios Stavros), which having been recently restored and whitewashed, shines against the dark peaks of the Lasethe range bounding the view above and behind it, as a bright star resting upon the mount, and as if intentionally placed by the Cretan Christians as significant of the rising cross, thus elevated conspicuously over the recently fallen minarets of the towns (Spratt 1865, vol. I.269).

It is interesting that Spratt saw such huge symbolic meaning in this small chapel – literally for him a beacon church proclaiming the triumph of Christianity.

The major revolt of 1866 had a double effect on the landscape of Crete in general and that of Sphakia in particular: first, churches as well as houses were again destroyed all over the island[98]; and second, Turkish forts were constructed from 1868 onward, often in extremely conspicuous locations, such as Ag. Roumeli, the Anopolis Ridge, and Askyphou. The fort on the Anopolis Ridge was close to AN CH 1 Ag. Aikaterini; according to local legend, the Turks first tried to build the fort on top of the church but every time they began there was another accident, until finally they resigned themselves to a slightly different spot to the

---

small display about Dhaskalogianni and his Revolt inside it.

[97] 1821: Burning of houses, churches, trees in Asphendou, Impros; destruction in Brosgialos, Khora, Komitadhes, Mouri, Loutro (Mourellos 1950, II. 400–401). Khora, Impros, Kallikrati, Askyphou burned (Lamprinakis 1890, 55, 57, 58). Mouri 20 people killed (Lamprinakis 1890, 54). Destruction of Sterni (5.02) (Papadhopetrakis 1888, 19). Loss of flocks and ships by Anopoli (Pashley 1837, II.311; Papadhopetrakis 1888, 21). Meeting of revolutionary council in Loutro: Spanakis n.d. II.

1824: Upwards of 2000 olives in Anopoli burned in 1824 (Pashley 1837, II.243; Raulin 1869, 72–4), which may account for the peculiar lack of older, larger olive trees in the Anopolis plain. Great number of burned and ruined houses at Anopoli (Pashley 1837, II.242).

1828: legend of Dhrossoulites in Frangokastello – see catalogue entry for FK CH 7 Ag. Nikitas; cf. footnote 41.

[98] 1866: Khora houses ruined in 1866, but restored by 1890 (Bourchier 1890, 193).
Destruction of churches:

> Tomadhakis 1974, 161: 204–9 (= *Kr.Chron.* 8 (1954), 7–43), list of churches damaged in 1866–9. Stillman 1966 [1874], 131–138: Samaria: Stillman 1966 [1874], 131–138: church, with tiles, [in Samaria area], Byzantine?, is the only church on Crete, outside line of permanent occupation, which had not been desecrated (in phase three of the insurrection); Stillman 1976 [1867], Appendix C: 20 December 1866 General Assembly (at Sphakia) to Stillman: p. 131 'All the churches and other sacred edifices have been profaned and destroyed, all the villages and habitations have been burned or demolished entirely, and forests of fruit and other trees burned.'

west of the church.[99] Nor did the destruction end in the 1860s; at least one traveller to Crete saw many recently desecrated churches in the 1890s.[100]

As for Sphakia itself, its boundaries changed. Under the Venetians, the eparchy had ended just east of Patsianos; Pococke saw the wall dividing Sphakia from Rethymnon. In 1867, however, Sphakia was enlarged to include one more commune with three villages, Kapsodhasos, Skaloti, and Argoule.[101]

As we have already seen, two new churches were built in Frangokastello during this period, in Kapsodhasos (1836) and in Patsianos (1848). My hypothesis is that the first eikonostasia may have been built in the later 19th c., beginning the trend of marking boundaries of ever decreasing territorial units which continued into the 20th c. Specifically, I have suggested that three icon stands in Anopolis (AN IK 4, 5, and 16) may be 19th c.

A traditional practice involving churches, nearly all of them exokklisia, is first attested directly in the 20th c. but almost certainly goes back at least to the Turkish period: this is xekatharisma, the 'cleaning out' after cases of suspected perjury in cases of theft (chiefly animals but other property as well). Suspects had to take an oath that they were innocent in a church; three of the Sphakiote churches are exokklisia located on actual commune boundaries. Clearly, both the boundaries and the notion of churches as structures making them visible are built into the practice of xekatharisma. Xekatharisma is discussed in greater detail in the next section, where details of the relevant churches are given.[102]

5.5 Sphakia in the 20th Century

The 20th c. saw huge changes in Sphakia as elsewhere in Greece, but on the whole it is the economic changes rather than the political ones which are reflected in the landscape. The short period of Cretan independence with Prince George as High Commissioner; the complete incorporation of Crete into the modern Greek state; two world wars separated by the Exchange of Populations; the Junta; the advent of PA.SO.K (PAnelliniko SOkialistiko Kinima, ΠΑνελληνικό ΣΟσιαλιστικό Κίνημα Panhellenic Socialist Movement) – none of these is legible

---

[99] There are Turkish forts in several locations in all three of these places (Ag. Roumeli, Anopoli, and Askyphou). In Ag. Roumeli the most conspicuous is the big one on the west side of the foot of the gorge. In Anopoli, it is the fort on the ridge near the church AN CH 1 Ag. Aikaterini; for the associated legend, see Fielding 1953, 210 and cf. catalogue entry for AN CH 1. In Askyphou, the more conspicuous fort is the northern one. For a *church* built soon after the departure of the Turks, see again the church on Mt Lykavittos in Athens, discussed above.

[100] Bickford-Smith 1898, 70–72.

[101] Pococke 1743–45, II.1, 241: 'To the east of the castle they shewed me the foundations of a wall, which, they said, was the boundary between the territories of Sfachia and Retimo.'

[102] Animal theft was certainly part of life in Sphakia before the 20th c.; Papagrigorakis 1959, no. 6, presents a document of 1788 which discusses it. But I know of no pre-20th c. documents which explicitly mention xekatharisma as a way of resolving conflicts over animal theft.

in the landscape. Only the entry of Greece into the EU can be read there, because of the economic consequences of this political move.

Four main economic developments have marked Sphakia. First, rural emigration has resulted in the death of the summer/winter village system, which can be seen in deserted or partially deserted settlements at both 'middle' and 'down' altitudes.

The second is road-building, which destroyed old links between villages and created new ones. For example, the village of Mouri was on the way from Askyphou to Anopoli, because that was the route of the main footpath; but the main car road takes a different route, more or less due south of Askyphou. Thus even if Mouri had not been strafed by Germans in World War II it would almost certainly have 'died' as a village. And in Frangokastello the new village of Ag. Nektarios, built on the car road, has effectively replaced the old village of Kolokasia/Ag. Georgios, which was bypassed. [103]

The third economic change has come through European Union subsidies for shepherding and farming. People no longer have to leave Sphakia in order to make a decent living, but the old agro-pastoral system involving the use of summer pastures 'up' in the White Mountains is dying out.[104]

Fourth, the advent of serious tourism in Sphakia has meant new prosperity for locals, seen in the construction of new private houses in inland and coastal villages, as well as rent rooms, tavernas, and hotels, chiefly on the coast.

At least some of the significant changes in the landscape must still be sacralised, even when there are no invaders, or perhaps more accurately, especially when invasive changes are welcomed with open arms. It is striking that the power of icons remains crucial, both in churches and eikonostasia, and in purely secular settings.[105]

In terms of new placements for sacred structures, metal eikonostasia are now used to mark both crossroads and accident spots on car roads, just as they were built to mark them on monopatia and kaldirimia. But contact with the supernatural, benign or otherwise, is far less likely to be mentioned as the reason for erecting them. Older people talked freely and matter-of-factly to me about their fears of exotika such as dhaimones at crossroads, or neraïdhes at the edges

---

[103] The village of Samaria in the homonymous gorge was more or less dead by 1962 when the Forest Service bought out the local families in order to establish the National Park of Samaria; there were at the time only three old people living there. The broken ceramic font whose fragments were found by the Sphakia Survey outside Ag. Georgios in Samaria (1.22) could be seen as evidence for the decline of the village – no more baptisms, because no more children living there. (It could also be that the ceramic font was replaced by a metal one before everyone left.)

[104] See Nixon and Price 2001 for a discussion of pastoral transhumance in Sphakia.

[105] Examples of icons in purely secular settings: the box office of the then new and very smart Attikon movie theatre in Khania, 1997; one of the smaller offices in the new Athens airport, opened in 2001. But note the icon stand without an icon, FK IK 3; and cf. the memorials in Plymakis 2001b, 80–83, all without icons.

of villages (e.g. AN IK 9). By contrast, younger people, if they mentioned exotika at all, were rather shamefaced about 'superstitious' beliefs. Indeed, neraïdhes generally have metamorphosed from extremely dangerous creatures, lurking at the margins of safe, civilised village space, to (good) 'fairies', who might grant a wish to a child: in 2002, a supermarket in Kastelli Kissamou outside Khania sold a toy mirror which told children that the neraïdha in it would grant their wishes. And a gift shop in Kythira, also seen in 2002, was called Neraïdha without any fear of frightening customers!

Similarly, new exokklisia and eikonostasia are built in areas made accessible, and therefore economically viable, by roads; they make important resources (pastoral, touristic) visible, just as their predecessors did. The following have already been mentioned above: the church near Askyphou built on land now used as pasturage; the icon stands AN IK 7, near an EU-subsidised sheepshed (hypostego, υπόστεγο) and AN IK 17 where land is now used for pasturage; and the church at Ta Marmara below Aradhena where tourists now go swimming, and can even spend the night in the new rent rooms. Thus even though icon stands are no longer apotropaic, at least not of exotika, they are still apotropaic or 'thankful' in connection with accidents or their prevention. They are still needed, and so are the exokklisia – but for personal rather than public marking.

As areas like Sphakia become increasingly less self-sufficient, and more dependent on the external world, so too the landscape is marked differently: during the 20th c. ever smaller boundaries are marked by eikonostasia: first the space between neighbourhoods, and then the space right outside private houses. The new concrete 'church' eikonostasia are designed to be plugged into the householders' electrical system, instead of having candles which could be lit by passers-by. It is also important that these new eikonostasia are bought in garden centres, rather than in 'holy shops'. Thus collective space is less important, while individual space is emphasised.

The reflection of this shift from collective to individual in contemporary material culture has implications for archaeological analysis, which cannot be discussed in detail here. But it is worth noting that there are other material correlates of the shift, in addition to the changing placement of icon stands: Kenna discusses the change from family vaults in fields to more individually differentiated memorials in village cemeteries (Kenna 1991, 117f.); communal facilities in villages, such as ovens and fountains, have been replaced by electric stoves with ovens, and piped water in individual houses; and the pottery used for eating and drinking has changed from a repertoire of large bowls and dishes from which people ate shared food directly, to a system with individual place-settings. This change from a self-sufficient way of life, which required co-operation within villages, to a more individual lifestyle where people depend more on the outside world, has also been noted by du Boulay.[106]

---

[106] The shift from collective to individual was also mentioned above in connection with name days

Along with the decline of co-operation and the rise of individualism came signs of secularisation in 20th c. Greece, perhaps heralding the beginning of separation of the Greek Orthodox Church from the modern Greek state. For example, civil (rather than religious) marriage became legally possible in the 1980s; and while Greek identity cards (taftotites, ταυτότητες) still give the holder's religion, it is now possible for people to say that this might not be a good idea, in a way that once would not have been possible.[107]

The placement of Greek (national) government signs marking the beginning and ending of villages could be seen as a material sign of this secularisation. I have yet to see a single church or icon stand erected to accompany these signs.[108] Does this mean that the old forcefield of villages, which required sacred marking, has been superseded by modern boundaries, which do not? And similarly, the boundaries of the new demes are marked only by signs, again put up by the Greek government; I have seen no churches of icon stands sacralising these new, larger-scale boundaries. Is this lack of sacred structures another sign of secularisation?

I suggest that in both these cases, villages and demes, the important factor is local perception of external authority and internal responsibility, and that this perception may well be something that has not changed very much. The communes were always the largest units whose boundaries were marked by churches, built (as far as we can determine) by people who lived and worked in those communes. We have already seen that the Venetians were surprised by the resistance to their plans offered by people living in the communes around Navarino, who clearly expected to control their own destiny (cf. p. 73 and n. 91; Davies 2004, 109). Churches marking eparchy boundaries are relatively rare, and may well mark them only accidentally. Thus churches such as Prophitis Ilias (1.04) and Ag. Pnevma (2.37) were probably built to mark the border(s) between adjacent communes, which happen to lie on either side of the line between two eparchies, not the border between the eparchies. It is scarcely surprising, then,

---

and birthdays (p. 21 and n. 22). The communal oven used by villagers in Pitsidhia (Mesara) for baking bread and paximadhi, still in use in the 1980s, was destroyed (to khalasane, το χαλάσανε) in order to free up central space in the village for new houses; M. Kadhianakis 2004. The magnificent Venetian fountain in Siva (Mesara) built of cut stone and adorned with sculpture, incorporated basins for drinking water, areas for washing clothes, and troughs for animals; it is now maintained as a historic monument. Du Boulay talks about the time before and after people in Ambeli went to Katerini (on Euboia) during the Greek Civil War (1974, 242–249, especially 247–249).

[107] The menu for formal Cretan wedding feasts remains exactly the same, whether the marriage is civil or Orthodox: boiled meat served with pilaphi and lemon is followed by roast meat with potatoes. But it still matters which religion you declare in Greece, as witness the enormous and violent controversy over Karakasidhou's 1997 research, which suggested the possibility of non-Greek, non-Greek Orthodox (in this case Slav) input to Greek culture.

[108] I have seen the reverse: FK IK 1, put up in 1982, is now accompanied by no fewer than six signs, including a national government road sign, and an EU trail sign (E4); see FIG 3 and catalogue for details.

FIG. 3: FK IK 1. Icon stand of Ag. Ioannis Khrysostomos at intersection, with six signs (road signs, E4 trail sign, hotel signs). October 2003.

that the boundaries of the new demes have not been marked with churches or icon stands: demes, like eparchies, are not seen as units within local control, but rather as areas created and maintained through higher, external levels of government. And so also for the Greek government village signs: these too are imposed from outside, and are thus unlikely to receive sacred marking by local insiders.

In both Anopoli and in Frangokastello we can see that the scale of sacred marking has decreased, with ever smaller units now being sacralised, down to the level of individual houses. As we saw above, this change is one of several signs of a shift to greater individualism, and contrasts strongly with the construction of ever-bigger governmental units. But secularisation may not be the right word to apply to these changes in the sacred landscape. It is not so much that the landscape has become more secular, but rather that the perceived level of responsibility for sacralising it has become even more local than before. Whose sacred landscape is it? A century ago it would have 'belonged' to communes and villages. Now, at least some aspects of the sacred landscape seem to belong to individual householders.[109]

---

[109] In terms of 'large-scale' uses of the sacred landscape, FK CH 7 Ag. Nikitas is now the focus of a very deme-oriented festival, marked by the inclusion of larger and more varied groups of people,

But one larger-scale practice involving sacred markers continued well into the 20th c.: xekatharisma (ξεκαθάρισμα), the 'cleaning out' of disputes over animal theft, in which suspected perjurors had to take an oath that they were innocent in a church. In the early 20th c. there was a special meeting (sygkentrosi, συγκέντρωση) near Khora Sphakion at the church of Thymiani Panagia (8.01). Animal theft had become so rampant that existing methods of keeping it in check, which presumably already included xekatharisma, had failed. Politicians and others outside the eparchy met with local shepherds to try to eliminate the problem. Their attempts were not successful, however: both theft and xekatharisma continued well into the 20th c., both in Sphakia and in other parts of Crete. One informant said that there was a xekatharisma in Sphakia as late as the early 1990s (at Ag. Astratigos, 3.20); both practices continued in other parts of Crete as well (see below on Herzfeld).[110]

Six churches in Sphakia have been mentioned as suitable for xekatharisma, four of them exokklisia (1.17, 3.01, 6.03A, 8.01). Three are on commune boundaries: Ag. Astratigos (3.20, in the village of Aradhena on the edge of the gorge separating it from Anopoli), where the most recent xekatharisma within Sphakia was done; AN CH 5 Timios Stavros (6.03A, on the boundary separating the communes of Anopoli and Khora Sphakion); and Thymiani Panagia (8.01, on the boundary separating the communes of Impros and Asphendou). The fourth church, Ag. Pavlos (3.01), sits on the shore between the villages of Ag. Roumeli, Ag. Ioannis, and Aradhena, though not on either of the relevant commune boundaries. The fifth, Ag. Zoni, is just outside the village of Vouvas (8.05). The sixth church, Ag. Nikolaos (1.17) near the Y of the Samaria Gorge, is later, 19th c., rather than Venetian; it may mark a crucial line between the village of Samaria and the Omalo Plain to the north which became important towards the end of the Tourkokratia.[111]

---

coming from longer distances, and by car. The annual saint's name day service on 15 September 2004 was attended by six priests, including a bishop; people from various villages (e.g. Khora Sphakion and Vouvas as well as the two closest ones, Patsianos and Kapsodhasos; children bussed in from Khora Sphakion; representatives of the police and coast guard, the latter in dress uniform; and men in suits (seldom if ever worn by village men) representing various levels of government; see catalogue entry for FK CH 7. At the highest level of Greek government, broadcasts of the prime minster and other top politicians going to church and cracking eggs at Easter are still de rigueur on Greek national television.

[110] For the practice of xekatharisma, see S. Kelaïdhis 2003 [1960], 23–30, P. Kelaïdhis 1981, 106–15, 1982, 154–5. Both write as though the practice were no longer common in Sphakia. Mr Kanakis Geronymakis also gave me oral information about xekatharisma in 2004.

[111] S. Kelaïdhis and P. Kelaïdhis, op. cit. discuss all except the last of these churches; S. Kelaïdhis is the only one to mention Ag. Pavlos.

Ag. Nikolaos, Samaria Gorge (1.17): the 19th c. construction of this church suggests that the use of resources in this area had changed; the church is not on a commune boundary, but may mark some crucial line which had become relevant to the use of the Omalo Plain to the north.

Ag. Pavlos (3.01): the location of this church has been discussed in some detail above on p. 62.

Xekatharisma for Sphakiote shepherds could also be done outside the eparchy, for example at the church of Ag. Nikolaos in the area called Kerameia, at the roots of White Mountains (on the north side), in the eparchy of Kydhonia.[112]

Herzfeld's anthropological work establishes that animal theft and xekatharisma were commonplace in the late 1970s and early 1980s in the area around the village of 'Glendi' near Rethymnon. His research has provided a positive social reason as to why animal theft – a practice which has seemed negative to outsiders and insiders alike – has continued to occur: it can be a way of forming alliances between men ('we steal to make friends'). Alliance-building also helps to explain the existence of supra-regional churches for xekatharisma: they provided another place for shepherds to meet. People from 'Glendi' used a nearby exokklisi for xekatharisma (Ag. Georgios at Dhiskouri), but they also used at least three supra-regional churches for it, Ag. Nikolaos in Kerameia, already mentioned; Ag. Georgios near Dhramia, on the border between the eparchies of Apokoronas and Rethymnon; and Ag. Georgios in the gorge of Selinari near the town of Neapoli in eastern Crete.[113]

Ag. Astratigos, Aradhena (3.20): protects the dangerous, gorge-side eastern edge of the village of Aradhena; see also p. 81 above; cf. also Fielding 1953, 213 for this church.

Timios Stavros, Mouri (6.03A) = AN CH 3.

Thymiani Panagia (8.01), located 500m south of the village of Komitadhes across a major revma: see also Spanakis 1991, 1.308.

Ag. Zoni, Vouvas (8.05), underneath overhanging crag, cf. Plymakis 2002b, 174); miracles reported here, Papadhopetrakis 1888, 29. Kanakis Geronymakis is the informant for the use of this church for xekatharisma, because of its miraculous icon (pers. comm. 2004).

[112] The church of Ag. Nikolaos in Kerameia is in the eparchy of Kydhonia (nome of Khania). Herzfeld 1990b, 312 discusses the use of this church for xekatharisma by people living in Rethymnon nome; Geronymakis (pers. comm. 2004) by people living in Sphakia.

[113] A negative inside view of animal theft: S. Kelaïdhis categorises animal theft as one of the three scourges of Sphakia, along with the abduction of women, and the practice of vendetta (2003[1960], 21–47.

Herzfeld on animal theft and alliance-building, 1985, 174–194; xekatharisma, 1985, 194–205; 1990a, 114, and 1990b. Kondylakis in his novel *Patouchas* (1987 [1891], 44 describes serial sheep theft as a way of maintaining a kind of equilibrium.

Churches used by Glendiots for xekatharisma:

Ag. Georgios at Dhiskouri, near the village, Herzfeld 1990b, 309, 310; cf. Spanakis (n.d., 154–155) notes that Dhiskouri is between the villages of Leivadhia and Veni, and mentions the role of the wonder-working icon in the church of Ag. Georgios for xekatharisma

Ag. Nikolaos in Kerameia, Herzfeld 1990b, 312, and cf. Spanakis n.d, 206–207 for the area of Kerameia

Ag. Georgios in Dhramia, Herzfeld 1990b, 309; Spanakis n.d., 165 notes that the area was inhabited mainly in the winter months, by people from Sphakia who left for their mountain villages in the summer

Ag. Georgios in Selinari Gorge near Neapolis, Herzfeld 1990b, 309, 310

Other churches used for xekatharisma: monastery of Ag. Georgios at Karydhi, southwest of Vamos, Herzfeld 1990a, 114.

Saints with xekatharisma churches (in addition to Ag. Georgios and Nikolaos, and the Sphakiote

While insiders and outsiders agree that a suitable church for xekatharisma must contain a miraculous icon (thavmatourgi, θαυματουργή, literally wonder-working), there is little detailed discussion of the precise location of such churches. Herzfeld (1990b, 306) describes them in general terms as 'remote and deserted'. He makes an important observation when he says that the monastery church of Ag. Georgios at Dhiskouri near Glendi is 'accessible to all the surrounding villages but removed from them all' and therefore 'neutral territory' (1985, 204). But the location of several of these churches on or near important boundaries suggests that these invisible lines also play a role in the selection of churches for xekatharisma. Indeed in some cases these boundaries may be the very ones broken by animal theft – similar to the situation described in the document of 1435 discused above (p. 69).[114]

This does not mean that everything stays the same: the landscape in Sphakia, sacred and otherwise, is changing, and in a changing landscape, decisions have to be made about the old and the new. Churches, both inside and outside villages, are often the last structures to be maintained and used after settlements have been deserted. In most parts of Sphakia, the annual leitourgeies are still held, recalling past kin and other relationships, and re-animating old patterns of land use. The actual distance between exokklisia and the nearest village(s) from the participants in these services have to to travel is no predictor of whether a church will be maintained, nor is the visibility of the church; the major determinant is the strength of the perceived connection with the area. Whitewash, at least nowadays, does remain a crucially visible indicator: a church which is no longer whitewashed is no longer part of a landscape in current use. We saw earlier (p. 57) that the two churches in the Trypiti Gorge, Prophitis Ilias (1.04) and Ag. Nikolaos (1.01) were both maintained. Indeed, up to the year 2000 at least, the annual service was still celebrated in Prophitis Ilias, even though the only settlement here was abandoned in the Turkish period, and the only economic use of the Trypiti Gorge, by people from Ag. Roumeli, consists of winter pasture for goats, plus beehives. The two churches are accessible only by boat, and, furthermore, while Prophitis Ilias remains conspicuous by land and by sea, Ag. Nikolaos is effectively invisible, because it lies behind a high cliff near the bottom of the gorge. In this case, out of sight is not out of mind: Ag. Nikolaos, like

---

saints listed in note 111 above): Timios Stavros and Ag. Phanourios; plus St John the Divine at one church 'near the south coast', Herzfeld 1990b, 309.

And note also that one quarter of a stolen sheep was commonly promised to Panagia in village church at Myriokephala (just east of Sphakia) if a raid was successful, Herzfeld 1990b, 308.

[114] Herzfeld does say that in order to assure secrecy, Glendiots and Tholiots may choose to do xekatharisma in 'a small and almost deserted church in the tiny village that lies between their respective communities' (1985, 204), implying that this church sits in a line separating the two villages. It is interesting that xekatharisma is not mentioned in the document of 1435, but it would be unwise to say definitely that it must therefore be a later practice.

Prophitis Ilias, still remains a node in the local public memory network (cf. again Carruthers 1998, 54–55).

A vivid example of memory and forgetting in the landscape comes from three churches in the area of Khora Sphakion. Ag. Apostoloi (6.18) and Ag. Pavlos (6.23) were mentioned above in connection with the pasturage treaty of 1435, and should therefore date to the earlier Venetian period. The former is a relatively large, architecturally complex, and extremely conspicuous church at the top edge of a still inhabited neighbourhood of Khora, frequently mentioned in discussions of Byzantine architecture and frescoes; the latter is a cowshed (in architectural terms) of similar date, also marking the boundary line discussed in the pasturage treaty, on the old route from Khora Sphakion to the small settlement at Ta Dhikhalomata, which has been deserted since 1900. Yet Ag. Pavlos was still in use (just) in 1992 when we last visited it, while Ag. Apostoloi when visited in 2003 was beginning to slide into ruin – massive cracks in the façade, the chandelier fallen, and its glass pieces scattered on the floor. Scholars like us find it painful to see an architecturally and historically distinguished church like Ag. Apostoloi falling apart, but that feeling of connection belongs to us, not to the people who actually live in the neighbourhood of Mesokhori, for whom the boundary marked by this particular church is no longer relevant. Ag. Pavlos, on the other hand, was maintained partly because people in Khora Sphakion still felt a connection with the summer village of Kaloi Lakkoi to the north. Maintaining the church was a way of making it clear that that landscape was also still alive and in use.

The third church in the area of Khora Sphakion is the small chapel of Ag. Antonios (6.07), in a very conspicuous location 100m north of the neighbourhood of Bros Gialos. It is now completely ruined and doorless, functioning mainly as a casual shelter for sheep and goats. Just below the chapel is a bee enclosure, in which both older and modern wooden beehives and a beekeeper's protective suit were abandoned. Chapel and bee enclosure lie above the old footpath to the neighbourhood of Georgitsi to the west, which has been abandoned for some fifty years. Settlement in Khora Sphakion has shifted from higher up to lower down, and tourists have replaced bees as one of Khora's resources. This part of the local landscape is economically dead, and the church has died with it.

In the Frangokastello study area, the two 'dead' churches of FK CH 4 Ag. Astratigos (8.38) and FK CH 5 Ag. Ioannis Vokolos (8.48) point up some of the same issues, and also raise others. Both are relatively close to the village of Patsianos; Ag. Ioannis Vokolos is only 250m southwest of the village, and Ag. Astratigos lay on a footpath and is now visible near a car road. Yet the other nine churches have remained in use, and most have even been refurbished: FK CH 1 Ag. Theodhoros has been repainted, FK CH 7 Ag. Nikitas has a new gate. Even FK CH 2 Ag. Ioannis Prodhromos (8.25) – much farther away from Patsianos and a short climb after the car road peters out – is still standing, and in good order. Once again, economic activity gives us some clues as to why some churches are maintained, while others are neglected. Bees are kept near Ag. Theodhoros; Ag.

Nikitas lies in the vibrant touristic area by the sea; and there is still shepherding near Ag. Ioannis Prodhromos, perhaps because of the spring above it.

The issue raised by these and other churches is that of responsibility, touched on earlier in the discussion about increasing scales of authority and government, and decreasing scales of areas to be marked with sacred structures. While householders now take sole responsibility for 'their' eikonostasia, whose responsibility is it nowadays when churches (or 'shared' icon stands) fall apart? This is an area which would repay further research, but I can suggest two kinds of local answers to this question. In some cases, people are certain that the maintenance of exokklisia is the responsibility of the state, specifically the Ephoreia of Byzantine and Later Antiquities. Thus if a church falls down, it can be seen not as descration by ruin and collapse, but as the result of inefficient (national) government – certainly not something that locals need to do anything about. For example, when local people discuss the collapse of the frescoed church of Ag. Ioannis Vokolos, they say things like 'Why didn't the Ephoreia fix that church up? It's a disgrace that *they* [emphasis mine] let it fall down, etc.'

In other cases, local people simply take responsibility for repainting and refurbishing churches themselves (Ag. Theodhoros, Ag. Ioannis Prodhromos, Ag. Nikitas as above). Once again, what determines the maintenance or neglect of a church is the strength of the perceived connection with it. A final piece of evidence for this assertion can be seen in the restoration of exokklisia. The church of Ag. Spyridhon on the north edge of the village of Ag. Ioannis (3.08) was restored in 1991. It had been a roofless ruin like the two 'dead' churches of Ag. Astratigos and Ag. Ioannis Vokolos; a metal icon stand had been put up inside it. Moreover the village itself was nearly deserted. There had been no school for some time, and very few people lived year round in Ag. Ioannis. The construction of the bridge over the Aradhena Gorge, complete in the late 1980s, made for a jump in land prices in the area of Aradhena and Ag. Ioannis, but not for an increase in permanent residents.

Yet a group of people, including residents of other villages in Sphakia and Ag. Ioannis 'expatriates' living in Khania and even further afield in Montreal, raised the money to restore Ag. Spyridhon. The number of different surnames (six) suggests that they are not all members of the same kin group; both women and men were involved. Inside the church, a plaque records the list of people who contributed the money or labour, and a framed photograph shows what it looked like when roofless and ruined. My interpretation is that the donors found it so painful to see one of their own churches ruined and destroyed – a church representing part of their locally distinguished heritage – that they needed to make the church 'live' again. In other words, however people react, however responsibility is assigned, everyone understands what the demise of an exokklisi means: it is the visible disintegration of a particular landscape, a break in continued communication of memory, heralding the eventual death of the meaning associated with it. If a church dies – if a node in the public memory network ceases to function – then that particular part of the landscape dies as well. To restore a church is thus to resurrect both the meaning of the landscape around it, and to reconnect it to the public memory network for that area.[115]

The public display of inscriptions such as the donor list for Ag. Spyridhon raises some important questions about the construction and preservation of memory. Inscriptions in older churches in Sphakia are relatively rare: the early 14th c. church of Ag. Georgios (8.03) below Komitadhes is unusual in having painted inscriptions recording the names of the founders, Emmanouil Skordhylis and Georgios Phorogeorgos, as well as the name of the fresco-painter, Ioannis Pagomenos. In 20th c. Sphakia, it became more common to display written information about donors on plaques in churches. In the case of Ag. Spyridhon, the inscription makes it clear that this was a restoration rather than a new church, but no explanation for the restoration was given. Thus although it has become more common for specific donors to be recorded, it is still uncommon to give a specific explanation for restoration or construction; Ag. Nektarios between Skaloti and Argoule, discussed below in the paragraph on gender, remains exceptional. Increased literacy does not mean more or different information being written and read in churches and icon stands.

It is sufficient, then, for the particular explanation for building/restoring a church or erecting an icon stand to be known to the builders and the people they choose to inform at the time, even though people are aware that this information can be forgotten relatively quickly, and that in any case human memory is fallible. For example, no one I talked to in Anopoli could remember which saint AN IK 16 was dedicated to, let alone who dedicated the icon stand and why; the major kaldirimi on which it stands went out of use less than 50 years ago.

I conclude that as in earlier periods, it is the general meaning of a church or icon stand which remained important in the more literate 20th c.; specific explanations relating to builders and donors of churches and icon stands are not, in most cases, important enough to be remembered in the longer term. The grammar of location works whether or not you can remember or 'know' the total history of a church or icon stand. The mere presence of the structure in a particular location tells you that there is something important about that place – that is why it is there. No further explanation is required.[116]

---

[115] The whole issue of responsibility would bear further investigation. Herzfeld (1991, 57–58 and cf. 160 and 273 n. 2) has studied the difference in local response to buildings in Rethymnon defined as 'Venetian' or 'Turkish' (Venetian was always better than Turkish). But in the case of churches there is absolutely no doubt that these structures are part of Greek, Orthodox life. The selectivity in their preservation/restoration is therefore all the more interesting. For the restoration of another ruined church, see note 52 above on Ag. Dhimitrios outside Kapsodhasos. For similar issues in the restoration of churches in the area of Paliochora on Kythira, see Diacopoulos 2001; the author is one of three members of the Australian Paliochora-Kythera Archaeological Survey who are of Kytherian descent. Cf. Kenna on the restored church of Panagia Kalamiotissa, Anaphi (2001, 200–201).

[116] In section 5 below I discuss related issues of memory. People did volunteer fairly precise

Finally, it is possible to say something about gender and how it relates to the construction and restoration of churches and icon stands for the 20th c. Anthropological research reports a very rigid ideology of separate physical and metaphysical spheres for women and men in modern Greece, including religious life. For example, men are priests and sing in leitourgeies in churches; women are not priests, and sing laments (moirologia, μοιρολόγια) outside at funerals).[117] My own observations suggest that nowadays at least women and men have more flexible roles to play; whether this greater gender flexibility was always part of the creation of the sacred landscape, or whether it has to do with changing gender roles in the last decades of the 20th c., I cannot say, although I suspect the latter.

The gender of specific saints is irrelevant in terms of location, as we saw earlier. The selection of specific saints is not obviously related to the gender of the donor(s). Both women and men can be involved in the decision to erect a church or an icon stand. Both women and men can contribute to the construction/ restoration of churches and icon stands, as in the example of Ag. Spyridhon. Both women and men can be memorialised by a church; for example, the church of Ag. Nektarios between the villages of Skaloti and Argoule was built in 1984 by a son in memory of his mother, and dedicated to a male saint; and the church in Askyphou was built to commemorate the donor's uncle, mentioned earlier. Women can certainly bear some of the responsibility for maintaining sacred structures; this assertion is however based on my seeing one woman repainting one icon stand in Anopoli.

At the end of the 20th c., churches and icon stands, new and old, were still very much part of the landscape. Their use and deployment had changed, but their architectural vocabulary and their location, in spatial terms, remain the same. Outlying churches in particular remain a very clear index of economic activity and resources.

---

information about the more remote past, as in the case of the ancient city of Anopolis, probably because they had learnt about it formally in school; cf. Nixon 2001. But when I asked how old AN CH 1 Ag. Aikaterini was, people said that it had been there 'for years'. Similarly, the specific date of the church (for which there is no evidence) said to underlie AN IK 11 was unimportant; the important thing was to mark and remember this earlier significant structure. And no one ever linked an older church to a particular kin group, even though presumably some of them might well have been constructed by members of one or two extended families. Thus in the case of the recently ruined church FK CH 5 Ag. Ioannis Vokolos people in Patsianos did <u>not</u> say, for example, well, all the members of that kin group have left the village, and that's why there is no one to look after the church any more.

[117] Alexiou 2002; Seremetakis 1991; and cf. du Boulay 1974, chapters IV and V on gender roles in Ambeli (Euboia). It is important to realise that *ideology* may insist on rigid gender separation but that *reality* is often rather different. Thus for example, the traditional ideological place of women was in the house, and that of men was outside it (du Boulay 1974, 129) – but in reality women did hard physical labour in fields and vineyards (du Boulay 1974, pl. 4 facing p. 90, showing a couple loading harvested oats onto a donkey).

5.6 Natural and Cultural Landscapes

It is time now to reconsider the 'natural', environmental constraints that affect the location and distribution of outlying churches and icon stands. It is almost certainly the case that the dissected terrain found in many parts of the Greek world, and strikingly in Sphakia, might favour the development of small, conspicuous structures, simply because they can be seen from multiple viewpoints, often over long distances. Here I discuss two environmental questions relating to the landscape of Sphakia, the relative lack of sacred structures in the summer pastures (Madhares), and the different distribution of churches and icon stands in Anopoli and Frangokastello.

The first question relates to the almost total absence of sacred structures in the 'up' level of the summer pastures (Madhares), such as those above Anopoli; see TABLE 4 for the contrast between this area and other parts of Sphakia. There are in fact only two, the church of Ag. Pnevma (2.37); and an icon stand just below the peak, set up to commemorate the death of Nikolaos Platsidhakis in 1998 (Plymakis 2002a, 27–32). Ag. Pnevma performs the familiar boundary-marking function known at 'middle' and 'down' levels. At 2264 masl, it marks a multiplicity of boundaries, relating to life at 'middle' altitudes: between two eparchies (Sphakia and Apokoronas, on the south and north sides of the White Mountains); and between three communes in Apokoronas, whose southwestern boundaries converge here. It could be explained as a way for an exokklisi to prevent disputes over contested terrain, by making boundaries visible over long distances (cf. the discussion of xekatharisma above in sections 5.4 and 5.5 on Turkish and 20th c. Sphakia). Only its altitude is exceptional. But why are there not more churches and icon stands in the Madhares?

I propose two different answers, one functional and one phenomenological. The functional explanation has to do with the natural environment of 'up' altitudes which is, in local terms, extremely unnatural, compared with those of 'middle' and 'down'. First of all, there is permanent snow for much of the year, but running water is scarce. Second, there is little soil of any kind, except in the small basins between the conical hills, where plants suitable for grazing manage to survive; potatoes can also be grown here. Third, not only are there no olive trees (perceived by many Greeks as emblematic of the culture of 'home'), there are no normal trees at all: those that grow here have adapted to cold and to browsing, and tend to be small and low, if not actually 'flat'. In short, the resources considered necessary to sustain life year round are missing from the Madhares. Although the area was certainly used in the Byzantine–Venetian–Turkish epoch, as in earlier periods, its resources are not sufficient to merit 'systematic' marking with churches.

And finally, there is the disorienting mist (i omikhli) which makes it impossible to see anything. No church or icon stand would be the slightest help to you. If there is mist, you either know where you are and which way to go, or you do not. In fact you need to wait in a safe place until the mist has cleared, otherwise you are likely to die, either quickly, by a fall, or slowly, by cold and exposure. In short, 'up' is a place where at any moment the landscape can turn on you, with the odds against your survival.

The phenomenological explanation is linked with perceptions of 'up' altitudes. In a landscape unmarked by any natural homely features, it is perhaps not surprising that there are few cultural homely features either. Traditionally, women and children did not go 'up'; only men and boys old enough to walk long distances took sheep to the Madhares.[118] Thus 'up' has no connection with family life. The only structures in the summer pastures are the huts for cheese-making (mitata) which often have a small room in which shepherds sleep. The mitata are made out of local stone, as houses are, but their form is different, and they are not white-washed. Moreover they almost never have icons; I have seen only one. Now, if a house without icons is 'a shelter for animals' (du Boulay 1974, 54), then mitata canot be proper houses.[119]

I conclude, therefore, that although women and children could go up to the Madhares, although 'proper' houses could be built there and equipped with icons, and although churches and icon stands could be constructed there by women and men as they are below, none of these cultural things happens because the very environment up there is felt to be too risky, too unnatural and too deficient. There exists a strong contrast beween the unmarked, unsanctified, dangerous, male landscape of 'up', and the fully human altitudes of 'down' and 'middle', where churches and icon stands create a safe, sacralised landscape for families.[120]

The second environmental question relates to the different distribution of churches and icon stands in Anopoli and Frangokastello. I believe that we can account for this difference by considering the relationships between particular systems of sacred marking on the one hand, and particular types of environment on the other.

---

[118] There are good reasons for women of child-bearing age to avoid direct contact with animals: the zoönoses which can cause spontaneous abortion. But this contact has to be managed at the 'down' and 'middle' altitudes ; it is not simply that women escape this contact by not going to the Madhares in the 'up' altitude. See Nixon and Price 2001.

[119] Confirmation of the idea that mitata fall into the 'shelters for animals' category comes from the following observation: the only place in Sphakia where I have ever seen a pornographic image of a human female openly displayed was on the wall of a mitato in the Madhares above Anopoli.

[120] It is quite wrong to assume that women (and children) are somehow immobile, and needed to stay 'at home' where 'home' is a single fixed place, because they always used to move from 'down' to 'middle' or vice versa, e.g. from the winter village of Khora Sphakion with its four neighbourhoods to the summer village of Kaloi Lakkoi; it was only the 'up' altitude above Kaloi Lakkoi, with its summer pastures and mitata, to which they did not move; cf. Nixon and Price 2001, 403–404. Moreover much women's work is solitary e.g. collecting brush or plants needed for textile production; Dimen 1983, Nixon 1999. And women in later life, at least in other areas, may travel for religious reasons, for example, to visit shrines; Hirschon 1983.

The environment of Sphakia, as in much of Crete, consists of dissected terrain with discontinuous stretches of arable and a broad altitudinal range. But it is clear even from diachronic comparisons that the environment of Crete does not evoke a single sacred response. In other parts of the island where there is more evidence for sacred landscapes, it is immediately obvious that the grammar of location for Minoan religion is different from that of the Graeco-Roman period, and that both are different again from the grammar of location for the Byzantine–Venetian–Turkish sacred landscape.

The environment does not determine the language(s) of sacred marking, but it does have an effect on how a particular language is deployed or 'spoken'. My view is that in the case of Sphakia, what the environment can, and in the case of Sphakia does, determine is how a particular language of sacred marking is used in micro-landscapes such as those of Anopoli and Frangokastello. But the link between environment and sacred landscapes is neither direct, nor unmediated by other factors, of which the particular grammar of location is paramount.

We can see the effect of the Byzantine–Venetian–Turkish grammar of location in two ways. The first is to do with resources. Religious systems will tend to sanctify, among other things, the means of subsistence in their original culture – as Christianity from the beginning sanctified bread, wine, olive oil, and sheep – but it is not always necessary for places of worship to be physically related to those means of subsistence in terms of their location.

In the Byzantine–Venetian–Turkish system, however, it seems that it *is* necessary to mark some resources on site: from the beginning, there is a compulsory combination of locations for sacred markers, outside as well as inside settlements, with the largest territory being the commune. In general it may be that free land-holders controlling relatively small properties will tend to construct a grammar of location not only sanctifying their mode(s) of subsistence, but also marking particular resource areas where they occur in the landscape.

Thus mountain plains consisting of alluvial basins punctuated by rocky outcrops are more likely, in Sphakia at least, to have non-nucleated settlements with churches placed on the rocky outcrops; as a result, the multiple neighbourhoods of Anopoli have more internal, liminal spaces requiring marking by icon stands, with a smaller number of churches outside neighbourhoods. Larger plains with uninterrupted stretches of arable, such as Frangokastello, are more likely to have nucleated villages with a greater number of exokklisia and a smaller number of icon stands. Other micro-landscapes show similar patterns: the Askyphou Plain is like that of Anopoli, while the fertile Amari Valley (Rethymnon nome) with its distinguished exokklisia resembles the Frangokastello Plain.[121]

---

[121] Askyphou has already been mentioned as one of several mountain plains in Sphakia with non-nucleated villages; p. 33; for its icon stands, see p. 54, TABLE 4 and p. 58. Cameron 2003, 341–343 lists no fewer than six exokklisia with datable frescoes in the eparchy of Amari, including Ag. Anna, with

The second way in which the Byzantine–Venetian–Turkish grammar of location affects the deployment of sacred structures in the dissected terrain of Crete is the insistence on a particular kind of visibility, and often intervisibility, of churches and settlements. The village of Anopoli lies in a part of Sphakia where resources are thinly spread; it cannot be seen from other villages, nor can it be seen from the sea. Only the beacon church of Ag. Aikaterini AN CH 1 makes the village visible over long distances by land and by sea. The Anopolis Ridge, a natural feature, interrupts sightlines to village churches for people approaching from below, hence the placement of icon stands such as AN IK 4, 6, and 16 at closer range.

In the general area of Frangokastello, where resources are more generously distributed, their visibility is heightened by exokklisia. FK CH 2 Ag. Ioannis Prodhromos and FK CH 11 Ag. Georgios are intervisible: standing at either one, you can look along the study area from west to east or east to west, and you can see nearly all the churches in between them, as well as the two villages of Patsianos and Kapsodhasos. In both cases, it is important for settlements and resources to be made visible by the small structures characteristic of this particular system of sacred marking. The micro-analysis of small sacred landscapes such as Anopoli and Frangokastello within a larger system provides a level of detail which illuminates the whole.

---

some of the earliest wall-paintings in Crete (late 12th c.), Gerola 1993, 299 and n. 505; and the cruciform church of Ag. Paraskevi, Gerola 1993, 210 fig. 182 (plan), 212 fig. 190 (photograph) of the pl. 14.2 (colour drawing of fresco with inscription of founder, Khortatzis family).

6

CONCLUSIONS

6.1 Defining and Claiming Sacred Space:
the Grammar of Location

I would like now to discuss the grammar of location which underlies the placement of individual outlying churches and icon stands. A brief comparison with sacred landscapes in other periods may be helpful (see also section 6.3 below on recurrent patterns in sacred landscapes, with TABLES 8 and 9). Peak sanctuaries in the Minoan period lie on relatively low hills near settlements; in Sphakia Survey terms, they lie at down or middle altitudes, like the outlying churches of Prophitis Ilias discussed above (in section 3.2). Cretan temples in the Iron Age can mark the boundary between two poleis, as well as occurring within them. These are relatively simple 'grammars' to understand, in spatial terms. The grammar of Late Roman basilicas has not been fully understood, although it is true to say that many of them are near the sea, in settings reflecting the safety of coastal locations in the Roman period.

But outlying churches and icon stands are different. There are more of them in a given landscape, and their relative density can be highly variable and may co-vary with local patterns of land-ownership[122]; they have a broader range of locations; they mark a wider variety of features, whose spatial logic I have attempted to unravel, and they come with explanations which may not always explain why they are exactly where they are, but which nonetheless need to be taken into account.

I will return to the question of explanations below. For now I want to look at the idea of continuity within sacred landscapes, because I feel that it has obscured important issues connected with the Byzantine–Venetian–Turkish sacred struc-

---

[122] Kenna 1976, 1994–95, 454 (more than 70 outlying churches on Anaphi, about two per square mile); Tinos has over 700 outlying churches, and there are several in each village as well, Dubisch 1995, 62, though their seemingly greater number may be because of the poor preservation of earlier structures and sacred area.

tures discussed here. It is true that some outlying churches (and this applies more to them than to icon stands) do lie on or near Minoan peak sanctuaries (e.g. the church on the peak sanctuary on Kythira), or on temples, or on Late Roman basilicas, or in one case in Sphakia, a temple and basilica (Panagia on the coast below old Ag. Roumeli, 1.28).

But what looks like continuity of location, I would submit, is not that at all. It is rather an overlap in locational grammar, which is a very different thing.[123] The language of Byzantine–Venetian–Turkish outlying churches happens to include suitable locations for peak sanctuaries, temples, and Late Roman basilicas, but it is a different language with its own grammar. The grammar of Byzantine–Venetian–Turkish exokklisia is a way of expressing the capabilities of the landscape (hence the emphasis on resources such as water and good land), and it also belongs to the language of contested terrain. Each icon-bearing church declares the value of some part of the landscape, while claiming it on behalf of Hellenic Christianity. To begin with, these claims were made against the perceived threat of the Arabs (both Dhigenis Akritis', and the Spanish Saracens of Crete). In terms of location, this meant a number of early coastal exokklisia, as exemplified by Ag. Pavlos (3.01), on one of the outside edges of Sphakia. Sacred marking of the landcsape continued in the Venetian and Turkish periods. Over time, the externality of the disputed units usually decreased, and more and more the claims were internal. In the 20th century and afterwards, every exokklisi still has the potential to make a conspicuous declaration about local and 'national' claims to sacred space in particular, and the overall landscape in general.

Some may think that I am overstating my view that outlying churches and icon stands are part of a Hellenic Christian attempt to lay claim to the Greek landscape, an attempt which can itself be securely located in time and space. Let us therefore look at some examples of what happens when Greek sacred space is threatened and invaded. In the past, temples were turned into churches, and then into mosques, as in the case of the Parthenon (Travlos 1971, 456–457; Nixon 2004, 435–439). Pagan landscapes were often aggressively Christianised in late antiquity, as in the case of Aphrodisias (Cormack 1990, Smith and Ratté 1995; and for the general phenomenon cf. Price 1999, 164–71). Churches changed into mosques were often changed right back again after 1821, or whenever the Turks left a particular part of Greece.

---

[123] Hasluck in his *Christianity and Islam under the Sultans* (1929) spends a considerable amount of time on the question of cult continuity; in his view it is dangerous to assume that two cults in the same location necessarily represented any kind of direct continuity from the older to the younger: 'In the case of urban cults particularly a special *caveat* must be entered against the arbitrary assumption that, because a church was taken over by the conquerors and used as a mosque, the *religio loci* was transferred with the building' (p. 6). And further on p. 8, he notes that although churches and mosques are both congregational religious buildings, they do not share an identical assemblage of functions. He does not, however, develop any ideas about the grammar of location affecting whole sets of religious buildings in a particular time and place.

But one of the most compelling examples is far more recent: the Rock War (Petropolemos) of Kalymnos which took place in 1935, when the island was under Italian occupation (Sutton 1998). The Italian governor wanted to separate the dioceses of the Dodecanese from the Patriarchate in Istanbul. The Kalymnians thought that Papal authority was to be imposed on Orthodox churches, and they feared a de facto conversion to Catholicism. When a local priest was interrupted during a liturgy in early 1935, he was first protected by the largely female members of the congregation, and then smuggled off the island by them. The Kalymnians then closed all churches on the island for two months. In early April, there was a rumour that the Italian administration was going to open the churches; bells announcing services were to be rung at the main church in the harbour of Kalymnos, near the water's edge. Women gathered in the harbour square (plateia) to prevent the bell-ringing, and were galvanised into further action, in defense of their church and their religion, when they heard them being rung. Later the Italians interrupted a procession of women by attacking a group of nuns and smashing their processional cross. On the third day after the beginning of the uprising, women gathered in the harbour plateia once again, and stoned the Italian soldiers gathered there, while additional Italian reinforcements were attempting to disembark. The churches remained closed for two years with service being held in secret, until in the end the Italians gave up the attempt to make the Dodecanese autocephalous.

The Rock War was the largest protest against the Italians during their 30-year rule of the Dodecanese. The women who protested achieved both a victory, and 'the right to raise high the banner of Orthodox faith and tradition' (Kapella [1986, 102], cited in Sutton 1998, 91). Moreover, Sutton notes that the incident is connected locally to other perceived religious threats, both older (the legend of the Cave of the Seven Virgins, a story of women's bravery during the Tourkokratia) and more recent (a small group of Jehovah's Witnesses proselytising on Kalymnos). The women's response to the Italian challenge was very precisely located in space, focussing as it did on first on the church with the interrupted service, and then on the main church of the island right by the sea, where invaders actually arrived (Sutton 1998).

The grammar of location for churches and, later, icon stands is a Byzantine–Venetian–Turkish phenomenon, which has some spatial overlap with earlier sacred landscapes, but a significantly different meaning. The grammar of location for Byzantine–Venetian–Turkish churches makes it possible for people to define, maintain, and use sacred space in a culturally appropriate way, and to declare their position in the landscape. The only Venetian church in Sphakia was inside the fort at Frangokastello (FK CH 12), and there was never a mosque anywhere in the eparchy. But I would submit that churches in Sphakia, as elsewhere, can be seen as positive declarations of allegiance to Hellenic Christianity, as well as responses to real threats from historically known invaders (Arabs, Venetians, Turks; and cf. Dubisch 1995 on Tinos and again Sutton 1998).

Reading the landscape of Sphakia through the language of churches and icon stands can give an accurate view of threats, real and perceived, to local (and national) definitions of sacred space. At the beginning of the period, points in the landscape seen as vulnerably valuable or dangerous will receive the protective marking they require. The kind and degree of value or danger may change but the basic nature of the markers does not. In this particular system, you still nearly always need a container for an icon in order to mark things properly, even if that container is only a relatively small icon stand.

6.2 Locations and Explanations: Spatial and Social Views of Sacred Landscapes

In this book I have argued that there are consistent spatial patterns which explain the location of exokklisia and eikonostasia. Specifically, I have distinguished four major types of location – resources/new activity, visibility, liminal areas, earlier significant structures – all of which can be deduced through the spatial analysis of these sacred structures within the landscape. I have also suggested that there may be a recurrent ratio of settlements to exokklisia, such that there is a 'package' of one settlement to around two outlying churches. In areas with more resources, of whatever type, there will certainly be more settlements and more exokklisia, but the settlement:outlying church ratio remains the same, as the comparison of Regions 4 and 8 shows (see again TABLES 4 and 5, plus TABLE 6 comparing Sphakia and Kythira).

It is true that one of my aims was to find, use, and test the kind of material evidence which any archaeologist could use for robust and reliable analyses of sacred landscapes, both in Byzantine–Venetian–Turkish Sphakia, and in other times and places. The reality of archaeology is that being able to interpret material evidence in this way is of fundamental importance. This is not to say that I have ignored the explanations for churches and icons stands available to me in Sphakia, i.e. the oral information provided by local people, and documentary evidence from legends, documents, and maps. I have classified these, too, into four major types – human boundaries, supernatural contact, specific events and places, and vows. But it was difficult to find a robust way of combining the two categories of information, in terms of incorporating explanations into an originally locational archaeological analysis.

Some people may think that in the end I have somehow privileged location over explanation, indeed that I have overemphasised a rational view discernible only by academic outsiders, while dismissing the 'irrational' experience of the people who actually live in the landscape. For example, it might be easy for some people to say that the four types of location were functional and pragmatic, while the four types of explanation were fanciful, superstitious, and ultimately irrelevant to archaeology. The ultimate example of this blind pragmatism would be to use the information about the locations of outlying churches, and to a lesser extent icon stands, merely to help find archaeological sites, both Byzantine–Venetian–Turkish and earlier; see Appendix 4 for further discussion. But the whole question of location and explanation is more complicated, and more interesting, than that.

Before I began the first major phase of analysis for this book, I recalled the common archaeological fantasy that if we archaeologists could only speak to the people whom we know only from material evidence, we could know so much more. I thought rather smugly that studying sacred structures which people were still building would enable me truly to understand the sacred landscape of which they were a part.

After the first major phase of field work for this book, I was frustrated by what I then saw as a gap between the grammar of location, revealed from actual evidence of churches and icons stands on the ground (i.e. perceivable through normal archaeological means); and the oral explanations which local people gave me, which explained why a sacred structure was built, but not where it was built. This discrepancy, as I thought of it, was not what I had expected, and I didn't like it.

TABLE 7 will show the sort of thing I mean. It includes churches and icon

TABLE 7: Locations and explanations revisited.

	LOCATIONS	EXPLANATIONS
Ta Marmara church (pp. 24, 55, 78, 97, 100, and 124) Region 3	*1. resources/new activity* beach where landowner brought tourists by boat and built rent rooms	*?!* 'because he wanted to build a church'
Askyphou church (pp. 24, 78) Region 7	*1. resources/new activity* area now used for pasture, on new dirt road	*3. event* in memory of landowner's uncle
AN CH 2 Ag. Nektarios	*3. liminal area* just outside neighbourhood of Kambos	*3. event (future)* expatriate who wanted a place to be buried here
AN IK 9 Ag. Panteleimon	*3. liminal area* edge of neighbourhood, jct of two footpaths	*2. supernatural contact* dream that neraïdhes would kidnap wife here
FK CH 7 Ag. Nikitas	*1. resources/new activity* good arable; *4. earlier significant structure* LR basilica	*3. event* church was built at same time as fort
FK IK 3 Vranakis Memorial	*1. resources/new activity* side of paved car road (straight stretch with poor visibility), near large group of tourist establishments	*3. event* death in car accident here
icon stand below Skaloti (pp. 31, 51) Region 8	*1. resources/new activity* shore area with some arable (stous Lakkous tis Skalotis) where fishing done	*3. event* death by drowning during fishing here
Tinos, Church of Panagia (1822) (Dubisch 1995, 134–136); above, pp. 29–30, 94	not enough information	*2. supernatural contact* vision of Panagia tells nun to dig in a field and build a church here

stands from the two study areas, from other parts of Sphakia for which I have both locations and explanations, and from the island of Tinos. It is true that most explanations stress the 'here-ness' of something – it was here that a nun had a vision of the Panagia, it was here that there was a fatal accident, it was here that the boundary between two communes lay. The church or icon stand shows exactly where something significant happened or was, as Herzfeld has correctly pointed out (1990a, 116–117). And it is also true that there is a recurrent theme of danger connected with the icon stands – stories about demons at junctions, neraidhes, and accidents, actual or averted, do reveal the dangers of specific liminal spaces, and therefore help to explain why an icon stand is precisely where it is. One icon stand in Anopoli (AN IK 9, liminal in location, explained by malign exotika), and another in Frangokastello (FK IK 3, linked with economic activity, explained by a fatal accident) suggest that people should be careful in these three particular places. But if explanations are given for the construction of outlying churches, they usually explain why the church was built, but not where it was built. Thus the church of Ag. Ioannis Prodhromos (FK CH 2), built close to the line separating two communes, is typical of others in having no 'border' information in its explanation. Even the legends associated with FK CH 7 Ag. Nikitas explain the location of the basilica (on the site of an ancient city's altar), but say nothing about the placement of the later church (see catalogue entry for a summary of these legends). And the explanation given for the construction of the exokklisi at Ta Marmara contains no spatial information whatsoever.

Another common explanation given for building outlying churches is that they commemorate a family member. Such explanations do not, however, include a specific reason for the actual placement of the church. Further questioning will usually establish that of course the church is built on land belonging to the family, but not why the particular plot was selected. Only outside observation can add that the location is usually determined by new activity. Clearly, then, accounting for the specific location is not always a high priority for local explanations; the point is to construct a visible memorial for one's relative in a suitable place, and the definition of a suitable place – on a piece of family land that ensures at least some visibility for the church – is perhaps too well understood to require explanation. The very visibility of churches and icon stands, essential for the preservation of memory, was never mentioned as a reason for building a church in a particular place, even though local people use these sacred structures in order to orient themselves accurately in the landscape.

In general, therefore, there seemed to be almost a complete dislocation between the two categories of location and explanation. Structures erected because of events do not have similar locations. Structures erected because of resources do not have similar explanations.

My next step was rueful recall of the archaeological fantasy described above. We would indeed know more if such conversations were possible, I thought, but we would not necessarily learn what we expect from them. How paradoxical (I continued) that people who live in the midst of a symbolic system – even when they are the ones who construct it – cannot always see it for themselves. It is the outsiders, I thought loftily, who are better able to see the patterns, whether they are anthropologists studying the present, or archaeologists studying the past. In other words, I was reverting to the old chestnut: 'If anthropologists were goldfish, the last thing they'd see was the water they swam in'.[124]

At this point, I had a choice to make. I could simply have given up on any attempt to reconcile location and explanation – indeed one anthropological colleague suggested that I do precisely that. After all, I had stressed that the 'grammar of location' was susceptible to external observation and basically consistent over time, whether or not we have access to local explanations, present or past. You could say that in establishing and reinforcing this principle, and in deducing the grammar of location for exokklisia and eikonostasia, I had therefore done my job as an archaeologist.

But serious archaeology has for some time included the attempt to get 'beyond subsistence and dating', and to find methodologically sound ways of getting at meaning. Once I knew that explanations routinely included information not immediately knowable through an analysis of locations – information which I hope I have already shown has added hugely to the nuance and depth of the picture presented in the chronological sections above – I could not exclude them.[125]

And even if I had viewed my archaeological responsibilities in this way, studying all of the second millennium A.D. including the 20th c. for my work on the churches and icon stands – a century not included in the larger archaeological survey in Sphakia, which ends with the departure of the Turks in A.D. 1900 – meant that I was taking on a different, and ethnoarchaeological, kind of responsibility for my enquiry. I felt that I couldn't simply give up on locations and explanations, and that there must be a different way of looking at these questions, a way of finding a link between them so that a view based on locations could be amplified and refined by information from explanations.

Once again, comments from colleagues helped me to find a different and better perspective. First, John Bennet, another archaeologist with anthroplogical leanings, pointed out that my questions were spatial, whereas the answers I got were social; I was interested in landscape and my informants were interested in people. And second, Renée Hirschon, an anthropologist, suggested that it was important to know whether local people were themselves aware of things like

---

[124] It is to some extent true that people within a symbolic system do not necessarily perceive all of it fully. See Appendix 3 for a discussion of two Greek attempts to distinguish location and explanation. But I do not for a moment believe that people outside a symbolic system, whether anthropologists or archaeologists, automatically get everything right.

[125] The phrase 'beyond subsistence and dating' is the subtitle of Charles Redman's influential book *Social Archeology* (1978).

commune boundaries – in other words, was it that they simply didn't know where these boundaries were nowadays, or was it that they didn't see this information as relevant in explaining why churches and icon stands were built where they were?

My initial reaction to these comments was that as an archaeologist I had to be spatial – archaeologists really cannot usually talk to the people whose material culture they are investigating – whereas I couldn't see why my informants had to be only social in their answers. Why couldn't they be both social and spatial? But eventually these comments enabled me to ask a new and different question: is there any evidence that local views of the sacred landscape overlap at all with the locational view that I was putting forward? And it was then that I could move forward again.

In this next section I want to discuss how my own view of sacred landscape in Sphakia overlaps with the views of local people, in terms of the following factors: the overall significance of outlying churches and icon stands; their use in orienting people as they move within the landscape; their underlying association with important features of the landscape; the performative aspect of exokklisia and eikonostasia; the meaning of their condition (regular maintainance, or ruinous neglect); and finally, their value in learning, knowing, and recalling the landscape.

In the early stages of this research, I began to ask local people about specific examples of outlying churches and icon stands. Now of course we had been asking people for local information from the beginning of our work in Sphakia – water sources, the placement of agricultural terraces, the mitato system, footpaths and kaldirimia, and toponyms for the archaeological and other sites which we were exploring. But the conversations about exokklisia and eikonostasia were different. People were really pleased that I was asking about these structures: at last I was asking about something of real importance to them. They were impressed by my growing knowledge of churches and icon stands, especially when they saw that I was familiar with those not on car roads, which therefore require a fuller knowledge of local topography than merely driving around could ever provide. Indeed, people even volunteered information as well as answering questions, so that my picture of the churches and icon stands in their area could be as complete as possible.[126] People were genuinely pleased to be giving me information about something which had longterm meaning for them, and was also relevant in the here and now. It was the status of the outlying churches and icon stands as sacred structures in the local landscape which made them important; their actual age was irrelevant. As someone who could recognise the overall significance of these structures, I was therefore worth talking to.

---

[126] In our research people living in Sphakia nearly always answered direct questions, but they tended not to volunteer archaeological information, preferring to wait until we had already noticed something before commenting on it.

At the very beginning of this book I described how I had unconsciously begun to use outlying churches in order to orient myself in the unfamiliar landscape of Sphakia while participating in the overall archaeological survey project (p. 2). In my conversations with people, it was clear that they, too, used outlying churches and icon stands as landmarks, for example by mentioning individual churches as reference points when giving directions. In this case their own 'native' experience of these structures as points of orientation dovetailed with my newcomer's experience of their landscape. Again, it is important to remember that Sphakia as an area of highly dissected terrain and relatively low population is potentially dangerous for anyone, permanent residents and transient researchers alike. Anything that can help you find your way safely will be useful.

But to return to visibility: local people never used the abstract noun visibility (in Greek oratotita, ορατότητα), much less intervisibility (dhioratotita, διορατότητα), as an important quality in selecting a spot for a new church or icon stand. Thus when I asked about the then new church at Ta Marmara, people would never say that when Mr Orphanoudhakis built the church at Ta Marmara he chose a spot so that people could see it from different areas, by land and by sea. But when I asked how to get to X or Y, people would give directions in the following form: go along this path or road until you can see the church of Ag. Ioannis or the icon stand on the road to the Madhares (AN IK 6).[127]

Similarly, it is true that when asked about the location of a church or icon stand, people never mentioned resources as the explanation for building a sacred structure in a particular place. But occasionally, during longer conversations about small areas, it became clear that people did associate resources, often a cluster of resources, with a particular outlying church. One example is FH CH 2 Ag. Ioannis Prodhromos, which I knew lay very close to the commune boundary between the villages of Kolokasia/Ag. Nektarios and Patsianos, as well as an important route between them. I was talking about the bog near Kallikrati and people started listing other 'wet' places near Frangokastello, including Pano Nero, the spring near Ag. Ioannis. So the church of Ag. Ioannis made several significant landscape features visible. It remains, true, however, as we saw earlier, that visibility itself was never discussed.

As for commune boundaries, they were never mentioned as a reason for placing a church in a particular spot. But this does not mean that people didn't know where they were: they did, and particularly if they were born before 1960.

---

[127] It is interesting that the visibility of AN CH 1 Ag. Aikaterini was never mentioned, even though it is one of the most usefully visible churches in Sphakia in terms of orientation. I do not know if this omission is linked to the continued presence of the adjacent Turkish fort, whose existence cannot be mentioned because of the local chronology of desire which says that 'the Turks never set foot in Sphakia'. It is all the more surprising as the church is built on and among older structures, whose date *is* generally known and discussed. The Thick Wall (pakhy toikhos) not far away was mentioned over and over again by inhabitants of Anopoli; cf. Nixon 2001, 81–82.

People are almost always keenly aware of anything, including boundaries, which affects their economic life; they just didn't talk about them as I would have done, that is, in relation to the churches. Now that the commune boundaries have been superseded, there is less reason than ever for people to mention them.[128]

It is not enough to mark the landscape: it is essential to perform it as well. Thus the yearly services at exokklisia on the name day of the saint are more crucial than one might think for such anniversaries. Similarly, the lighting of oil lamps, candles, or incense burners in or near eikonostasia is an important sign of their continuing use and significance. Exokklisia (and also eikonostasia) are not functioning properly unless they are used – indeed the landscape of which they are a part is not functioning properly unless these sacred structures are used. The practical use of the landscape is thus made visible by ritual acts at regular intervals in outlying churches, and to a lesser extent at icon stands. The structures are there all the time, but it is their liturgical use which, so to speak, lights them up in the landscape, and provides the link between here and now, and here and then, for the community, however that community is constructed.[129]

Since the second half of the 20th c., many of the people at an annual leitourgia may well not be permanent residents in the nearest village or even in the general area. I know of people living in Khania who went every year to the service at Prophitis Ilias in the Trypiti Gorge, near an area still used for bee-keeping and pasturage, though no one has lived there for 200 years. People express anxiety about the retirement of the 'area priest' in Sphakia who has for sometime now taken responsibility for taking the services at remote churches. 'When Papageorgi retires,' they say, ' no one will do the leitourgeies at the exokklisia any more'. The services at exokklisia are performative in the sense that they represent the use of the church and of the surrounding landscape: no service, no church, no landscape.

---

[128] Geronymakis 1996, 10 gives the boundaries relevant for the commune of Asphendou; these were defined in 1956. Asphendou has borders with the communes of Askyphou, Impros, and Patsianos. The boundaries consist of lists of toponyms, given on p. 13, shown on the map at the end of the book. Geronymakis does not say whether the 1956 boundaries differ from those of earlier periods. Cf. also the catalogue entry for FK CH 2. Manolis Kadhianakis, whom I interviewed in April 2004 about churches in the southwestern Mesara, knew exactly where the local commune boundaries were; he was at that time nearly 90.

[129] Cf. Carruthers 1998, 55–56 on the importance of processions in early Christian Rome:
'During Easter, for example, each major basilica (the Lateran, Santa Maria Maggiore, St Peter's, San Paolo, San Lorenzo, Sancti Apostoli, Santa Maria ad Martyres) was visited in the order of the importance of the saints in the city's life. The journey thus provided a walk-through, in processional order, of the city as memorized network, for clergy, laity, and neophytes alike. Each basilica was a node of this network, a site for memory-making: and at other seasons, other churches were incorporated into the stational schemata.'
Of necessity the performance of a *landscape* such as Sphakia is different, in that it is the cumulation of many liturgies throughout the *year*; a larger space requires a longer time for the necessary set of performances.

The performative aspect of exokklisia explains the significance of ruined churches: quite simply, they represent a ruined landscape. As an outlying church begins to fall apart, so also the surrounding landscape disintegrates. People know very well what it means when churches goes out of used or area allowed to fall into disrepair and ruin, even if they are not able or willing to articulate the meaning to themselves or to outsiders. In some cases, as we saw earlier, the church or icon stand is allowed to fall apart. That particular part of the landscape is no longer significant enough for the effort to be made to maintain its sacred marker. The church (and the landscape features which it marked) can be forgotten. In other cases, it can be too painful to let a church remain in ruins, and a campaign is launched to restore it, often by 'expatriates', as in the case of the church of Ag. Spyridhon in the village of Ag. Ioannis, where there are now very few permanent residents (pp. 85–86). Or it may be that a new phase of economic activity restimulates the desire to keep a church in good condition, as in the case of AN CH 5 Timios Stavros, which was nearly engulfed by gorge gravel when it was restored in the later 20th c. There may in some cases be tension between 'expatriates' who want to preserve the landscape as they remember it, and locals who can afford to forget some aspects of the area in which they actually live – but there is general agreement on the meaning of a ruined church.

And finally, it is possible to summarise a particular piece of landscape by recalling the exokklisia, as well as the villages, within it. I have heard people 'telling' a landscape by naming the outlying churches along with the settlements, and I have found myself doing the same. It is possible to visualise an area, its dimensions and resources, simply by naming its churches, and where relevant its icon stands.

To sum up, local people know that exokklisia and eikonostasia are importantly visible in the landscape, and that they provide a means of orientation and navigation. They know that these structures are directly associated with important features of the landscape, such as economically important resources and boundaries. They know that it can sometimes be important to mark earlier significant structures; and they also know that the presence of an earlier significant structure can confer additional prestige on a later one. Local people know that performing the landscape through liturgy, as well as marking it through structure, is necessary to keep the landscape as they use and experience it alive. They know very well what letting a church or icon stand fall into ruin means for a particular piece of landscape, and they are perfectly capable of choosing whether to maintain or to neglect individual structures – whether to remember or to forget individual pieces of landscape. Local people know that a landscape can be learned, known, and recalled by listing its churches and icon stands. Local chronologies of desire are thus constantly made and remade.

If local people do not tell outsiders about the links between churches and icon stands on the one hand, and resources, visibility, and boundaries on the other, it is not because they aren't aware of the connection – it is simply that accounting for the specific location is not a high priority for local explanations. Or, to put it another way, explanation is in the eye of the beholder: it all depends on your view of the landscape, and what you are trying to explain within it. This statement doesn't mean that local people are not aware of the importance of resources, visibility, and boundaries. Of course people know that these things are important – their economic survival depends on such knowledge.[130]

But all of this functional, pragmatic information is out in the open, literally visible on the ground, where anyone, even a newcomer, ought to be able to see and understand it. Local people may not explicitly connect locations and explanations in what they say, but they do know about both. What they tell you in their explanations is what you as an outsider could not know otherwise: the specific 'here-ness' which a sacred marker icon presents for memory or forgetting. This is precisely the kind of information which spatial analysis cannot tell you directly. But if you have both spatial and social knowledge of the churches and icon stands – the nodes in the local memory network, as Carruthers puts it (1998, 56) – then you can know the whole physical and metaphysical landscape of that area.

In Sphakia, local people explain churches and icon stands in social rather than spatial terms – these structures preserve the memory of specific ancestors, they remind people of danger, they recall supernatural encounters, they commemorate a vow. The sacred structures tell the informed viewer that here in this spot, right here and not somewhere else, is something which is important for them to remember. Though specific explanations for the structures can be forgotten, the general memory of the structures cannot.

The grammar of location is expressed by a structural language so that particular locations are made individually memorable by structures of a general form. These structures make the social and spatial aspects of the landscape visible, memorable, and sacred. They are both individually and collectively mnemonic of the landscape: taken singly, each church or icon stand carries a particular bundle of significance; taken together, they summarise the landscape. If you know the locations of churches and icon stands, you know what you need to

---

[130] Scholars are sometimes surprisingly patronising in their reaction to the necessary competence of people in societies 'less complex' than their own. Consider Binford, commenting on the Nunamiut, a group of indigenous hunters in North Alaska:

> Probably one of the first things to strike the reader is that there is an unrelenting demonstration that the Nunamiut behave rationally in their treatment of animal foods. This rationality is facilitated by a *truly remarkable* knowledge of animal anatomy. It is facilitated by a general outlook that is future oriented. (Binford 1978, 453, emphasis mine).

There ought to be nothing remarkable about people's expertise in matters on which their survival depends. And this from someone who can cope very well with the unexpected in informants' comments; cf. p. 39, where he describes how he had to change his research strategy on discovering that expressing personal food preferences was not culturally inbuilt for the Nunamiut.

know about the area and its physical capabilities. If you know the explanations for them, you know the society 'on the ground'. In this case, the churches and icon stands pin the social landscape to the spatial one, making the two congruent. Or to put it another way, the spatial and social aspects of the landscape are two sides of the same coin, and the link between them is made visible and memorable by sacred markers in the form of outlying churches and icon stands.

In earlier sections (Introduction, 3.4.1, 5.3, 5.5, 6.1), I spoke of the grammar of location and I wish to return to this theme now. The language of the outlying churches and icon stands is relatively simple, and relatively imprecise. It is made up of two different standardised units, exokklisia and eikonostasia, deployed in various locations in the landscape of Sphakia in various ways over time. The two types of sacred structure encode social and spatial aspects of the landscape, but they do not make precise statements – a church built in memory of an ancestor does not look significantly different from a church constructed because of a vision. To understand what a particular church 'says', the viewer must already know something about locations and explanations. Just as accounting for the specific location is usually a low priority for local explanations, so also the definition of a suitable place – on a piece of family land that ensures at least some visibility for a church, in the liminal area between neighbourhoods – is perhaps too well understood to require explicit discussion.

Even so, people do have a clear and consistent definition of 'a suitable place' which coincides with my own outsider's observation. Thus whatever churches mark, they mark it in the same way, to the extent that one can predict where a church would be built in a particular area, were it to come into the appropriate kind of use. Moreover, both outlying churches and icons stands are part of a visible system of marking the landscape which is recognised by everyone; people share the same grammar of location, and can use it to make landscape statements understood by everyone else. It is also true important that in this 'language', the medium constitutes a large part of the message – that is, the sacredness of the structures is an important part of the statement they make in the landscape, and perhaps compensates for the imprecision mentioned earlier. Certainly it is clear, and important, that the kind of memory being marked in the landscape is always a sacred one of a particular kind.

I turn now to the value of outlying churches and icon stands in learning, knowing, and recalling the landscape. Gosden and Lock have explored what they call prehistoric histories, distinguishing between genealogical history, which uses links with known ancestors, and mythical history, which works with information about the more distant past. Both types of history can co-exist at the same time, and both can be made manifest through ritualised actions at specific landscape features. Thus features in the landscape – in this case, the landscape of the Ridgeway in south Oxfordshire, from the late Bronze Age to the Romano-British period – can be thought of as the manifestation of social relationships,

relationships which physical effort, as well as rhetoric, can keep socially active (Gosden and Lock 1998).

What Gosden and Lock say about prehistoric landscapes in southern England can be applied to post-prehistoric landscapes in Crete. In other words, outlying churches and icon stands in Sphakia are also landscape features which can be thought of as the manifestation of social relationships, relationships which need to be kept active through 'physical efforts', such as the maintenance of these sacred structures, as well as 'metaphysical' work, including rituals such as the burning of incense, the lighting of candles and oil lamps, and church services.

That it is possible to apply, and apply directly, an analysis based on a prehistoric landscape to a 'post-prehistoric' landscape is important. Indeed, the only disagreement I have with Gosden and Lock is their suggestion that you have to be 'prehistoric', i.e. illiterate, in order to mark landscape in this way. People in any culture who live intimately with a landscape will be inscribing their social relationships on it. I suspect that the only conditions are close connection with a landscape, and a certain amount of control over it. Literacy is more or less irrelevant. For example, in landscapes where people do agriculture on a small, local scale (free land-holders vs slave labour on large estates or latifundia), there will probably be marking on a scale that reflects both intimate knowledge of a landscape, and the power to make decisions about its use – such as the exokklisia and eikonostasia which form the subject of this book.

One sign of that intimate knowledge is the naming of every distinguishing feature. Both small-scale agricultural societies and hunter-gatherers do this kind of topographic naming; it is important for both groups to know every lump and bump in the landscape. Many of these names will be purely 'natural' – compare the preponderance of natural names in the perambulation document discussed above, Treis Elaies (Three Olive Trees), or in other landscapes, Nine Elms. Landscape names like these – topothesies in Greek (τοποθεσίες) – may also be used to locate events, e.g. sto Aeroplano, 'at the airplane', near the ancient site of Kommos in the Mesara, where an airplane crashed during World War II. Topothesies may also indicate, in a way that Gosden and Lock's work more or less predicts, the presence of older human activity, as in the case of the toponyms recorded by Xanthoudides in the early 20th c. for some of the Early Bronze Age Mesara tholos tombs.[131]

---

[131] I heard the toponym 'sto Aeroplano' from workmen at Kommos Excavations in the later 1970s. The excavated area was on one of the hills known as Tou Spanou ta Kephalia, 'at the heads of the bald one'; these hills were so named because of the lack of ground cover; Shaw 1977, 204. Three examples of early 20th c. topothesies for sites where Xanthoudides excavated Early Minoan tholos tombs: To Minares (the minaret) near the place called Hagia Eirene; Tou Mpaïrami to Papouri (Bairam Hill) at the site of Porti; and oi Trokhaloi (the stonepiles/ruins) near the village of Kalathiana; (1924, 21, 54, 81). Two of these topothesies incorporate Turkish words, minares (minaret) and bayram (Muslim holiday, especially the major one at the end of Ramazan). We can see that there is definite time depth in these topothesies, new ones being added to old for particular reasons. At Kommos, sto

Indeed it is important to realise that even in literate societies these topographic names are seldom written down. I know of only one map giving local toponyms in Sphakia, and that is the map published by Geronymakis for the commune of Asphentou, which includes names such as Pano Nero (high water, the spring above FK CH 2). Other examples are a mixture of natural and 'historic': Vigla (watchpoint, usually a high conical hill, ultimately from Latin vigilia), Phokospilios (seal cave), Tourkolakkas (pit of the Turk), tou Sarakinou o Volakas (the Saracen's Boulder, where according to Geronymakis a Saracen was probably killed, pers. comm. 2004), and Batsinela (blackberry).[132]

I know of no other maps for topothesies for any other part of Crete or the wider Greek world. Traditionally these names were passed down orally from older people to younger ones, as part of the local knowledge essential for surviving in a particular landscape. But people's survival no longer depends on this kind of knowledge, and so the names are gradually being lost. If there is no one to 'tell' the landscape to future generations through the topothesies, then the names, and the information which they encode, will be lost.

We saw above (pp. 102–104) that in the Greek case, churches and to a lesser extent icon stands can serve as summaries and mnemonics for local landscapes. The topothesies give the microsopic detail of a particular landscape; the churches,

---

Aeroplano referred specifically to a World War II plane crash, but even without that knowledge, the term 'aeroplano' has a realtively narrow chronological range; Tou Spanou ta Kephalia is much harder to date. In the case of the tholos tombs, it is important to note the exotic nature of the Turkish names for these 'outlandish' sites, even if we cannot immediately understand the meaning. The use of Turkish in these toponyms cannot be earlier than the time in the Venetian period when Turkish words began to be known in Greek (G. Morgan 1960). Note also that Xanthoudides recorded topothesies, not ownership, 'the plot of so-and-so', which is how localities are most often identified by Greek archaeologists nowadays when explaining where archaeological material was found. The kind of name gives a clue as to who is doing the marking. Topothesies go along with intimate familiarity with the land, not with 'prehistoric' societies per se. For a detailed study of the sacred landscape of a hunter-gatherer society (which unfortunately does not discuss the naming of individual landscape features explicitly), see Peter Jordan's study of the Siberian Khanty (2003); cf. also Smith 1990 on the role of landscape features in the cults of early saints in Brittany. And, finally, note the kind of place-centred narratives recorded by Basso 1996, where named landscape features were used to instruct the people who live among them. I have not come across this particular use of Greek topothesies; either it is something which people did once do, but don't any more, so we are too late to get it; or the stories relating to saints and exotika are another version of the same thing. In all these cases, close knowledge of the landscape is fundamental.

[132] List of names in Geronymakis 1996, 10–13; foldout map in back of book. Number for topothesies mentioned in text: 61 and 308 Vigla; 69. Phokospelios; 84. Tourkolakkas; 260a. tou Sarakinou o Volakas; 281. Batsinela (note the proximity of moisture-loving Blackberry to the spring at no. 285); 284. Ag. Ioannis Prodhromos (FK CH 2); 285. Pano Nero; and note again 290. Dhigenis (p. 64, n. 75). Peristerakis (1991) gives lists of Sphakiote toponyms by village; he compiled these by going to villages and asking local people to tell him the toponyms relevant to their area. Because the toponyms are given in alphabetical order, and the book does not include any maps, it is not possible to locate most of them in real space.

the general outlines. As knowledge of topothesies begins to fade, the exokklisia and icon stands have become the only permanent markers which preserve any part of this intimate knowledge of a particular landscape, and the names for individual features within it. These sacred structures are therefore a fundamental part of our view of Sphakia – and every other part of the Greek world – where they have been built.[133]

This view of landscapes and the individual features within them can be applied to areas like Sphakia in the 2nd millennium A.D. Southwestern Crete in this period was not strictly prehistoric, but was and is certainly an area in which literate memory has played an intermittent role. There are two scales of memory, or as Gosden and Lock would put it, two historical scales in Anopoli and Frangokastello. One is smaller and more personal, represented by icon stands and newer outlying churches, which typically recall individual people from particular local families. They can also be connected with protection from present, local dangers. This small-scale memory is short-term, because the details of who precisely is commemorated will eventually be forgotten, even though the memorial structure remains in the landscape.

The second scale of memory is larger-scale, and linked mainly (though not exclusively) to older outlying churches. These older structures represent the grand narrative of borders and boundaries, whether of territory or of Orthodox Christendom. They are a form of long-term memory made visible in the landscape. If they go out of use, then both the memory and the meaning which inspired them are lost and then forgotten.

In between the two scales of memory is an intermediate stage of forgetting, in which literally historical, i.e. written history, becomes mythical. The church of Ag. Apostoloi (6.18), discussed above (p. 84) is an example of this transition from history to myth. No one now remembers the pasturage document written in 1435 which records the importance of Ag. Apostoloi as a boundary landmark. Indeed the existence of published documents about the significance of the church in the local landscape is entirely irrelevant. The resources and boundaries encoded by the church are no longer memorable, so people can forget all about the significance of the church, and indeed can let it fall apart before their very eyes. Thus in general when people forget what a particular church or icon stand means, the forgetting can be seen in the increasing dilapidation of the church. We can

---

[133] In connection with the names of topographic and other features, Harriet Blitzer quoted in Younger and Rehak 2001, 465 says rightly that this is the kind of knowledge of the self-sufficient life about to disappear for ever. If you don't have someone to 'tell' you the landscape then the names will be lost; cf. Zarinebaf et al. 2005, 146 n. 127. Cf. also Bryer and Winfield on the change from older Greek names to newer Turkish ones in Turkey (as a result of the post-Exchange of Populations chronology of desire which wishes to suggest that Greeks did not live in Turkey after antiquity). As Bryer and Winfield point out, 'the Pontic Turks have been deprived of their own past in a way even more radical than the departiure of the Pontic Greeks in 1923 (1985, vii).

thus track memory and forgetting through the physical condition of the churches (and sometimes icon stands).

The two scales of memory and forgetting are shaped by particular chronologies of desire: not all ancestors are commemorated, not all conspicuous landscape features are marked. The relatively recent past provides an interesting example of the changing adjustments to memory and forgetting. For example, the idea that 'the Turks never set foot in Sphakia' – that is, that Sphakia managed to escape the Turkish yoke and to survive as a beacon of freedom – is an important one. As a result the large, conspicuous Turkish forts all over Sphakia, in locations actually called Koule (the Greek version of the Turkish word for fort) present difficulties for local memory, to the extent that some of them cannot always be 'seen'. According to a legend recorded 50 years ago by Fielding, Ag. Aikaterini AN CH 1 is a triumphant Christian marker whose powerful saint prevented the Turks from building a fort on top of it; the fort is nearby but does not encroach on the church. This fort could then be seen – because the church won out. But the conviction currently held by at least one person from Anopoli that only the forts in Askyphou were Turkish, while the Turkish fort near AN CH 1 Ag. Aikaterini was actually Venetian, suggests that this fort cannot now be 'seen' for what it actually was and is.[134]

It is important that researchers, too, never forget the huge selectivity of memory. The past always matters, but what people choose to remember is what is important to them – the salient features of their own landscapes, both internal and external. It is chronologies of desire which determine which pasts are remembered and which are forgotten. The selection of salient features will thus vary from period to period. What people might tell outsiders about them in their explanations is what is salient or memorable to them, at that particular time. The scales of memory, the kind of memory, may well be different in different periods, again because of changes in chronologies of desire.

The relationship between the social and spatial aspects of landscape is intrinsically interesting. In addition, the notion that social and spatial aspects of the landscape do have some kind of direct relationship is an important one for archaeologists working only with the latter, and wanting to reconstruct the former. In analysing the spatial aspects of a landscape (the locations, as I have called them here), you can begin to get clues for learning the explanations. The question is how far you can push the link between social and spatial, a link which may not be very precise in its physical form, as we saw above in the discussion of the grammar of location.

---

[134] Fielding 1953, 210. For general discussion of 'the Turks never set foot in Sphakia', see Nixon 2001, 81–82. Herzfeld (1991) on the Cretan preference for Venetian over Turkish structures was mentioned in n. 115. The person from Anopoli had apparently seen a book about Venetian forts in Sphakia (which do exist) and was convinced that the fort near Ag. Aikaterini fell into this category; I am grateful to Marina Pyrovolaki for this information.

In the case of Sphakia, the sacred dimension of the relevant structures would be recognisable, as would their relatively small scale, which is in keeping with the scale of most buildings in settlements. It might also be possible to suggest that dispersed landscape markers might correlate with dispersed resources and dispersed patterns of landholding. It would certainly be possible to suggest that visibility was a prime consideration for many structures. It might be possible to suggest that there was a link with ancestors, on the principle of Gosden and Lock's genealogical history. It would certainly be possible to trace the slow but certain shift from general collective markers of larger units, built of lcocal materials, to particular markers of personal space, imported from outside the locality, as I have done here and cf. the material changes mentioned in section 5.5 on 20th c. Sphakia).

In this section I hope to have demonstrated the importance of integrating locations and explanations. Even where it is no longer possible to talk to the people who inhabit and inscribe a particular landscape, it is still possible to look for, and to interpret, clues that will contribute to a social as well as a spatial view of landscape. Specifically, I suggest that it is useful to separate locations and explanations as rigorously as possible. I suggest further that many of the same kinds of locations and explanations can be applied to other times and places. The next section will show how using locations and explanations can help us to understand and to compare other sacred landscapes, both synchronically and diachronically.

6.3 Recurrent Patterns in Sacred Landscapes
(TABLES 8 and 9)

Future work will be able to look at the subject of recurrent patterns in sacred landscapes in more detail. Here I want to make some brief synchronic and diachronic comparisons, in order to show how the factors of locations and explanations discussed in relation to second millennium A.D. Sphakia can be applied to other times and places, and to demonstrate the value of making systematic comparisons through the application of consistent variables (cf. Nixon and Price 2001).

TABLES 8 and 9 (locations and explanations) compare four different religious systems and sacred landscapes, in terms of what we know about locations and explanations: Minoan palatial religion; ancient Greek religion; modern Greek Orthodoxy as seen in Sphakia; and Northwest France since Christianisation. The length of time represented by each of these systems, a millennium plus or minus a few hundred years, is very roughly equivalent.

But there are major differences among the four religious systems, in terms of the type of religious system; territorial extent; scale; and the material or architectural form of sacred structures. Some have an enormous total territorial extent (ancient Greek religion; Christianity in the two forms included here) and a correspondingly large scale overall (religious adminstration and personnel, and the relevance or not of literacy; number of religious structures). Minoan palatial religion, on the other hand, is basically a Cretan phenomenon (total area of the island ca 8300 sq km) with activity in other areas such as Kythira and Thira. The forms of sacred structures vary greatly. In Minoan palatial religion, architecture often seems less important than natural settings such as hilltops and caves for sanctuaries outside settlements; in the other three systems, structures of particular and very different types, usually with a large range in size – cathedrals, temples, calvaires, etc – are a fundamental part of the system. All four religious systems look different, and can therefore be visually distinguished from one another.

It is all the more interesting, then, that although there are inevitably many gaps in evidence and analysis, there is also enough information to suggest that different religious systems do use similar types of locations and explanations in order to construct and account for their sacred landscapes. Because the same factors recur, it is possible to compare the different systems, and as a result to learn more about them.

To begin with locations, it is immediately clear that not enough work has been done on the correlation of sacred structures and the resources they sometimes mark; people will mention the presence of water (springs, rivers, the sea) but almost never anything else (arable land, pasturage, etc).

Comparison of the role of visibility in the systems studies here, however, is immediately fruitful. Both Minoan palatial religion and ancient Greek religion use a range of visibilities, from high (peak sanctuaries, temples on akropoleis) to low (sacred caves whose location must be known; the Kamares Cave on Crete is exceptional is having a mouth large enough to be visible over most of the Mesara Plain). Visibility in Minoan palatial religion seems to be mainly important by land (though note the little seaside sanctuary near Mallia, Dessenne 1949), whereas in both ancient Greek and Orthodox Greek religion, visibility by sea as well as land is extremely important. But Orthodox Christianity has a narrower range, though a critical deployment, of visibility. Everything in this system must be out in the open, so caves are no longer used, though rock shelters may be turned into churches.

There is plenty of work to be done on intervisibility in all four systems. The little we know already is tantalising – that the Minoan peak sanctuaries can be intervisible (Peatfield 1994, 25; Soetens et al. 2003); that there are important sightlines all over Phokis, involving sanctuaries as well as forts (McInerney 1999, C. Morgan 2003); that the coastal sanctuaries on Kephallinia and Ithaki may have been intervisible (Randsborg 2002, vol. 2, map on p. 16); that Orthodox churches are frequently intervisible, with beacon churches providing long distance

TABLE 8: Locations: recurrent patterns in sacred landscapes.

RELIGION	SCALE & NO. OF STRS	1. RESOURCES	2. VISIBILITY	3. LIMINAL LOCATIONS	4. EARLIER SIGNIF STRS
Minoan, palatial	small scale strs; relatively scarce (as far as we know)	peak sanctuaries in the middle of an area's resources; some encls mark springs	a range of visibilities from high (peak sancts) to low (most caves)	?	relationship may be in terms of 'seeing' earlier sacred strs rather than being on top of them
Ancient Greek	range of scales (large temples, small shrines)	water	high vis by land and sea; also low vis (caves still used)	mtn ridges, edges of settlements, junctions in routes	yes; Gk temples on Minoan bldgs; Gk cults on tombs; etc
Christian/Greek Orthodox (Sphakia)	small and relatively numerous (e.g. 2 outlying ch/sett); cathedrals elsewhere	x	x	x	x
Christian/Roman Catholic (NW France)	ranges from fewer, larger cathedrals to smaller, multiple strs (e.g. calvaires)	water; landscape research not really done, tho'	?	edges of settlements, junctions in routes	Celtic pre-Christian

TABLE 9: Explanations: recurrent patterns in sacred landscapes.

RELIGION	SCALE AND SCOPE OF AVAILABLE EXPLS	1. HUMAN BOUNDARIES	2. SUPERATURAL CONTACT	3. SPECIFIC EVENTS AND PLACES	4. VOW
Minoan, palatial	limited literacy; some discussion of religion in Linear B	some peak sanctuaries? (tho' most seem to be in middle of territories)	?	?	?
Ancient Greek	inscriptions in/on sacred strs provide most literary expls	large-scale (borders between poleis); small scale (crossroads)	x	x	x
Christian/Greek Orthodox (Sphakia)	inscrr in/on sacred strs, maps; oral info	x	x	x	x
Christian/Roman Catholic (NW France)	inscrr in/on sacred strs, maps; oral info	city and territory boundaries	many	x	x

References for Tables 8 and 9.

PALATIAL MINOAN:

Locations

1. *resources*: sacred enclosures near springs, e.g. Kato Simi, Rutkowski 1986, 115
2. *visibility*: intervisibility of Ioukhtas and Kophinas, Peatfield 1994, 25; hierarchy of local and regional peak sanctuaries, (different ranges of visibility), Watrous 2001, 195-196; seaside sanctuary at Malia, Dessenne 1949

Explanations:

1. *human boundaries*: Kamares (sacred) Cave as boundary marker for territory of Phaistos, Watrous et al. 2004, 285

ANCIENT GREEK RELIGION

Locations

1. *resources*: water, Cole 2004, x, 186
2. *visibility*: by land and by sea, Morton 2001; intervisibility of sanctuaries on Kephallinia and Ithaki, Randsborg 1995, 2002, vol 2: 16 map of sanctuaries on Kephallenia; 2002, vol. 2, 16 (and cf. Randsborg 1995, 94–102); sight-lines across Phokis, including the sanctuaries of Artemis Elaphebolos at Kleonai/Kalapodhi, and of Artemis Dhiktynna, McInerney 1999, 288–289, 347; and cf. C. Morgan 2003, 113–120
3. *liminal locations*: Cole 1994, 2004, 48, 179; Nixon 1995; Parker 2005, 68
4. *earlier significant structures*: Coldstream 1976; Snodgrass 1980, 38–40; Nixon 1991; Alcock 2002 esp. 108ff. for Hellenistic Crete; Prent 2003

Explanations

1. *human boundaries*: Nixon 1991; Schachter 1992; de Polignac 1994; Erickson 2002, 82-83; Cole 2004, 48–49; Chaniotis 2005
2. *supernatural contact*: mark of Poseidon's trident left visible in Erekhtheion, Pausanias I.xxvi.5 and Dinsmoor 1975, 187–188; cult of Demeter established at Eleusis because the goddess was there, *Homeric Hymn to Demeter* lines 97, 318, 356, 490
3. *specific events*: sanctuary at Olympia established because chariot race between Pelops and Oinomaos happened there, Price 2004, 115–116; thank offering to Zeus, Poseidon, Athena, all gods, and the river Euros, from someone who was endangered and saved on this spot (Greek, tode to topo), Milner 1998, 69, no. 150
4. *vow*: thank offering to a goddess for children and grandchildren, Milner 1998, 69, no. 49

MODERN GREEK ORTHODOX (SPHAKIA): this monograph

ROMAN CATHOLIC (NW FRANCE):

Locations

1. *resources*: wells, fountains, Martin 1983, 305
2. *visibility*: calvaire on a hill, Castel 1980, 10; density of monuments suggesting intervisibility, Gueguen 1993, 195ff.; marking of routes pilgrimage and other routes, Pichot 2002, 239
3. *liminal locations*: bridges, Martin 1983, 305; crossroads, Martin and Martin 1977, 36; Castel 1980, 12; cf. Limbourg Brothers [ca 1415], 21
4. *earlier significant structures*: Christianised menhir of Saint-Duzec at Pleumeur-Bodou, Déceneux and Mingant 2001, 18

Explanations

1. *human boundaries*: of places of asylum, Martin and Martin 1977, 33 and 36; property boundaries, seigneurial or princely estates, parishes, Martin 1983, 298-299
2. *supernatural contact*: miracles e.g. of Saint Samson, Martin and Martin 1977, 31
3. *specific events*: commemoration of battles, Martin 1983, 303
4. *vow*: prevention of plague or fire, Martin 1983, 307; cf. Gueguen 1993, 32

visibility between villages and areas (p. 25). As far as I know, visibility has not been studied systematically for Northwestern France, but the various atlases show that the density of sacred monuments implies some intervisibility (Castel 1980, 10; Gueguen 1993, 195ff.).[135]

The three later systems use sacred structures to mark various liminal points, and Minoan palatial religion may have done the same. Similarly, all three later systems make use of earlier significant structures, from Greek temples built on Minoan structures, to Orthodox churches on Roman basilicas, to French calvaires set up on (and sometimes incorporating) Celtic monuments. It may have been important for some Minoan sacred areas to 'see' earlier places of significance, rather than be on top of them, but this is a suggestion which requires further work.[136]

To return once again to the coincidence, or not, of sacred structures of different periods in the same place, Minoan peak sanctuaries and exokklisia do sometimes coincide, because both systems sometimes make use of 'Prophitis Ilias'- type locations at ca 600 masl. But systematic comparison quickly reveals that they represent very different landscape systems. It is true that our list of peak sanctuaries is far from complete (Watrous 2001, 195–196), but even so there are far more exokklisia than there ever were peak sanctuaries – for example, it is unlikely that there were ever two peak sanctuaries per settlement as there may have been two exokklisia per settlement in the second millennium A.D. (see section 4.3 above for discussion); and the exokklisia use a wider range of locations than peak sanctuaries do. It could be said that many peak sanctuaries and sacred caves had a wider significance than most exokklisia, whose meaning is usually very local. In addition, peak sanctuaries are only one type of site in the Minoan sacred

---

[135] In Attica, mountain and cave sanctuaries are popular down to the 5th/4th c. B.C., and then again in the Late Roman period; note that eight of the 10 mountain sanctuaries on Parker's map are at Minoan peak sanctuary altitudes, i.e. 650 masl or lower. In the interim period, people preferred even lower hills with an 'acropolis function'. See Parker 2005, 60–61 and 69–70, and Fowden 1988, 55–57. One of the reasons for these shifts could be a change in preference for different kinds of inter/visibility. In mediaeval France, the Limbourg Brothers' picture for March (n.d. [circa 1415], 19, 21) shows a crossroads near Chateau de Lusignan and a church, conspicuously marked by a calvaire visible from both. The picture is composed so that this intersection is itself conspicuous, in the middle ground.

[136] It may be possible to show that visibility was a resource affecting the pattern of settlement in some areas. For example, the Agiopharango, south central Crete, is a prosperous place in the Early Minoan period (with some rich and extremely interesting tholos tombs), but more or less deserted by the Late Minoan period, when the rest of Crete including the nearby Mesara Plain was highly active. The resources of the Agiopharango had not changed. But the desire in later Minoan Crete for visibility and intervisibility at increasingly longer scales may have adversely affected settlement in this gorge, which can provide only limited visibility between different areas within it, and almost none outside it. The tholoi themselves can be seen only from very short distances within the gorge. I am pursuing this topic in further research (Nixon, in press). For the coincidence, or not, of exokklisia and earlier archaeological sites, see Appendix 4, with TABLE 13.

landscape system: when Minoan sacred caves are factored into the equation, the two systems overlap even less. And finally, it is extremely interesting that there is little if any coincidence of ancient Greek religious structures at Minoan sacred sites: the use of sacred caves continues or is renewed in the Iron Age, but temples in Crete are seldom if ever built on peak sanctuary-type/'Prophitis Ilias'-type hills.[137]

In terms of explanations, there is a great deal of information about human boundaries, supernatural encounters, events, and vows for the three later systems as the references for TABLE 9 make clear. With literate cultures, it is often the case that more is known about explanations, usually from documents, than about locations, because the basic landscape questions have not been asked, for example, whether the choice of site for a sanctuary correlates with the presence of significant resources. The comparison in TABLE 9 between the largely non-literate culture of the Minoans and the three later literate cultures considered here immediately opens up an important set of questions about 'explanations' in Bronze Age Crete, some of which may be archaeologically answerable.

One of my aims in writing this book has been to show that it is necessary to consider religious systems holistically. Studying individual sacred structures is important, but it is crucial to consider them as part of an assemblage. In particular, landscape work makes it possible to join up the two sides of the coin, spatial locations and social explanations, and to get a more nuanced view of sacred landscapes in other times and places.

In the case of Bronze Age Crete, specialised studies have helped us to understand individual features of Minoan sacred landscapes, such as peak sanctuaries (Peatfield 1983, 1992). Rutkowski has discussed all categories of recognised Minoan sacred sites, though as separate categories (1986); and Jones (1999) has compared some aspects of peak sanctuaries and Minoan sacred caves. Adams (2004) has looked at the different concentrations of ritual objects in the regions of Knossos and Malia. But we still do not really know much about the nature and constitution of Minoan sacred landscapes. For example, is there such a thing as a typical palatial sacred landscape, and if so, what elements were 'required' for it? Can we recognise characteristics for pre- and post-palatial sacred landscapes?

This lack of holistic work on Minoan sacred landscapes is particularly clear in discussions of possible border sanctuaries. Iron Age Greek sanctuaries and later outlying churches were used to mark boundaries of various scales on Crete, between poleis and communes. Archaeologists suspect, with good reason, that Minoan palaces controlled more or less definite territories, and have tried to reconstruct their boundaries; Cherry (1986, 21) produced one of several maps

---

[137] Not only are there no Greek *structures* at peak sanctuaries, I know of no Greek *use* of peak sanctuaries. For Greek use of other Minoan features, see the references given for TABLE 8. The relationship between Greek forts and sanctuaries has yet to be explored.

attempting to define boundaries for all palace centres known at the time, through Thiessen polygons. Comparison with evidence from the two later cultures on Crete already mentioned suggests that these palatial borders could well have been marked by sacralised points in the landscape. Working within the relevant territory, Watrous and Hadzi-Vallianou have recently suggested borders for the Phaistian state; one point along their proposed line is a sacred site, the Kamares Cave (2004, 284–287), and this suggestion has duly been noted for TABLE 9. They may be right, but it is difficult to say one way or the other, in the absence of a general, landscape-based discussion within the field of Minoan archaeology. Can boundaries run below ridge-lines? Evidence from the Pylos tablets, used to reconstruct the line between the Hither and Further Provinces along Mt Aigaleon (Chadwick 1976, 43–44) might suggest otherwise. Are there other sacred caves which might have marked boundaries in Minoan Crete? Can peak sanctuaries mark borders, as well as suggesting territorial extent, which is not the same thing? These are some of the questions which a more holistic approach could help to answer. A first step would be some landscape reconnaissance to see if any Minoan sacred sites lie on or near the boundaries generated by the Thiessen polygons.

So also for the Iron Age. There are some ancient Greek landscapes with good assemblages of sacred structures (of various periods, including Byzantine–Venetian–Turkish!) which would benefit from this combined approach. Mantineia (Hodkinson and Hodkinson 1981), Arkadhia (C. Morgan 2003, Jost 1985), Phokis (McInerney 1999, C. Morgan 2003), Kephallinia (Randsborg 1995, 2002) all have small but substantial sacred landscapes with good dates, plus a distinguished body of scholarship, which would repay further study along the lines suggested here. And to return to the final comparison made in TABLES 8 and 9, the landscape dimension would add so much to the study of Christian structures in northwestern France.

Though there are inevitably many gaps, these comparisons give enough information to confirm the idea that different religious systems use religious monuments, of whatever kind, to sacralise their respective landscapes in remarkably similar ways. Given these recurrent patterns, it is all the more important for researchers looking at a particular places and times to discern the specific grammar of location that underlies the deployment of sacred structures, both large and small. Continuity of religious use is once again something which definitely has to be proved, not assumed. The combined study of the spatial (location) and social (explanation) will help us to obtain a much better understanding of all these sacred landscapes and the cultures that produced them. Equally, this work will help us to contextualise the particular chronologies of desire that determine sacred landscapes, which as we have seen, as most likely to emerge and change at times of social change (Alcock 2001, Nixon 2004). It is especially important to be aware of the general factors governing the emergence and development of sacred landscapes, in order to avoid any form of triumphalism in connection with individual belief systems.

6.4 Summary Conclusion

In this book I hope to have shown the value of applying the methods of archaeological survey to a post-processualist study of two particular sacred landscapes in Sphakia. I have attempted to show that outlying churches, village churches, and icon stands relate to one another as well as to the landscape which they mark so conspicuously. The study of sacred structures, in particular the outlying churches, has revealed developments not datable, or perhaps not even detectable, by other means. Looking at the Byzantine–Venetian–Turkish landscape in the context of an archaeological survey has demonstrated the value of the enforced consistency mentioned at the beginning of this book. Because we collected information about all periods from the time that people arrived in Sphakia until the end of the Turkish period, we have been able to observe and compare the development of two smaller areas within the eparchy. The comparison of Anopoli and Frangokastello has shown that the two areas developed differently, and that there is more play in the landscape, even in the difficult and potentially 'determinist' environment of Sphakia, than might initally be suspected. The use of site trajectories has once again been a crucial tool for testing and extending comparisons. A truly diachronic approach has been valuable in exploring the Byzantine–Venetian–Turkish sacred landscape; its similarities and differences with previous sacred landscapes in Sphakia, particularly that of the the Late Roman period; and its own development over a millennium. The context of an archaeological survey has therefore made it possible to combine our field data with the work of other specialists in a truly diachronic and consistent manner.

Because people continued to build churches and icon stands in the 20th c. (and continue to do so in the 21st), it has been possible to ask people who live there about these structures and their meanings in the landscapes of Anopoli and Frangokastello. Including the 20th c. has enabled me to consider both spatial and social factors affecting this and other sacred landscapes. The combination of local knowledge and documentary evidence on the one hand, and traditional archaeological work based on spatial analysis on the other, has meant that we now have a better idea about the work of memory in Sphakia, and by extension, in other parts of the early modern and contemporary Greek world. I hope that further research, both archaeological and anthropological, will add more details to the picture that I have sketched here.

APPENDICES

Appendix 1: Recording Methods:
Studying Outlying Churches and Icon Stands
(FIG 4)

The present study was done in two parts. First came a more general or 'macro' phase, which included the main period of Survey fieldwork (1987–1992), during which time Byzantine–Venetian–Turkish data were collected and some churches, mostly those in villages, were recorded. We did some hard thinking about how to approach the Byzantine–Venetian–Turkish epoch, with its far greater complement of structural remains, and how to make meaningful comparisons between it and the Prehistoric and Graeco-Roman epochs (Nixon et al. 2000; cf. also Nixon and Price 2001). At the same time, I began to get a general picture of patterns in the location of individual churches and icon stands, inside and outside villages, throughout Sphakia. This general picture is presented in chapter 4 above.

The information gathered in the macro phase was interesting but it pertained to individual structures. I realised that in order to study the development of the Byzantine–Venetian–Turkish sacred landscape, I would need to do a 'micro' study, i.e. to consider a set of outlying churches, icon stands, and villages in at lesat one part of Sphakia, and to analyse them in relation to one another, over time. I decided to look at two areas within Sphakia, the two areas in which we had done the most fieldwork, and on which we had focused many of our analyses: the mountain plain of Anopoli ('middle'), and the coastal plain of Frangokastello ('down'). My analysis of the sacred landscapes of Anopoli and Frangokastello is presented in chapter 4.

In 1996 I recorded nearly all icon stands and most of the outlying churches in the two areas on the short forms originally developed for Survey sites (FIG 4). Some churches had already been recorded in enough detail during earlier field seasons, e.g. those in Anopoli, recorded systematically in 1992.

Information recorded on the short form included the following: sketch plan, including orientation (variable for icon stands); external features; surnames and dates of people buried in the cemetery, if any; other items left in the vicinity of the church or icon stand (e.g. empty oil bottles, candles stubs, the remains of an old

SPAKIA SURVEY: Site Summary

Recommendation

Site number

Date found   Site name

Date recorded   Site chronology

Location

General comment

Site condition (include environment, construction, cultivation, etc.)

Site size   PhotoColor

PhotoB&W

Structure comment

Pottery comment

Non-ceramic finds comment

FIG 4 : Sphakia Survey Short Form.

epitaphios, piles of ceramic rooftiles pulled off when a new cement roof was installed); the name of the deity or saint, established from the principal icons; the amount and type of church furnishings. Dating evidence for construction and decoration could be obtained in various conventional ways, such as building inscriptions; graffiti; or the presence of spolia built into a church, visible inside, or re-used e.g. as the base for the altar.

I also learned to record the date of the most recent newspaper, perhaps used to cover the bottom of an icon stand; or, in a church, to line the candle-stand (bagaz), or to absorb drips from bottles of olive oil onto the floor; and to check the dates of any visible coins, in order to establish a rough date for the most recent use of a church or icon stand.

As with other sites, environmental information was also recorded, e.g. the proximity of water and other resources.

With the benefit of hindsight, I would have added a systematic way of recording visibility and intervisibility, but otherwise the forms worked well, and were consistent with the other site recording done by the Survey.

In addition to filling in the forms, I interviewed people in both areas. In Anopoli I went to most icon stands on my own in 1996, and consulted people in three neighbourhoods about their location (Kampia, Kampos, Limnia). I completed the mapping of the icon stands in Anopoli with Simon Price in 1998. We visited the last of the peripheral churches in 2003, thanks to Mr George Dourountakis who organized the key for us. In Frangokastello I visited most of the exokklisia in 1996 with Mrs Popi Koukounaraki, who accompanied me in my rented car, and introduced me to the priest in Patsianos. I also discussed my research with other people in the area. I completed the recording of the Frangokastello icon stands, again with Simon Price in 2003. We attended the giorti (festival) of Ag. Nikitas in September 2004 (PLATE 20).

In 1999, I visited one of the larger funeral parlours in central Khania, as these shops also sell ecclesiastical equipment such as icons, incense burners, and candle stands, and their owners can advise on prices for metal icon stands and prefabricated concrete churches. I saw the newest icon stands, in the shape of little churches and made of concrete, on sale in a pottery workshop outside Rethymnon in 2000, and in Vrysses, just outside Sphakia, in 2003.

Appendix 2: Altitude and Site Trajectories
(TABLE 10)

Two aspects of our work on the Survey are directly relevant to this study: altitude and site trajectories. By the time I started doing my focused work on outlying churches and icon stands, we had already established that altitude was crucial for understanding the landscape of Sphakia in any period.

In Sphakia, our work has shown that three different altitudes are important: 'down', i.e. on or near the coast, 0–249masl; 'middle', ca. 250–1199 masl; and 'up', 1200+ masl for example the Madhares, the high summer pastures in the White Mountains, at 1800m. Land and resources at each of these altitudes can be, and have been, exploited in different ways at different times over the Survey's 5000–year time span. In terms of the Environmental Zones distinguished by the Survey, 'down' includes Coasts/Coastal Plains; part of Lower Slopes, and part of Gorges; 'middle' includes part of Lower Slopes, part of Gorges and Cliffs, and all of Mountain Plains; 'up' consists of Upper Slopes, Mountain Desert and Madhares.

'Up', 'middle' and 'down' are our terms, derived from Sphakia Survey fieldwork. But the old commune (koinotis) boundaries suggest that the idea of up-middle-down is implicit in local concepts of the landscape, if not explicitly acknowledged. The dissection of Sphakia by gorges running north-south has already been mentioned. Eight of the nine old communes in Sphakia also run north-south, and each one includes some land at all three altitudes. One example is the commune of Aradhena, with coastal land, two villages at the middle level (Aradhena and Ag. Ioannis), and land higher 'up' in the White Mountains. Having land at more than one altitude permitted communes to maximise their resources. An eparchy like Sphakia, with relatively few resources had fewer, larger communes, and fewer people; eparchies with greater resources (especially arable land), such as Kissamos, had more, smaller communes usually including land at only one altitude, and a much higher overall population.

The area of an eparchy is no predictor of the number of communes within it: Kissamos is the second largest eparchy in terms of size, but had the highest number of communes. Apokoronas is the smallest of the five, but had the third highest number of communes. A topographic map makes it clear why this is so. The more mountainous the eparchy, the lower the number of communes, regardless of area, as shown in TABLE 10.[138]

Altitude has consequences for settlement patterns in Sphakia, in that it gives people choices. In some periods, people prefer to live 'down' on the coast; in others, they prefer to live inland and upland, at the 'middle' altitude. In the Byzantine–Venetian–Turkish period, there is no permanent settlement at the 'up' level, though this altitude is used in the summer. Similarly, outlying churches and icon stands are found only at the 'down' and 'middle' levels, with two exceptions discussed above (Ag. Pnevma plus a much more recent icon stand, p. 88). An

---

[138] Nixon and Moody et al. 1994; Nixon and Price 2001 describe several north-south 'slices' of Sphakia. The exception to this rule for defining communes in Sphakia is Askyphou, which has land at two altitudes (up and middle); it traditionally had strong links with coastal areas to the north and south as well. On the relationship between resources and wealth in the ancient Aegean, see Nixon and Price 1990. It is worth pointing out that when we ourselves divided Sphakia into eight regions for the purposes of focussing on particular areas, we instinctively replicated some of the commune boundaries. We did this in 1988, well before we published Nixon and Moody et al. 1994 (first presented 1992); see the website, Nixon and Moody et al. 2000 for a map of the Survey's regions.

explanation for this altitudinal distribution – specifically, why the sacred landscape should mirror the settlement pattern – is given in section 5.6 above on natural and cultural landscapes.

The use of site trajectories, which means tracking the development of individual settlements in order to make diachronic comparisons, is also an important part of our work on the Sphakia Survey and makes it possible to compare sites over time in a rigorous way. Careful assessment of major and minor phases makes it possible to get a sense of the range of different patterns of settlement development within different parts of Sphakia. For example, if two sites have

TABLE 10: Eparchies in the Nome of Khania, arranged in ascending amount of area per commune.

NAME OF EPARCHY	AREA (KM²)	NO. OF COMMUNES	AREA PER COMMUNE (KM²)
Apokoronas	313	34	4.9
Kissamos	513	60	5.84
Kydhonia	613	51	12.01
Selino	447	16	27.9
Sphakia	472	9	52.6

similar trajectories, e.g. an Early Minoan-Middle Minoan phase followed by Hellenistic and Turkish phases, then the more detailed information (site size, etc) should show whether all three phases at the two sites are really comparable. I originally developed this approach of looking at setttlements for other areas and periods of Crete and have further refined it for the Survey (Nixon 1987, 1991; cf. Nixon and Moody et al. 1994). In investigating outlying churches and icon stands, it is important to know how the Byzantine–Venetian–Turkish settlement pattern is changing and developing over the millennium involved.

Appendix 3. Two Greek Assessments of Locations and Explanations for Icon Stands
(TABLES 11 and 12)

Khatziphoti (1986) and Plymakis (2001b) both include lists on the locations and explanations for icon stands, and these lists permit us to get an idea of how people within the culture see these structures. Khatziphoti explicitly attempts to separate locations (topoi anegersis, τόποι ανεγέρσης) from explanations (aities anegersis, αιτίες ανεγέρσης). Khatziphoti simply has one list (reason[s] for construction and placement, aphormi anegerseos i topothetiseos, αφορμή

TABLE 11: Khatziphoti 1986: locations and explanations for icon stands.

LOCATIONS	EXPLANATIONS
Khatziphoti 1986: 23	Khatziphoti 1986: 20–22
L1. dangerous turns on national highways	E1. in memory of deceased family members
L2. dangerous turns on other roads	E2. for fatal car accidents
L3. places where there were car accidents = E2, E3	E3. for 'rescue' from a car accident
L4. squares in settlements	E4. for protection
L5. sidewalks near churches	E5. for guard posts at borders
L6. enclosures or corners of house gardens	E6. at the location of an older (ruined, rebuilt) church
L7. fields	E7. for additional reinforcement outside churches or near restored churches
L8. crossroads (roads)	E8. for reasons of worship, to indicate the way to a monastery away from a main road, i.e. type of crossroad = L8
L9. crossroads (road plus railway)	
L10. edges of bridges	
L11. border posts = E5	
L12. military bases: inside or outside, near guard posts	
L13. mountains	
L14. inside and outside monastery enclosures	
L15. hills/ridges near monasteries	
L16. harbour jetties/moles	

ανεγέρσεως η τοποθετήσεως), combining location and explanation; TABLE 11 shows her list, numbered and arranged by me according to location and explanatiopn. Plymakis has two lists, one for external areas and one for internal areas (though many of his examples are simply icons rather than spaces combining icons and candles, oil lamps, or incense burners); see TABLE 12.

There is considerable, but not total, overlap in Khatziphoti and Plymakis say about icon stands. In terms of the analytical categories used in this book for locations, both authors mention liminal locations and earlier significant structures; neither Khatziphoti nor Plymakis comments explicitly on resources, nor on visibility, but then these are not always as important for icon stands as for churches. In terms of explanations, they both list human boundaries, supernatural contact (usually an attempt to establish it), and specific events such as accidents, though not of course using these precise terms. Only Plymakis explicitly mentions vows.

In terms of the strict separation of location and explanation applied in this book, both authors blur the categories. Thus Khatziphoti includes border posts in both location (L11) and explanation (E5). She also classifies icon stands on a main road signalling the presence of a monastery on a side road as an explanation (E8),

TABLE 12: Plymakis 2001b: locations and explanations for icon stands.

LOCATIONS	EXPLANATIONS
EXTERNAL AREAS	EXTERNAL AREAS
Plymakis 2001b: 23	Plymakis 2001b: 23
	1. accidents or criminal actions
	2. in places of sacrifice or deaths from military events
	3. for protection, divine help, blessing (eulogia) or exorcism, agricultural matters
	4. to express thanks or to fulfill some other vow
5. at present or past (ruined) places of worship (churches)	
6. cemeteries	
INTERNAL AREAS	INTERNAL AREAS
Plymakis 2001b: 85-92	
1. inside houses	
2. on seafaring vessels	
3. on vehicles – buses, military vehicles	
4. in other places (clinics, hospitals, factories	
5. in churches (on templa)	

when it is also a category of crossroads (L8). Though Khatziphoti's and Plymakis' lists are interesting – and their catalogues of specific icon stands invaluable – they are not as useful, in terms of helping to establish general analytical categories for location and explanation, as the work of Kyriakidhou-Nestoros (1975); cf. p. 11 above.

Appendix 4: The Correlation of Outlying Churches with Archaeological Sites
(TABLE 13; PLATES 1 and 6)

During our work on the Sphakia Survey, I realised that in some cases, outlying churches can be very good predictors for significant archaeological material, because they are so often built in areas with good resources. In areas like Sphakia where resources are sparsely distributed across the landscape, it is not surprising that the same 'resourceful' places are used, though not necessarily settled, in more than one time period. Icon stands, because they are less often associated with resources per se, are less often useful as predictors, and have not been considered here.

TABLE 13 tabulates outlying churches in Regions 3, 4, and 5, plus the study area in Region 8, and the presence of other material (20th c., Byzantine–Venetian–Turkish, Graeco-Roman, and Prehistoric); see PLATES 1 and 6 for the location of the churches. As the map in PLATE 6 shows, 3.03 Panagia and 3.03 Ag. Ioannis count as two outlying churches, and 5.03 Azogyres/Ag. Athanasios and Ag. Eleftherios are counted as one (because the latter is a Late Roman basilica, rather than a VT outlying church). For Region 3, Gerola (1961, 47 no. 211) notes the presence of a church to the Panagia at a location called Gialos, which was ruined when he saw it in the early 20th century. We did not locate this church and I have not counted it here.

There is ancient material (Graeco-Roman or Prehistoric) at nine out of the 14 Region 3–4–5 outlying churches (64%). Similarly, there is ancient material at seven of the 11 churches (63%) in the Region 8 study area. The sample is small, but it does suggest that there is a much better than average chance of finding ancient material at or near outlying churches.

The table includes two other Sphakiote churches, Ag. Triadha (6.06), and O Khristos (8.05A). The church of Agia Triadha (6.06) near Khora Sphakion is a particularly clear example of outlying churches as predictors for significant archaeological material. As mentioned above (p. 24), it lies at the top of a large terraced enclosure on a southeast-facing slope, well above the main footpath from Khora Sphakion to Anopoli. The terraces were relatively broad and therefore easier to cultivate than most. We went to look at this area in 1990 because the presence of the church suggested to me that there might be resources around it which people in earlier periods might also have wished to use. We were rewarded by some of the most interesting Prehistoric and Graeco-Roman material in the area of Khora Sphakion, both near the church (Final Neolithic-Early Minoan and Early Minoan pottery, several pieces of obsidian; Roman pottery and a cistern), and at two other sites in the vicinity (6.04, 6.05).

And in another example, our desire to investigate a location called Ta Livadhia (The Meadows) (8.05A), mentioned in a Venetian document, was heightened by the mention of a church. When we visited the area in 2003, the precise location of the toponym was still known to people in the nearby village of Komitadhes, and we found Prehistoric and Graeco-Roman material (Late Minoan III, Archaic, Hellenistic and Late Roman pottery), as well as evidence for Venetian (and later) occupation.

The church at Ta Marmara (Region 3, at the foot of the Aradhena Gorge) was discussed in the main text (p. 24). Ta Marmara is an example of a marginal area which has been 'almost a site' in more than one epoch. A sherd solidly dated to the Early Minoan period was found here; and a church was built in the locality, but only after three decades of tourism along this stretch of coast.

And finally, a brief glance at churches in the Agiopharango, also included in TABLE 13, confirms that the link between exokklisia and earlier material is not merely a Sphakiote phenomenon: all four of the religious establishments in the gorge coincide with rich ancient material of various dates (Blackman and Branigan et al. 1977, 54, 66, 73, 77; 1982; Vasilakis 1989–90, 26–38, 49, 62–66; Vasilakis 1992, 213–215 with figs 30.1 [ground] and 30.2 [aerial], both photographs showing both tholos tombs and monastery; Vasilakis 1999/2000, 85, 88, 91, 93, 97).

Given that churches are often built where there are good resources, and given that people in the past were also interested in good resources, this relationship is perhaps not surprising. Let me re-emphasise one last time that I am not talking about cult continuity, but rather about the possible repeated use of similar resources within small areas, use which may have been continuous but need not have been. In future archaeological surveys, the correlation proposed here between outlying churches (and in some cases perhaps also icon stands) could usefully be factored into sampling strategies.

TABLE 13: Outlying churches as predictors for earlier periods. Data from Regions 3-4-5; two churches in Region 6; study area in Frangokastello; plus Agiopharango (Southern Mesara).

NAME OF CHURCH	LOCATIONS	OTHER 20TH C.	OTHER BVT	GR	PH
3.01 Ag. Pavlos	water, route	x	x		
3.03 Panagia and Ag. Ioannis	arable outside village?	x	x	x	x
3.12 Prophitis Ilias	boundary between Ag. Ioannis and Aradhena	x	x	x	x
Region 3. Ta Marmara	tourism	x			x
4.19 AN CH 2 Ag. Nektarios		x	x		
4.21 AN CH 1 Ag. Aikaterini	post-Turkish beacon		x	x	x
5.02 Sterni/Ag. Vasilios	deserted settlement		x	x	x
5.03 Azogyres/ Ag. Athanasios & Ag. Eleftherios	deserted settlement (LR basilica?)		x	x	
5.11.8 Metamorphosi tou Sotiros	terraces		x	x	
5.11.2. Ag. Antonios			x	x	
5.11.1 Ag. Kharalampos	LR basilica?		x	x	
5.21 AN CH 3 Timios Stavros			x	x	
5.22 AN CH 4 Glyka Nera	water; continuation of coastal path		x		
6.03A AN CH 5 Timios Stavros	commune boundary. spring	x	x		
6.06 Agia Triadha	terraced arable	x	x	x	x

NAME OF CHURCH	LOCATIONS	OTHER 20TH C.	OTHER BVT	GR	PH
8.05A Ta Livadhia/O Khristos	route jct; 'wetspots' and cultivation	x	x	x	x
8.18 FK CH 3 Ag. Pelagia	route jct; 'wetspots' and cultivation	x	x	x	x
8.24 FK CH 1 Ag. Theodhoros	W entrance to plain	x		x	x
8.25 FK CH 2 Ag. Ioannis Prodhromos	commune boundary; spring; route				
8.32 FK CH 12 San Marco	church for V fort		x		
8.38 FK CH 4 Ag. Astratigos	LR basilica, settlement			x	
8.48 FK CH 5 Ag. Ioannis Vokolos	arable				
8.50 FK CH 7 Ag. Nikitas	LR basilica	x	x	x	x
8.50 FK CH 8 Ag. Kharalampos		x	x	x	x
8.51 FK CH 6 Ag. Athanasios	commune boundary	x			
8.55 FK CH 9 Ag. Ioannis/Lakko	route; wet area			?	
8. 59 FK CH 10 Prophitis Ilias	N edge of plain	x	x	x	x
8.71 FK CH 11 Ag. Georgios	marker for W side of Skaloti	x	x	?	
Moni Odhigitria	arable to N and S; visibility			?	x
Ag. Sophia (Gialomonokhoro)	settlement; enough water for a V mill		x	x	x
Ag. Kyriaki	spring			x	x
Ag. Antonios	well near sea		x	x	x

CATALOGUE OF OUTLYING CHURCHES AND ICON STANDS

This catalogue is divided into two main sections, one each for the study areas in the Anopolis and Frangokastello Plains. Within each section, the outlying churches come first and the icon stands come second. The outlying churches and icon stands in each area have their own numerical sequence; AN CH 5 is an outlying church in Anopoli; FK IK 3 is an icon stand in Frangokastello. There are five outlying churches and 18 icon stands in Anopoli, and 12 outlying churches and five icon stands in Frangokastello.

The locations of the outlying churches and icon stands in each area, along with other relevant features, appear on the maps and aerial photographs for Anopoli (PLATES 1 and 2) and Frangokastello (PLATES 3 and 4). On the maps, churches and icon stands are distinguished by symbols: a triangle for a church, filled for an outlying church, outlined for an 'inlying' church in a village; a circle for an icon stand. Individual outlying churches and icon stands are numbered. The numbers correspond to the numbers used here in the catalogue.

Throughout the catalogue, as elsewhere in the book, Sphakia Survey site numbers are given, in the format 4.20 (Ancient Anopolis) and 8.32 (the Venetian fort at Frangokastello). These are the numbers used on the Survey website, at http://sphakia.classics.ox.ac.uk. They are repeated here to facilitate quick consultation of the website, which includes many colour illustrations of the sites discussed.

Not all icon stands have their own site numbers. In this case I have given the name of the nearest site, church, or prominent feature in brackets at the end of the first line of the entry.

The catalogue for Anopoli includes exokklisia and eikonostasia within the area studied here. It does not include all the exokklisia and eikonostasia in the commune of Anopoli. For example, the churches around Loutro are not catalogued, as they are part of a separate nexus within the commune, but they do appear on the map in PLATE 1. Ag. Pnevma (2.37) is also omitted; it lies within the commune, but is up in the Madhares, some distance to the N of the village. The catalogue does include three peripheral outlying churches (AN CH 3, 4, and 5) on the edges of the territory of the village of Anopoli, one of which (AN CH 5) lies on the commune boundary with Khora Sphakion. Similarly, the catalogue for Frangokastello includes only those exokklisia and eikonostasia within the study area. The commune of Patsianos extends farther N than the study area; the commune of Skaloti extends farther N and farther E.

Each catalogue entry contains information under the following nine headings: 1. Description; 2. Date; 3. Details and Measurements; 4. Icons; 5. Other Contents/Features; 6. Location; 7. Explanation; 8. Recorded; 9. Additional References. '4. Icons' was a heading designed mainly for icon stands, rather than churches. In '6. Location' and '7. Explanation'

I have put in the numbers used in the main text for the four major locations and explanations (pp. 22–31). In '8. Recorded' I have included visits before and after my own main recording (indicated by LFN for some sites with multiple visits).

And finally, the decision to publish a catalogue of these structures came relatively late. I have made every attempt to get as much detail as possible but inevitably there remain some gaps.

I. Anopoli
(PLATES 1 and 2)

OUTLYING CHURCHES

Outlying Churches in the Anopolis Plain

AN CH 1. AGIA AIKATERINI (4.21 SECTOR A); PLATE 7

1. Description: Small rectangular church near remains of Turkish fort on the hill at the E end, and highest point, of the Anopolis Ridge. The nearest neighbourhood is Riza, below and to the NE of the church. The view from Ag. Aikaterini is spectacular; equally this church can be seen for miles in every direction, from the N (descent from Madhares and village of Mouri); from the S (Libyan Sea); from the W (area of Aradhena and Ag. Ioannis); and from the E (Frangokastello, Khora Sphakion). Specifically, the church can be seen from FK CH 10 Prophitis Ilias, a distance of some 15 km. The Turkish fort has the same spectacular view, but far less of the same conspicuous visibility over long distances, as it is not whitewashed.

The church was preceded by various structures belonging to the classical city of Ancient Anopolis. The ancient city had two fortification walls. The outer wall, which may date to the Hellenistic period (Pendlebury 1939, 360), is best preserved just E of the church, and at the W end of the site (the so-called Pakhy Toikhos, or 'Thick Wall'). The builders of the church made a definite choice to put it on the hill, in a place of maximum visibility, where there were also conspicuous remains of an earlier, prestigious phase of Greek civilisation. This hill is bounded on E, N and W by ancient walling (width 1.50m–1.70m), which forms a substantial bastion at the SW corner (15 x 18m); possible tower at NE corner (wall 2m wide).

The construction of the church certainly obscured other ancient remains; we assume that there must have been significant public buildings here, the highest point on the ridge. The fact that the only figurine fragments from the ridge come from this area suggests that there was once at least a sanctuary here. W of the church and its hill is a flattish area, still full of ancient walling, stone piles, and stone tumble, presumably the remains of ancient houses.

Still further west, the Pakhy Toikhos has been a notable landmark since at least Venetian times: the ridge is labelled 'Pachidicho' on a drawing of 1631 by Monanni; Pashley 1837, 235, 242 recorded and drew it (cf. Deffner n.d., 151). This wall is indeed different from all other walls on the Ridge: larger stones, greater width, as well as better preservation.

The ancient city on the Anopolis Ridge was effectively deserted from early Roman times, though people still lived in the plain itself.

The Byzantine-Venetian-Turkish period saw the development of the non-nucleated village of Anopoli, with eventually ten neighbourhoods, again on the plain. The VT usage of the ridge has a very different focus from that of the Graeco-Roman period. The VT pottery found on the ridge suggests agricultural and pastoral activities rather than actual habitation. The stones on the flattish area W of Ag. Aikaterini were certainly tidied up at some point, presumably to increase the area available for browsing. The N-facing slopes of the Anopolis Ridge were terraced, and were used until within living memory. Even twenty years ago, people still went up onto the Ridge to collect snails from the stubble. Thus although the Anopolis Ridge was no longer inhabited, people living in the village below it were familiar with it and used it intensively throughout the VT period and well into the 20th c. as well.

The Turkish fort was built to the W of the church after the insurrection of 1866; it was not as definitively destroyed as others in the area in 1878 (cf. the Turkish fort near the neighbourhood of Kampia, wrecked and eventually turned into a mandra). That its construction would have been unpopular is an understatement; Fielding records a local legend that the Turks wanted to build the fort on top of the church, but every time they tried to set a single stone in place, Ag. Aikaterini herself intervened. When one of the Turkish builders tried to take revenge by defecating in the church, he excreted his guts instead, and died; Fielding 1953, 210.

Ag. Aikaterini is described locally as the church for Anopoli/Riza, even though all other neighbourhood churches in Anopoli are actually in those neighbourhoods. There are a couple of graves to the left of the door. Evangelia Tsourinaki, formerly of Anopoli, said that she thought there were once houses between Ag. Aikaterini towards Livaniana.

2. Date: Venetian-Turkish period? More likely middle-later Venetian, but cannot say for certain. Evangelia Tsourinaki was certain in 2004 that Ag. Aikaterini was there in the time of the Revolt of Dhaskalogianni (1770). Ag. Aikaterini is not, unfortunately, mentioned in the Song of Dhaskalogianni, which names only one church, Ag. Astratigos in Aradhena, and mentions the 100 churches of Khora Sphakion (Barmpa-Pantzelios 1947, l. 422; ll. 951–952).

3. Details and Measurements: Small rectangular church with apse; interior walls whitewashed. Bell tower on church.

4. Icons: Ag. Aikaterini, with tamata.

5. Other Features: Large enclosed terrace for church. Cistern.

6. Location:
   2. Visibility: Conspicuously visible position.
   4. Earlier significant structures: Church is built on and near the much older remains of the classical Greek city.

7. Explanation: None.

8. Recorded: 9.96.

9. Additional References: None.

AN CH 2. AGIOS NEKTARIOS (4.19 KAMPOS)

1. Description: Simple rectangular church with apse on car road running N from Anopoli/Kampos to Anopolis/Limnia. Graves to S of church. AN CH 1 Ag. Aikaterini is the only church visible from here.

2. Date: 1971–1975 (inscription in church).

3. Details and Measurements:

4. Icons: Main icon, with string of tamata, is to Ag. Nektarios (1846 –1920, beatified by the 1960s). Also Emmanouil of Sphakia.

5. Other Features: Graves (see below); garden with jasmine and roses; apothiki; ?cistern to NE; electricity.

6. Location:
   3. Liminal location: Outermost edge of Kampos.

7. Explanation:
   3. Specific events and places: According to the inscription in the church, Dhamoulis Orphanoudhakis (1909–1994) of Kampos was the prime mover in getting the church built and decorated, in memory of various Kampos families. Local people say also that he built the church because he wanted somewhere to be buried, and he got his wish: he was buried here in 1994.

8. Recorded: 7.9.96.

9. Additional References: None.

b. Peripheral Churches in the Anopolis Area

AN CH 3. TIMIOS STAVROS (5.21) NEAR LOUTRO

1. Description: Small rectangular church S of the coastal footpath linking Loutro with Khora Sphakion. The church was built onto vaulted mortared structures with an adjacent 2–room drystone structure; other walls below and S of chapel. The church sits slightly inland at 20 masl: it was not built right on the coast because it would soon have been ruined by waves swept up in winter storms. The bedrock here has been heavily eroded by salt spray.

   Some of the land above and N of the church was terraced, and is now browsed, i.e. its use has changed from primarily agricultural to primarily pastoral. The area of the church is SSE of Anopoli/Kampia. The 1:5000 map marks a footpath leading up from the area of the church, but not going as far as Kampia.

2. Date: VT and possibly V. Note that AN CH 4, which was built before 1639, also uses aeolianite.

3. Details and Measurements: Chapel has Gothic arch with internal rib; around door are cut aeolianite blocks (35 x 18cm) with 'braid' moulding.

4. Icons:

5. Other Features: Mortared vaulted structures by chapel, possibly for storage, presumably Roman.

6. Location:

    1. Resources: The church could have been built when the terraces were made.

    2. Visibility: It is conspicuous from the sea, and could also have marked the particularly rough coastline here (compare AN CH 4 which sits at one end of a beach).

7. Explanation: None.

8. Recorded: 26.6.87; 16.6.92. We never gained access to the interior of this church.

9. Additional References: None.

AN CH 4. AGIA PARASKEVI/GLYKA NERA (5.22); PLATES 8 AND 9

1. Description: On the coastal path at the W end of Glyka Nera (Sweet/Fresh Waters) Beach, a small ruined church with an icon stand built on top.

    The church was partly built onto the low cliff at this end of the beach; it sits at 15 masl. It is identified as a church of Ag. Paraskevi, and described as ruined in the 17th c. (Semitecolo 1639). Monanni in his drawing of 1631 labels the beach (Acque dolci, sweet waters), but does not mark a church here or anywhere else on this drawing. It may therefore have been ruined by 1631.

    The church is now buried by a 1.1m deposit of scree. It is said now to be 'a thousand years old'; it may indeed be EV if ruined by the earlier 17th c. (1622, 1639).

2. Date: Church before 1639 or possibly 1631; icon stand after church was ruined.

3. Details and Measurements: Church width 2m55, length 3m25, ending in apse; max internal height 3m35. All walls mortared stone; Gothic pointed apse window with aeolianite zig-zag moulding. Traces of plaster on interior.

Icon stand built on top of already ruined church (1m70m high x 1m32m wide x 0m65 deep); last whitewashed 30 years ago. No icon inside now, but interesting that locals say it is to Ag. Paraskevi, to whom the long-ruined church was dedicated.

4. Icons: None preserved.

5. Other Features: Attached to N end of apse is a wall (4.20m) attached to a small cave; this wall jogs out 55cm, to join a crosswall, 1.50m long.

6. Location:

    1. Resources: The church and icon stand mark the fresh water seep that gives the beach its modern name. Venetian galleys could beach here easily, and stock up on fresh water. There is sufficient fresh water here for people to try piping it in to Loutro (1992).

    The church and icon stand also show where the coastal path continues at the W end of the beach, where it rises from beach level to 'ground level'.

    2. Visibility: They would once have been conspicuous coastal landmarks; indeed the beach was once known as Santa Veneranda (Ag. Paraskevi): Semitecolo 1639.

7. Explanation: None.

8. Recorded: 16.6.92.

AN CH 5. TIMIOS STAVROS (6.03A) NEAR MOURI

1. Description: Simple rectangular church with apse, 500m W of Mouri (6.02) in the Ilingas Gorge at 880m. The church lies on the boundary separating the communes of Anopoli and of Khora Sphakion, which includes Mouri. The boundary starts at the mouth of the Ilingas Gorge on the coast and continues N through the Gorge.

The church stands just N of the junction of the main gorge and a smaller gorge on the W. It lies, very oddly, on the actual floor of the gorge (despite the existence of higher and more secure platforms nearby); ground level has risen round the church some 2m since construction. Early in 2003 the church was engulfed by cobbles and had to be dug out. A large cypress by the NW corner of church postdates the blocking of W door of church. Most trees are cypress, with prickly oak and maple.

Timios Stavros is one of the churches in Sphakia where those suspected of stealing animals used to swear their innocence (P. Kelaïdhis 1981, 106–15, 1982, 154–5); the others are Ag. Nikolaos (Samaria, 1.17), Astratigos (Aradhena, 3.20), Thymiani Panagia (8.01), Ag. Zoni (8.05); cf. pp. 76 and 81–83 where this practice is discussed at length.

The village of Mouri was effectively deserted after it was strafed by the Germans in World War II; it would probably have been deserted in any case once road-building started after the war. Today shepherds based elsewhere (e.g. Anopoli, Khora Sphakion) use the area for browsing. Bedding was stored in the church, presumably for a shepherd needing accommodation for the night.

The church is currently well-maintained, though we do not know if this maintenance has been continuous since the disruption of the 1940s; the day of Timios Stavros, 14 September, was certainly celebrated in 2003.

50 E of the church is a cave filled with fresh water (see explanation below). Diameter of cave ca 10m; depth of water 1m. A modern inscription affixed to it claims that this is where in 1367 the leaders of the Kallergi revolt of 1365 unsuccessfully took refuge.

50m SW of church there are three long-ruined structures: two 2–roomed houses, one with built-in cupboard, large stones used; a third upslope, with large prickly oak in middle. Sherds seen near houses include a good number of T sherds and two Graeco-Roman sherds. Old pear trees near houses; one very large olive tree S of church also in middle of gorge. These houses perhaps constituted a sub-neighbourhood of Mouri.

100m S of the church (i.e. near the spring) there is a footpath said to run up to the village of Mouri. The spring is visible from the top of the footpath on the western side of the Ilingas Gorge, but the church is not. It may be that the church is visible on the eastern side of the gorge, near Mouri but we did not have the opportunity of checking this. The spring is almost certainly not visible from the eastern side of the gorge.

Mr Georgios Dourountakis of Khora Sphakion organised the key of the church for us in 2003, and we are most grateful to him.

2. Date: VT, earlier than graffito of 1877; probably V.

3. Details and Measurements: Church is 9 x 4m, including apse of 1m. Three Gothic arches were built over (and therefore later than) the frescoes to serve as supports; one of these arches has a graffito of 1877. Roof now flat (and cemented); no sign of tile fragments from earlier roof, which is unusual (but similar to Ag. Pavlos in Sphakiano Gorge, 6.23). Bell of 1980, associated with major 1978 restoration of church (including building of shelter on S side for the annual festival).

4. Icons and Frescoes: Frescoes depict various scenes: Christ on W end; baptism of Christ; Kosmas, Christ and Damian; Apostles; scene with agrimi on S wall; ship and agrimi in apse. Gerola (1961, 48 no.215) says only that there are 'remains' of frescoes; Cormack (pers. comm. 2006) says that the frescoes date from the 15th to 19th centuries.

5. Other Features: Shelter built onto S side of church. Enclosed courtyard.

6. Location:
   1. Resources: The church marks the location of the cave with the spring. The spring and cave are visible from the top of the W side of the main ravine.
   2. Visibility: It may be that the church is visible from the ridge on the E side where the three hamlets of Koutsoura (6.03), Mouri (6.02), and Kavros (6.01) are.

7. Explanation:
   1. Human boundaries: The church marks the boundary separating the communes of Anopoli and Khora Sphakion.
   2. Supernatural contact: A family poem (P. Kelaïdhis 1983–4, 2 no. 105) relates that a Kelaïdhis, out hunting and in need of water, saw and shot a (miraculous) agrimi, which was standing beside a concealed source of water. In gratitude he gave up seafaring, and founded the church. The leaders of the 1367 Kallergi revolt are also thought to have taken refuge, unsuccessfully, in the cave where the spring is.

8. Recorded: 30.9.03.

9. Additional References: Faure 1979, 73, note 1; Plymakis 2001a, 210 (photo of agrimi in church fresco).

ICON STANDS

AN IK 1. ARADHENA GORGE (OPPOSITE 3.20 VILLAGE OF ARADHENA)

1. Description: Metal icon stand, painted blue, on the E side of the Aradhena Gorge, tucked into the first bend below the top of the gorge, on the main kaldirimi linking the villages of Anopoli and Aradhena. This kaldirimi remained in use until the bridge over the Aradhena Gorge was complete in 1987.

The houses and other structures of Aradhena lie along the W side of the eponymous gorge, with the 14th c. church of Arkh. Mikhail on the edge near the top of the kaldirimi (date of church, Gallas et al. 1983, 253–4). Also visible from AN IK 1 is the church of Ag. Vasilios further W (see PLATE 6 for the location of this church).

This icon stand is angled so as to be convenient for people going down to Aradhena and coming up to Anopoli. The glass window points up slope so as to be visible for people looking for the top of the path in the dark, e.g. when they were setting off before dawn to pick olives in the late autumn.

2. Date: 1976; see explanation 1 below.

3. Details and Measurements: Metal box with triangular roof with cross on top, on metal pole cemented to ground. Total H: approx. 1m20.

4. Icons: Ag. Antonios at back on left; Christ on at back on right; Ag. Varvara on left side, Ag. Georgios on right side. One holy postcard.

5. Other contents: incense burner, box with candles, bottle of oil, spray of jasmine; no coins.

6. Location:

    3. Liminal location: The Aradhena Gorge is deep. The kaldirimi, still in use until the bridge was completed in 1987, remains in reasonable condition; nonetheless this is not a place for carelessness, particularly when it is dark. The village of Aradhena sits right on the western edge of the gorge. This icon stand is the 'last outpost' of Anopoli, marking its outermost edge.

7. Explanations:

    1. Human Boundaries: The Aradhena Gorge marks the commune boundary separating the commune of Ag. Ioannis, which includes Aradhena, from Anopoli.

    3. Anna Kantounaki from Limnia/Anopoli said that this icon stand was put up in 1976 as a thank offering, because of an accident (on or near the gorge path) that didn't happen.

8. Recorded: 13.8.98; first seen by us in 1986.

9. Additional References: Plymakis 2001b, 25 (photograph).

AN IK 2. AGIA EIRINI KHRYSOVOLANTOU (W OF 4.19 KAMPOS); PLATES 10 AND 11

1. Description: Metal icon stand, now painted white, on the N side of the main car road leading W from Kampos/Anopoli; 0.2 km from Glymenos Café in Kampos. AN IK 2 contains several votive plaques (tamata); AN IK 12 contains one tama. Votive plaques in icon stands are highly unusual; these are the only two icon stands studied by me to have any.

    There is a large rosemary bush at the foot of the icon stand. Behind and to the NW is a well or cistern. The new (concrete) house to the E has a beautiful garden; its inhabitant may be the person who tends the icon stand.

2. Date: Later 20th c. Anna Kantounaki from Limnia/Anopoli said that there used to be an old stone icon stand here which was damaged and then replaced with this metal one.

3. Details and Measurements: Metal box with triangular roof with cross on top, supported on four metal poles in ground. Total H: 1m14. Currently white, formerly green, and pale green.

4. Icons: Three icons, all to Ag. Eirini Khrysovolantou (10th c. saint from Cappadocia in Turkey).

5. Other Contents: Tamata (votive plaques): two women, baby, girl, hand, female torso; glass with floating lamp on saucer, bottle of oil, box with lighter, wicks, glass vase with fake flowers, plastic doily/placemat as liner; coins.

6. Location:

    3. Liminal location: Currently on N side of main (paved) road leading W from Kampos/Anopoli. There is still a footpath E of the icon stand leading N to the old main path to Mouri and the Madhares (and probably continuing from the path from Gyro/Anopoli). If there was an older, stone icon stand, then it might have marked the junction of this northern path with the main path going W out of Anopoli, a junction which was destroyed when the car road was built. Ag. Eirini Khrysovolantou is a sufficiently 'old' saint for this to be possible.

7. Explanation: None given.

8. Recorded: 7.9.96.

9. Additional References: None.

AN IK 3. AGIOS ELEFTHERIOS (JUST W OF 4.19 KAMPOS)

1. Description: Concrete icon stand to S of main car road leading W from Kampos/Anopoli towards Ag. Dhimitrios/Anopoli, approximately 50m W of the Glymenos Café in Kampos. There is also a footpath running N-S along the front of the icon stand.

The icon stand lies E of an old house, unusual because of its size and enclosure wall, owned by an old woman but deserted by 1996. It faces E, away from the house and toward Kampos. This icon stand was accidentally destroyed by a truck between 2004 and 2005; it is unlikely that this icon stand will be replaced.

Date: Said to be 35 years old in 1996, so ca 1961. This is roughly the time when the main car road to Anopoli was built; cf. Doren 1981[1974], 148; he visited Anopoli in the 1960s when the car road ended at Anopoli, but he does not specify exactly where. It may well have stopped in Kampos, in other words just short of this icon stand.

3. Details and Measurements: Concrete icon stand with flat roof, painted white.

4. Icons: Five icons of Ag. Eleftherios, two or three of Ag. Georgios, one of Panagia, one of Ag. Ioannis Prodhromos.

5. Other Contents: Suspended oil lamp, bottle of oil, matches, charcoal, coins.

6. Location:
3. Liminal location: I was told that the old woman who owned the house built the icon stand, which would make it an early 'personal' icon stand linked directly to a particular house. The icon stand is certainly liminal in terms of protecting the outer edge of the house. (It could also have marked a junction in footpaths. Not entirely clear because of the difficulty of dating this stretch of the car road.)

7. Explanation: None.

8. Recorded: 7.9.96.

9. Additional References: None.
Note: This icon stand no longer exists. It was destroyed when a truck ran into it some time between September 2004 and September 2005.

AN IK 4. AGIOS GEORGIOS (AKA THE FRIDGE; WSW OF 4.12 GYRO); PLATE 12

1. Description: Large, whitewashed icon stand, on the footpath. Plymakis (2001b, 38) says that it is on the footpath linking the villages of Livaniana and Anopoli, SW of and closer to Anopoli. Also described locally as the place for a kolatso (snack) stop on the way from Livaniana to Anopoli. Another way of describing the location of AN IK 4 is to say that it lies between two sets of junctions in footpaths: 1. the junction of footpaths from Livanian and from a working area with multiple enclosures to the S, and 2. the junction of footpaths to the neighbourhoods of Ag. Dhimitrios and Gyro. AN IK 4 lies below and SW of split to Ag. Dhimitrios and Gyro; and above and NW of the junction of footpaths from Livaniana and Loutro.

2. Date: Earlier 20th c., if not older. Base cemented 7.8.72.

3. Details and Measurements: A tall upright 'monolithic' rectangle, wider at the bottom so that there is a convenient shelf below the metal-mounted glass window of the actual icon box toward the top. Not possible to tell what material lies under the whitewash. Window frame once painted blue. Total H 1m85; base is 1m x 1m. Base cemented 7.8.92.

4. Icons: Four icons of Ag. Georgios.

5. Other Contents: Lights, bottle of oil, matches, candles, newspaper lining dated April-May-June 1996. Metal mule shoe plate, broken bottles, whitewash brush nearby.

6. Location:
   2. Visibility: Because the icon stand faces out from Anopoli, I interpret it as part of the 'early warning system' for this village; cf. AN IK 5, 6, and 16.
   3. Liminal location: You cannot see either of the relevant villages (Anopoli, Livaniana) from this icon stand. Depending on the direction of the walker, AN IK 4 is the first indication that Anopoli lies nearby, on the N side of the ridge; as well as a confirmation that the walker is near the junction of the footpaths from Livaniana and the area due S.

7. Explanation:
   2. Supernatural contact: N. Glymenakis (teacher in Anopoli) said that the icon stand marks the footsteps of Ag. Georgios on his way from Gavdhos up to Ag. Thodhori in the White Mountains (1996); ditto A. Protopappadhakis of Kampos/Anopoli (1998). The area is known as 1. Tsi pates tou Agiou Georgiou (at the footsteps of St George); and 2. Ta Loumata (the revmas or small gorges).
   Plymakis says that the icon stand was built shortly after the time when Ag. Georgios (and his horse) left footprints in the bedrock: the saint had killed a wild beast threatening to tear apart either Crete or the island of Gavdhopoula (2001b, 68).

8. Recorded: 22.8.96.

9. Additional References: Plymakis 2001b, 68–69, with photographs of AN IK 4 and the prints left by Ag. Georgios and his horse.

AN IK 5. PANAGIA (SE OF AN CH 1 AG. AIKATERINI, 4.21 SECTOR A)

1. Description: Stone built icon stand with concrete cap and cairn on top, whitewashed, on main footpath linking the villages of Loutro and Anopoli, below and SE of the church of Ag. Aikaterini (AN CH 1), where the footpath divides, depending on the destination of the walker; one footpath goes NW to Riza/Anopoli, while the other went to the NE, and has been destroyed by the car road which goes to just below the church. The icon stand is on the E of the path, with its window facing W, and slightly downhill.

2. Date: Tempting to say that this icon stand is 19th c., though no definite evidence. Suggested date is therefore earlier 20th c.

3. Details and Measurements: Icon stand itself is square, 0.92m x 0.92m. Wooden door and frame, so door would have to be open if lights to be seen. Total H, including concrete cap, 1m49.

4. Icons: Two icons, both Panagia (Virgin Mary).

5. Other Contents: Oil, lights, incense, candles, matches, quick-lighting charcoal, plastic liner, coins. Newspaper stuffed in back behind icons, 17.6.93.

6. Location:

2. Visibility: this icon stand is part of 'early warning system' for Anopoli; cf. AN IK 4, 6, and 16. Once again, neither Anopoli nor Loutro can be seen from this icon stand.

3. Liminal location: Outermost edge of Anopoli.

7. Explanation:

8. Recorded: 26.8.96.

9. Additional References: None.

AN IK 6. AGIOS GEORGIOS LIMNIA EPANO (N OF 4.33 LIMNIA)

1. Description: Whitewashed stone icon stand E of the footpath leading N from Anopoli toward the village of Mouri to the NE and the Madhares (summer pastures) to the NW. It is below and S of the dirt road leading from Anopoli to Mouri and the Madhares. Plymakis says that it is on the mountain road to Ammoutsera in the White Mountains (2001b, 105). The local toponym for this area is sto Poro Lango, 'at the narrow place of the route'. The icon stand faces S, towards Anopoli. Looking S you can see almost the whole Plain of Anopolis – the Anopolis Ridge with AN CH 1 Ag. Aikaterini; the neighbourhoods of Riza, Gyro, Kampos, and probably Pavliana and Ag. Dhimitrios; the Ts'Asi basin; the Aradhena Gorge; the church of Prophitis Ilias W of Aradhena (see PLATE 6 for the location of Prophitis Ilias).

2. Date: Earlier 20th c. if not earlier still.

3. Details and Measurements: Whitewashed stone, with metal cross on top; metal frame with glass window. Total H: 1m57. Icon stand is built near lump of bedrock. Low stone 'wall' built to make a circles around it, possibly to protect it from the car road. Round, drystone structure built without mortar nearby, with opening on SSE.

4. Icons: Two modern icons of Ag. Georgios; one metal medallion of Panagia and baby Jesus. (Third icon of Ag. Georgios seen 12.9.04.)

5. Other Contents:
7.9.96: Oil lamp, oil in plastic bottle, incense in can; plastic bag with ?; lined with newspaper (13.7.95).
12.9.04: oil lamp, incense burner, incense, lighter, matches; coin (1 Euro cent, 2002); newspaper (17.4.04).

6. Location:

2. Visibility: As described above.

3. Liminal location: This icon stand lies at almost the last point where you can see the Anopolis Plain before you make the ascent to Mouri/ the Madhares. It represents the outermost edge of Anopoli.

7. Explanation:

2. Supernatural contact: Someone saw a ghost here and built the icon stand to keep it from coming back.

8. Recorded: 7.9.96; 12.9.04.

9. Additional References: Plymakis 2001b, 105 (photograph, top right).

AN IK 7. AGIOI KONSTANTINOS AND ELENI (N OF 4.33 LIMNIA)

1. *Description*: Metal icon stand outside hypostego (sheepshed) E of the main dirt road (which here follows the line of the old footpath) leading from Limnia/Anopoli to the village of Mouri and the Madhares, about 0.3 km N of the turnoff to Limnia. The window faces the S side of the road.

2. *Date*: Some time between the 1960s when the first car roads were made, and 1988 (painted graffito on wall of hypostego); probably after the EU subsidies for the construction of hypostega, so some time in the 1980s.

3. *Details and Measurements*: Metal box with 'pediment' roof and cross on top, on four metal legs on concrete platform. Roof is red, frame of window is blue, otherwise icon stand is painted white. Total H: 2m02, including cross, 24cm.

4. *Icons*: Konstantinos and Eleni at back, Ag. Georgios to right.

5. *Other Contents*: Lamp, matches, lighter, oil, paper napkins, coins. Broken incense burner on ground below.

6. *Location*:
   3. Liminal location: Just outside hypostego facing the road, presumably for protection of the sheepshed. The icon stand was put up by the person who built the hypostego, a member of the Orphanoudhakis family.

7. *Explanation*: None.

8. *Recorded*: 7.9.96.

9. *Additional References*: None.

AN IK 8. AGIOI PANTES (W OF 4.33 LIMNIA)

1. *Description*: Metal icon stand at the intersection of the side road to Anopoli/Limnia and the main road going N to Mouri and the Madhares. The icon stand is on the N side of the road to Limnia, facing S. About 2m00 to the W is a concrete pumping station.

2. *Date*: Some time after the 1960s when the first car roads to Anopoli were made. Cf. AN IK 3 above.

3. *Details and Measurements*: Metal box with pediment roof and cross on top, with four metal legs on a concrete platform; icon stand painted blue. Total H: 1m50 including cross.

4. *Icons*: Largest icon is Ag. Pantes (All the Saints); others to Ag. Spyridhon, Ag. Eirini, Ag. Ioannis Prodhromos, the Last Supper, Ag. Georgios, Panagia and baby Jesus, Ag. Nikolaos, and Prophitis Ilias. All icons in plastic bags.

5. *Other Contents*: Incense, incense burner, matches in box, oil lamp, bottles of oil, cloth, 1 nail, loose matches, coins. Plastic bag, newspaper in the bottom but date of newspaper not visible.

6. *Location*:
   3. Liminal location: Crossroads.

7. *Explanation*: None.

8. Recorded: 7.9.96.

9. Additional References: None.

AN IK 9. AGIOS PANTELEIMON (E EDGE OF 4.33 LIMNIA); PLATE 13

1. Description: Large, well-whitewashed icon stand now near refurbished (concrete) house and partly paved road at the E edge of the neighbourhood of Limnia, where two footpaths converged.

2. Date: 1948.

3. Details and Measurements: Probably stone under the whitewash. Window frame painted blue. Small compartment under the actual icon box. Total H: more than 2m00.

4. Icons: Ag. Panteleimon at back (biggest icon). Ag. Georgios on L. Both new. Small dark oval icons propped against Ag. Georgios.

5. Other Contents: Incense burner, oil lamp, oil bottles, floats for oil lights, matches. In compartment below, bottles, matches.

6. Location:
   3. Liminal location: The house was and still is at the outer edge of Limnia, near the intersection of two footpaths, and so in a doubly liminal and dangerous position.

7. Explanation:
   2. Supernatural contact: Anna Kantounaki, a widow, still lived in the house at the time the icon stand was recorded. When she and her husband were first married in 1947, he had a dream that a neraïdha (dangerous spirit; see Stewart 1991, 4–5; cf. 29–30 and 77–78 above) was going to come and take her away, so he built the icon stand. She is the sister of Khrysi Athitaki and they were both born in Limnia; see also AN IK 18, which is similar in appearance.

8. Recorded: 7.9.96.

9. Additional References: None.

AN IK 10. AGIOI APOSTOLOI (PETER AND PAUL) (SW OF 4.33 LIMNIA, N OF 4.19 KAMPOS)

1. Description: Icon stand in its own enclosure, on the E side of the car road linking Kampos and Limnia, 0.6 km S of the turning to Limnia, where the car road crosses the footpath linking Kampos and Limnia. The icon stand faces more or less due W onto the road.

2. Date: later 20th c.

3. Details and Measurements: Icon box (front 34, side 37 cm) with pediment on four-legged stand. Total H 1m30. Glass front of icon box broken in 1996 and repaired with plastic bag (bag disappeared by 2000). Cross on top made of two sticks and a piece of white cloth, tied on to the box with wire. Legs supporting box cemented to ground. Enclosure with gate is 1m56 square. All painted pale green at the time of recording.

4. Icons: Two icons to Peter and Paul.

5. Other Contents: Oil lamp, incense burner, bottles of oil, one or two leaves plus one dead carnation and one dead red rose.

On platform within enclosure: newspaper (date invisible); plastic bag with charcoal or incense, old bits of incense burner, can with incense, one dead red rose.

6. Location:
   3. Liminal location: This icon stand is placed at a spot where the car road crosses the old footpath leading N from Kampos to Limnia.

7. Explanation:
   3. Specific events and places: One person said that this icon stand was put up because someone was saved from an accident; another person said that it was put up by someone who lives in Limnia, and that it has nothing to do with an accident.

8. Recorded: 7.9.96; 2000 (slide).

9. Additional References: None.

AN IK 11. AGIOS GEORGIOS (4.19 KAMPOS); PLATE 14

1. Description: Painted prefabricated concrete icon stand in the shape of a church, on concrete stand, built into corner of fence around new house.

2. Date: 1997.

3. Details and Measurements: The icon stand has the shape of a cruciform church with dome and cross on top, plus a bell tower over the door. The church is painted white, with architectural details such as the moulding around the arched doorway and window frames in grey. The roofs of the church and the dome are painted orange in order to look like tiles.

4. Icons: The icon stand has Ag. Georgios painted over the door of the church. Icons of Panagia and Ag. Spyridhon at back.

5. Other Contents: Incense burner perched on concrete stand. (Not possible to investigate the inside of this icon stand in detail.)

6. Location:
   3. Liminal location: The icon stand is built into the corner of the fence of a new house near the boundary with an older house.

7. Explanation:
   3. Specific events and places: Roula Protopappadhakis, who lives in the new house, said that, according to tradition, there was once a church on this spot. They chose to put up an icon stand in the form of a church in order to commemorate the church. She also said that a German bomb fell near the church but not on it. They light the icon in the evening.

8. Recorded: 13.9.98.

9. Additional References: Plymakis 2001b, 113 (photograph, bottom left).

AN IK 12. AGIOI RAPHAIL AND NIKOLAOS; AGIA EIRINI (BETWEEN 4.19 KAMPOS AND 4.39 SKALA)

1. Description: Metal icon stand outside new house on car road E of Kampos; by 2000 superseded by concrete church on concrete pole.

2. Date: 1980s, to go with house? Newer icon stand, between 1998 and 2000.

3. Details and Measurements: Older metal icon box with plastic window, painted white, with red pediment and cross on top. Metal supports below attached to a single metal pole. Pebble enclosure around base of icon stand. Total H: ca 1m50.

Newer concrete icon box has blue kamara roof with blue bell tower and blue cross on top.

4. Icons: Ag. Raphail, Nikolaos, Eirini (older icon stand).

5. Other Contents: Older icon stand: bottom lined with foil. Plastic boxes with incense, wicks, matches, one tama (votive plaque) of a man; cf. AN IK 2. One coin. Incense burner on ground in little pebble enclosure.

6. Location:
   3. Liminal location: Outside a new house.

7. Explanation: None.

8. Recorded: 7.9.96; 2000 (slide).

9. Additional References: None.

AN IK 13. Agios Nikolaos (4.39 Skala)

1. Description: Metal icon stand, painted pale blue, NNW of two paved roads, one leading to a few new houses, the other to Mariana.

2. Date: Circa 1980; see explanation below.

3. Details and Measurements: Metal icon box and pediment roof with cross on top; glass window in centre of box. Mounted on four metal legs in concrete platform. Total H: Approx. 1m65.

4. Icons: Ag. Nikolaos in back; Ag. Savvas to right; two old and illegible oval icons hanging from the top; small icon of Panagia and baby Jesus; another illegible icon propped against icon of Ag. Nikolaos.

5. Other Contents: Lamp, burner, bottle of oil, two plastic containers (one with wicks and coins). Plastic sheet for lining.

6. Location:
   3. Liminal location: Junction of main road and side road leading to the neighbourhoods of Skala and Mariana; Skala is the closer of these two neighbourhoods.

7. Explanation:
   2. Supernatural contact: Deduced from conversation with a lady re-painting the icon stand, who also gave me the date: the icon stand was put up when 'their' road, the side road to Anopoli/Skala and Mariana, was paved because it is good to have icon stands at crossroads; I understood her to mean that icon stands give protection from dhaimones.

8. Recorded: 24.6.92; 7.9.96.

9. Additional References: None.

AN IK 14. AGIOS NIKOLAOS (BETWEEN 4.39 SKALA AND 4.56 MARIANA)

1. Description: Icon stand facing S onto main car road, near a crossroads in the old footpath system.

2. Date: ?1993. (Was there an earlier one here?)

3. Details and Measurements: Metal icon box with pediment roof and cross on top, painted blue. There is a stone to keep the door of the box closed. The icon stand sits on a square concrete plinth on a square concrete pillar, both white. Total H: 1m65. The icon stand is in front of a big outcrop of bedrock.

4. Icons: Two larger icons of Ag. Nikolaos at back, in plastic bags; one of Ag. Phanourios.

5. Other Contents: Glass lamp on paper napkin, wicks, incense, oil bottles with paper napkins, plastic lining on bottom. Incense burner on concrete platform.

6. Location:
   3. Liminal location: This icon stand is near a junction formed by the old footpath with double walls coming from Anopoli/Mariana, crossing the old main footpath to Loutro, and then looping back to Anopoli/Kampia.

7. Explanation: None.

8. Recorded: 7.9.96.

9. Additional References: None.

AN IK 15. O KHRISTOS (4. 54 VADHIANA)

1. Description: A whitewashed icon stand was built on what used to be the main footpath with double walls, leading W from Anopoli/Kampia, at a junction where a side road (then unpaved) ran up from the main car road to a new, two-storey house built in the 1990s. Further on, there is a hypostego (sheepshed). The house and the hypostego are both owned by the Phasoulakis family. There is a pumping station for the water system installed in the 1990s (many parts of Anopoli had no running water before then) to the right of the icon stand.

   At the turn of the millennium, a new concrete, church-shaped icon stand replaced the older one. By 2002 a protective case had been added. This newer icon stand is clearly related to the new two-storey house. The spur road leading up from the main road is now paved.

2. Date: Older icon stand: 20th c., before later 1980s; see details below. Newer icon stand there in 2000; with roof in 2002.

3. Details and Measurements: The older icon stand was built of stones underneath the whitewash; it is similar in form to AN IK 9. The window frame and cross on top are both painted blue. The cross is inscribed with the name Emm[anouil]. Ioan[nis]. Savioli in capitals. According to Thodhori Athitakis of Kampia, this man died in the later 1980s, so the icon stand was built some time before this date. Total H: 1m64.

   The newer icon stand is in the shape of a church with bell tower, like AN IK 11, but larger. It is painted grey, with lines to indicate 'stones'. The protective case is rectangular, with clear plastic walls and a solid red pitched roof.

4. Icons:
Older icon stand: Icon of Jesus with 'the healing lord' (o Kyrios therapevon) in back; Ag. Ioannis Prodhromos to right, Jesus to left.

5. Other Contents:
Older icon stand: Wicks, incense tin, matches, charcoal, oil lamp, burner, plastic, plastic lining. Newspaper underneath but date not visible. Discarded plastic lining and newspaper of 7.5.95 to right of icon stand.

6. Location:
3. Liminal location: The older icon stand was built at a crossroads in the footpath system; the old side footpath may have led to the neighbourhood of Anopoli/Vadhiana, now deserted.

The new icon stand, in the same location, still a crossroads, is linked only to the new two-story house. The older icon stand served as a collective marker, while the newer one has a function restricted to a single dwelling. Presumably the owners of the house felt that the older icon stand had to be removed, as it was literally inscribed with the memory of someone from a different family.

7. Explanation: None.

8. Recorded: 7.9.96; 9.00; 9.02.

9. Additional References: None.

AN IK 16. ? (NE OF 4. 49 KAMPIA); PLATE 15

1. Description: Large, formerly whitewashed icon stand facing SSE near the top of the main footpath leading up (and NNW) from the village of Khora Sphakion to Anopoli, where it splits into two. AN CH 1 Ag. Aikaterini and the top of the church in Mariana were visible to people coming up the main footpath, once they reached this icon stand. This footpath has seen little use since the construction of the road to Anopoli in the 1960s. Near the icon stand, along the line of the footpath, there are now some young pear trees, as well as the usual phlomis bushes (*P. fruticosa*).

This icon stand and its companion AN IK 17 are visible from the main car road as you come from Anopoli/Skala and Mariana toward Anopoli/Kampia. A dirt road now runs up from the main car road to AN IK 16 and its companion AN IK 17 (see next entry). This road is linked with the construction of the Phasoulakis hypostego, mentioned above in connection with AN IK 15.

2. Date: Earlier 20th c., if not earlier still.

3. Details and Measurements: Whitewash worn so that individual stones of icon stand can be seen. Wooden door and frame, i.e. no glass for icon box. Wooden pole on top presumably once part of a cross, with the horizontal element now gone. Total H; ca 2m00.

4. Icons: Old icon on wood, illegible. One empty glass frame.

5. Other Contents: Two glass bottles, one glass lamp suspended from top, one bottle of Azakh (Ajax), one little jar. No lining.
N.B. The debris around this icon stand included material markedly older than that seen around most others. Sherds: Turkish-modern, Turkish, Venetian-Turkish, nondescript

Graeco-Roman, and even one very possible piece of Prehistoric. Other: glass fragments, cans, a sponge; black plastic mesh, a broken walking-stick, part of a gate with rubber soles as hinges.

6. Location:
2. Visibility: The icon stand is the only sign of the village visible to people coming up the footpath from Khora Sphakion. Only when you reach this icon stand can you see any actual part of the village itself, and in this case what you see is the top of the church in Mariana. AN IK 16 is thus part of the 'early warning system' for Anopoli. Cf. AN IK 17.
3. Liminal location: This icon stand marks an important junction in the footpath system on the E edge of the non-nucleated village of Anopoli.

7. Explanation: None. No one had any idea which saint(s) this icon stand was dedicated to.

8. Recorded: 9.7.87; 8.9.96.

9. Additional References: None.

AN IK 17. PANAGIA (NE OF 4.49 KAMPIA); PLATE 15

1. Description: Blue metal icon stand at top of dirt road running up from main car road near Phasoulakis house and hypostego (see AN IK 15, 16), facing NNW.

2. Date: Later 20th c.; cf. AN IK 14.

3. Details and Measurements: Rusted blue metal icon box with pediment roof and cross on top with metal supports, attached to a single metal pole on a small concrete and stone platform. Total H: 1m35.

4. Icons: Two icons of Panagia with baby Jesus, one at back and one to left; one Ag. Aikaterini propped at back. Ag. Georgios on right; Jesus on left.

5. Other Contents: Oil lamp incense burner, oil bottles, incense in perished plastic bag, thread (for wicks?) in little metal dish, wet paper, coins of 1990, 1992.

6. Location:
1. Resources: Its position, more or less back to back with AN IK 16, but facing in to Anopoli, rather than out to Khora Sphakion, suggests a completely different view of this area from that implied by AN IK 16: literally inward- rather than outward-looking. It is still at a junction in the footpaths, but these are paths now used mostly by shepherds, not by everyone coming from Khora to Anopoli.

7. Explanation:
4. Vow or promise: Thodhori Athitakis of Anopoli/Kampia said that Evangelia Saviolis put this icon stand up as a tasimo (vow).

8. Recorded: 8.9.96 [festival of Panagia in Kampia].

9. Additional References: None.

AN IK 18. PANAGIA AND AGIOI THEODHOROI (4.49 KAMPIA)

1. Description: Well-whitewashed stone icon stand originally built in 1977 on open ground facing the main car road, opposite the Taverna Elvetia, near a footpath leading past the communal cistern and further along to the SW, the old neighbourhood of Anopoli/ Kampia.

In 1989 the owners of the taverna, Thodhori and Khrysi Athitakis, began to build a new two-storey structure (house for them on ground floor, more rent rooms up above). The icon stand was no longer in the right place on the plot of land, so they demolished and rebuilt it in 1990, in the same style, using the same metal elements, a bit further to the SE. The icon stand was built onto the new structure, and the gate to the small enclosed area in front of it is built onto the icon stand. It is still lit every evening when the Athitakises are in residence.

2. Date: 1977; rebuilt in 1990.

3. Details and Measurements: Old fashioned, whitewashed stone icon stand very similar in appearance to AN IK 9; the women in the two relevant families are sisters. Metal frame for door of icon box and metal cross on top painted yellow brown. Cross is incised with the initials ThAA [Thodhori Athitakis] and the date 1977. Total H: 1m60.

4. Icons: Panagia at back; Ag. Theodhoroi and Ag. Georgios on right; Ag. Ioannis Prodhromos on left.

5. Other Contents: Oil bottle on paper napkin, lamp on paper napkin, plastic liner.

6. Location:
   3. Liminal location: At the junction of the main car road and a side road as described above. An aerial photograph of 1980 shows that the main road was then paved only as far as the Taverna Elvetia. The icon stand marks the junction of a footpath with the end of the paved road.

7. Explanation:
   2. Supernatural contact: Both Khrysi and Thodhori Athitakis had each dreamt of the Panagia and Ag. Thodhori, and had thought of building an icon stand to the Panagia and Ag. Theodhoroi independently; they were delighted to discover their unspoken agreement.

8. Recorded: 22.8 – 7.9.96.

9. Additional References: None.

II. Frangokastello
(PLATES 3 and 4)

OUTLYING CHURCHES

FK CH 1. AG. THEODHOROS (8.24)

1. Description: Small rectangular church on NE corner of low hill or knob at the W edge of the central part of the Frangokastello Plain, at 44–64 masl. The church is positioned so that the main northern and inland footpath coming into the plain from the W passes right by it. (The main southern footpath runs along the coast, eventually passing FK CH 3 Ag.

Pelagia.) Ag. Theodhoros thus marks the W inland entry point to the plain. In addition. two footpaths join to the E of the knob to form a single path leading E to Patsianos.

There are agricultural terraces on the E slope of the knob. A dirt road now runs from the main car road down to the church; the water-loving shrub Vitex agnus castus grows in the little gully along its E side and around the E side of the knob. A small area on the dirt road linking the church to the main road is used for modern box beehives.

From Ag. Theodhoros several churches are visible: the two village churches of Patsianos, plus FK CH 4 Ag. Astratigos, FK CH 7 Ag. Nikitas, FK CH 8 Ag. Kharalampos.

Papadhopetrakis links the church with the so-called 'Bird War' (Polemos Ornithon), a Sphakiote uprising against the Venetians in 1570 (Papadhopetrakis 1888, 30; cf. Tomadhakis n.d.[ca 1965]).

2. Date: VT, and could be V before 1570, if the information about the Bird War is correct.

3. Details and Measurements: Exterior and interior cemented, with cursory whitewash. Exterior: bench along part of N side of church. Interior: Gothic vault; half buttresses; no wall paintings (or at least none visible now); new templo. Tamata on main icon.

4. Icons: Ag. Theodhoros.

5. Other Features:

6. Location:
3. Liminal location: At the W entry to the plain on the inland route following the roots of the mountains; two footpaths coming from the W join to form one of the main footpaths to Patsianos.

7. Explanation:
1. Human boundaries: The church is a few hundred metres E of the boundary between the communes of Asphendou and Patsianos.
3. Specific events and places: The priest in Patsianos said that there used to be a now deserted (Christian) neighbourhood of Patsianos here. Close to the site of the church, the Survey has found some ancient material (the latter mainly R-LR), but no sign of any BVT use other than the church, and the two agricultural terraces already mentioned. The only candidate for a neighbourhood in the general vicinity of Ag. Theodhoros is the Late Roman settlement site at Trokhaloi (8.23) to the SE, which has ruined walls and stone piles, as well as abundant LR pottery.

8. Recorded: 29.6.92; 6.9.96.

9. Additional References: None.

FK CH 2. AGIOS IOANNIS PRODHROMOS (8.25); PLATES 16 AND 17

1. Description: Church in highly visible position on the ridge NW of Patsianos Kephala, at 342 masl. From here, you can see *to the W*, the Loutro peninsula, AN CH 1 Ag. Aikaterini; two of the village churches in Ag. Georgios/Kolokasia; *to the S*, the N side of Patsianos Kephala, the village of Patsianos and its church, FK CH 3 Ag. Pelagia, 7 Ag. Nikitas, 8 Ag. Kharalampos, 9 Ag. Ioannis sto Lakko, *to the E*, FK CH 10 Prophitis Ilias and 11 Ag. Georgios, the 'lump' of Plakias, and the Paximadi Islands.

The church lies near the 1956 boundary separating the communes of Asphendou and Patsianos. Specifically, the church lies just W of the line between the village of Patsianos from the old village of Ag. Georgios/Kolokasia (and its successor Ag. Nektarios, built on the car road after World War II). The church was used by both villages as well as by people from farther afield.

Ag. Ioannis Prodhromos is on the footpath linking Ag. Georgios/Kolokasia and Patsianos. The spring Pano Nero lies at the foot of the cliffs above and NNW of the church; a hose ran up to it in 2004. The footpath leading to the spring continues to Kolokasia Kastro (8.31), where there are remains of fortifications (Byzantine or early Venetian) and an Early Iron Age settlement.

In 1990, the church in 1990 had large cracks in its walls, and the roof was about to collapse. It had been repaired and recently whitewashed by 2004. In the same year we saw well-maintained olive terraces at the same level as the church and below it; sheep were grazing above it.

2. *Date*: This church may be the one listed in 1637 under the village of Vraskas to the W (Khaireti 1968, under Vraskas).

3. *Details and Measurements*: No frescoes; arch slightly pointed.

4. *Icons*: 19th c. icons on the templo – Ag. Ioannis Prodhromos, Ag. Kharalampos, Panagia, Christ.

5. *Other Features*: Newspaper on window sill dated 23 August 2000; saint's day is 29 August.

6. *Location*:
    1. Resources: Nearby water source at Pano Nero.
    2. Visibility: The church lies in a highly visible position on the ridge separating two villages, and on the footpath between them.

7. *Explanation*:
    1. Human boundaries: The ridge mentioned above is also the actual boundary between the communes of Asphentou and Patsianos.

8. *Recorded*: 2.7.90; 1.9.96 (information collected locally, but no visit); 11.9.04.

9. *Additional References*: For the 1956 commune boundaries, see Geronymakis 1996, 13 (key to map; 284. church; 285. spring Pano Nero; 286. Kastri ['ereipia paliou kastrou', ruins of an old fort = our site 8.31 Kolokasia Kastro]; map at back of book).

FK CH 3. AGIA PELAGIA (8.18)

1. *Description*: Church and cemetery inside an enclosure, near the coast, above and N of an area where fresh water collects. In spring fresh water runs on the surface, and there are several small wells. Members of the Koukounarakis family told me that the area E and below the church was used intensively by people from Patsianos and Kapsodhasos until about 40 years ago. The presence of fresh water permitted the remote cultivation of tomatoes, beans, and okra in 'kitchen gardens'; the washing of clothes; and the watering of animals. Fielding, who saw women harvesting grain in this area one May in the early 1950s, comments on the lush vegetable gardens and countless fresh water streams below the church, and notes also that Ag. Pelagia is the patron saint of sailors (1953, 285–286). The church sits at the intersection of two major footpaths, the coastal route running NW-

SE (more or less exactly replaced by the car road), and one of the footpaths running S from Patsianos.

2. Date: VT, possibly V rather than later.

3. Details and Measurements: The church is built on a naturally flattish lump of breccia. Bell stand on (now cemented) roof of church. Enclosure has two gates, one on the N and one of the E, leading in from a one-room ruin.

4. Icons:

5. Other Features: There are two almiriki trees here (tamarisks), the larger one inside the enclosure; all the other trees in this area are carobs. Running water; electricity.

6. Location:
   1. Resources: Near a source of fresh water in an area used to grow garden crops before large-scale irrigation in the Frangokastello Plain.
   3. Liminal location: At junction of two major footpaths.

7. Explanation: None.

8. Recorded: 5.9.96; 9.4.99.

9. Additional References: None.

FK CH 4. AGIOS ASTRATIGOS (8.38); PLATE 18

1. Description: Smaller Venetian chapel set very precisely on bema of larger Late Roman basilica. The LR basilica was in the middle of a settlement, still marked by ancient terrace walls, structure walls, and stone piles, many marked by huge carob stools (up to 1000 years old?; Nixon and Moody et al. 1994, fig. 6 for the ancient terrace walls; Price and Nixon 2005). The V chapel was not part of a settlement; there are no other later walls or structures, and only two post-Roman sherds (1 V, seen by Hood 1967, 56 and 1 T). The V chapel has been a ruin for some time.
  The LR church and settlement lay in the western side of the Frangokastello Plain, closer to the coast than to the BVT village of Patsianos , in the middle of good arable land. Both the LR church and settlement and the V chapel had a view over the whole plain.

2. Date: V? (because of frescoes, and LR.

3. Details and Measurements: Early Christian basilica, dimensions 24.60m x 12.40m, including apse (chord 3.60m, radius 2.40m); internal colonnades (one column footing visible); central aisle 5.70m wide; door on N side, and narthex; fragments of mosaic floor said to have been found (plan in PLATE 18; the plans in Sanders 1982, 123 and Curuni and Donati 1987, 47 are wrong). Line on N wall shows end of each day's work. Basilica dated to 2nd half of 6th c. AD. Possibly a mosaic pavement.
    Basilica 'cut down' at a later date, and new V chapel built in sanctuary (bema) of the original basilica (as at FK CH 7 Ag. Nikitas, 8.50), and frescoes of geometric patterns added (14th c.?). One monolithic column of Proconnesian marble (2.10m tall) and base reused in chapel, and six pieces of other columns nearby; all presumably from original LR basilica; other limestone (poros?) stones also built into later church. The later church is long ruined, and poor quality walls were built to turn the basilica into a mandra. But even so everyone locally is sure that its name is Ag. Astratigos, also called Michael Arkhangelos

in some publications; the names Ag. Eustratios and Ag. Eustratigos found in some publications are erroneous. Gerola 1961, 49 no.229; Andrianakis 1982, 33; Andrianakis 1984, 76–7; Andrianakis 1998, 20–1).

4. Icons: Gone.

5. Other Contents: Gone.

6. Location:
   1. Resources: Good arable.
   4. Earlier significant structure: Basilica within settlement chosen for V church (because of use of local resources).

7. Explanation:
   3. Specific events and places: The church may lie in the area mentioned in a local legend. The area was a settlement originally called Patsianos (after a certain Patsos). After the settlement was ruined by Saracen and Algerian pirates (Papadhopetrakis 1888, 30), the inhabitants fled to modern Patsianos; the legend does not mention either basilica or church.

8. Recorded: 25.6.87; 26.6.88; 5.7.90; 8.93; 31.8.96 (LFN); 22.9.00.

9. Additional References: None.

FK CH 5. AGIOS IOANNIS VOKOLOS (8.48)

1. Description: Ruined church with cemetery 250m SW of Patsianos, on a major footpath leading from Patsianos to the coast via the 'West River' (gully to W of village). The church is said by Spiro Vranakis (9.96) of Patsianos to have been in reasonable condition until the mid 1960s, when something shifted in the cave beneath it.

   Pinelopi Koukounaraki (July 1999) said that this church was in an area where there was ploughing with oxen, hence the name Vokolos (cowherd). This church is near site 8.46 Khalasma (Patsianos) Alonia, where there are 14 threshing floors (alonia) for grain. Priest from Patsianos (September 1996) said it was Ag. Ioannis Chrysostomos.

2. Date: Wall-paintings suggest a V date.

3. Details and Measurements: Rectangular church with apse. Lunette above door on W. Stone plaque with cross above lunette. Frescoes, now in ruinous state, but dated to 14th c.; Gerola 1961, 49 no.223; Andourakis 1978, 13.

4. Icons: Gone.

5. Other Features:

6. Location:
   1. Resources: Arable; area now terraced for olives.

7. Explanation: None.

8. Recorded: 6.7.90; 5.9.96 (LFN).

9. Additional References: None.

FK CH 6. AGIOS ATHANASIOS (E OF 8. 51 KAPSODHASOS)

1. Description: Church and cemetery NE of Patsianos and W of Kapsodhasos, with new cemetery on other side of the ravine, below the bend of the dirt road to Kallikrati, on the main footpath from Patsianos to Kapsodhasos. People from both villages are buried in this cemetery.

2. Date: V (because of wall-paintings and graffito).

3. Details and Measurements: Two-centred Gothic vault, and arch over door; frescoes all over (which may date not long before graffito of 1426, perhaps ca 1420); dedicatory inscription; ancient tiles (Gerola 1961, 49 no. 224; Lassithiotakis 1971, 117–18; Andourakis 1978, 15–16; Bissinger 1995, 227–8).

4. Icons:

5. Other Features: Two cypresses about 20 years old (in 1996). No spolia. Electricity.

6. Location:
   3. Liminal location: The church lies on the main E-W footpath between the two villages, and marks a line between them.

7. Explanation:
   1. Human boundaries: The church is on the boundary between two villages (Patsianos and Kapsodhasos) and two communes. In some periods, it marked the eastern edge of the eparchy of Sphakia: under V and T rule Kapsodhasos was part of the territory of Rethymnon (in the commune of Ag. Vasileios). Basilicata 1629 (drawing) marks boundary between Sphakia and Ag. Vasileios running through the FK plain). Kapsodhasos was added to the new eparchy of Sphakia in 1867; Papadhopetrakis 1888, 30.

8. Recorded: 5.9.96.

9. Additional References: See above under details and measurements.

FK CH 7. AGIOS NIKITAS (8.50 = SITE NUMBER SHARED WITH AG. KHARALAMPOS); PLATES 19 AND 20

1. Description: Smaller V chapel set very precisely on bema of larger LR basilica, ca 150–200m from coastal cliff. The site is on or near the 'East River', a gully at its N end and a line of areas with 'wet' vegetation towards its S end, running S from the general area of the Kallikrati Gorge/FK CH 6 Ag. Athanasios, although no water is now visible on the surface. There is plenty of arable here, and coastal access would have been easy, even after the sea level became lower in later antiquity. The later church was not part of a settlement; the earlier basilica probably was.

   The earlier basilica fell into disrepair and was already ruined when the later church of Ag. Nikitas was built on top of it; indeed 1m of sediment had accumulated again its N wall. The frescoes preserved in the later church are dated to the second half of the 13th c. The later church had given its name to the area by 1340, when the area is referred to by the

Venetians as Santo Nicheta in 1340.[1] By this time the traditional/modern settlement pattern of the plain had more or less come into being. Because of piracy the local inhabitants asked the Venetians to build a fort on the coast, and the castle known as Frangokastello was constructed in 1371–74. In the early fifteenth century Buondelmonti also refers to the fort as 'Nichiton Sanctum' (1422 [1897], 103, 108 (long version), 1422 [1897], 140, 142 (short version); 1981, 114; cf. 101 (composite version)).

On 17 May 1828, Hadzimikhalis Dhaliannis and his men were slaughtered by Mustapha Pasha and a much larger group of Turks in the area between the church and the fort. Ghosts of the slaughtered Greeks -- the Dhrossoulites, or 'dew-shades' -- are said to appear every May at dawn, only to vanish at sunrise. They can still be seen, but only by the right people; Dawkins 1930, 34–35; Fielding 1953, 279 ff.; Llewellyn Smith 1965, 154–155.

Local legends say that the basilica was built on an altar of Victorious Apollo (Nikeios Apollon), which stood in the middle of an ancient city called Nikita. Athletic competitions were held here. Time passed and the basilica collapsed. According to these legends, the church was erected at roughly the same time as the fort; the latter was constructed with building material from the ruins of the ancient city. Ag. Nikitas was chosen as the saint for the new church because of the altar to Nikeios Apollo, and the name of the ancient city. The legends say that the church was destroyed twice by the Turks and rebuilt both times. The competitions held in the area of the church came to an end in the 18th c. after the Revolt of Dhaskaloghianni, which led to the depopulation of Sphakia (Papadhopetrakis 1888, 30–31; Splinis 1999, 14; cf. S. Kelaïdhis 2003 [1960], 98).

Dawkins retells a legend about Turkish pirates seizing a Christian girl who was washing clothes near the church; in one version of the story, it was Ag. Nikitas himself who brought her home again. Khrysoulaki-Paterou tells another version, with Barbary pirates as the abducting villains.[2]

The church remains in use today. In the 20th c. athletic and other competitions were added to the usual celebration of the saint's festival on 15 September. The first of these modern Nikiteia were held in the area near the church in 1956, and included various events: shooting, dancing; exhibitions of weaving and handicrafts, and of agricultural products such as cheese and honey. The account of the first modern Nikiteia explicitly links it with ancient competitions (P. Kelaïdhis 2003, 10; the illustration accompanying this article shows ancient Greek competitions). After a gap the tradition was revived in the 1990s (Splinis 1999, 14, with photograph of crowds; ([no author] 1999, with photograph of procession with icon), and continues into the 21st c. The saint's day and its accompanying

---

[1] The original publication of a Patmian MS of AD 1196 (Miklosich and Müller 1890: 6. 130–3, no. 6) referred to a monastery of Ag. Nikitas at Nisi, built probably in the 1180's. This was taken to be the church on the Frangokastello Plain (Tomadhakis 1980). However, a re-edition of the MS (Vranousi 1980: 206–16, no. 21), noting that the MS is damaged at this point, (cautiously) reads not 'Nikitas' but 'Nikolaos', and notes that there is an early church of Ag. Nikolaos (with paintings) at Nisi near Rethymnon. It is therefore not safe to use the Patmian MS as evidence for Sphakia.

[2] Dawkins 1930, 25. Dawkins adds a similar legend for the church of Ag. Nikitas near Tsoutsouros in the eastern Mesara, originally recorded by Spratt 1865, I.343–347. Khrysoulaki-Paterou's version is similar to the Tsoutsouros story (1986, 56–60).

celebrations, as observed by us in 2004, have become a deme event; cf. n. 109 on pp. 80–81 in main text.

2. Date: V (at the latest 14th c.), and LR (6th c.).

3. Details and Measurements: The LR basilica was excavated in 1980 and 1994 by the Byzantine Ephoreia. The church had two aisles (each ending in a pastophorion at the E end), an apse and narthex. Overall length 26.71m x 11.6m; middle aisle 4.50m wide; N aisle 2.34m wide; S aisle 2.28m wide; narthex 10.38m x 3.68m. Intercolumniation ca. 2.25m. Colonnade stopped 3.58m short of narthex, forming a wide open area at the W end. Sanctuary, separated by screen, in E end of central aisle (exactly under the B church); four column bases for baldacchino over the altar.

The basilica has a mosaic pavement which consists mostly of panels with geometric decoration; one panel features a billy goat nibbling spiralling stems (one with a pomegranate); another has a naturalistic rendering of a duck and a stork. A better version of the goat is found in the basilica at ancient Suia (modern Sougia). The mosaic at Ag. Nikitas dates to second half of 6th c. Another mosaic floor in narthex, by different hand, but of same date.

Various spolia from the first church survive, both here and in the nearby monastery of FK CH 8 Ag. Kharalampos: marble impost blocks (?) with cross decoration are re-used inside the later chapel; limestone base and Proconnesian marble base visible on floor; two columns re-used under B arch springs; column stump for altar; three Proconnesian marble columns outside church (one 2.06m long). Like the mosaic, they indicate a date in 2nd half of 6th c. (Pallas 1971, 243–5; Pelekanidhis and Atzaka 1974, 126, no. 114, pl. 98a-b; Sanders 1982, 123, 165; Andrianakis 1982, 33; Andrianakis 1984, 75–6; Asimakopoulou-Atzaka 1991, 44–45 fig. 3; Prof. K. Dunbabin, personal communication 1998; Andrianakis 1998, 16–19).

The later church of Ag. Nikitas is very roughly 5m25 by 3m75. Traces of frescoes survive (2nd half of 13th c), and a graffito of 1371 is preserved (Spanakis n.d., II.387; Gerola 1961, 49 no.227; cf. Lassithiotakis 1971, 118–19 (though the measurements given are questionable), fig. 447 photo of LR capital inside); Andrianakis 1984, 73, 77; Curuni and Donati 1987, 43–5l; Andrianakis 1998, 20.

4. Icons: Ag. Nikitas, Panagia, Khristos.

5. Other Features: A carob tree approximately 250 years old grows out of the apse of the older, larger LR basilica. New gateway erected in the late 1990s.

6. Location:
    1. Resources: Arable land; water.
    4. Earlier significant structure: Existence of the basilica in a well-resourced area used in the V period.

7. Explanation:
    3. Specific events and places: later church built at same time as fort and named after Ag. Nikitas because of name of ancient city; basilica built because of ancient altar to Apollo.

8. Recorded: 25.6.87; 4.7.88; 6.8.89; 7.8.89; 11.7.90; 13.7.90; 6.9.96 (LFN); 21.9.00; 14.9.04.

9. Additional References: None.

FK CH 8. AG. KHARALAMPOS (8.50 = SITE NUMBER SHARED WITH AG. NIKITAS)

1. Description: Double church with cemetery, and monastery just to the W with peribolos wall and gates, near coastal cliff E of the castle at Frangokastello. The immediate area is flat and fertile. The church lies on the main coastal footpath. It is visible from the sea.

Fielding reports that the Dhrossoulites (see above on FK CH 7) were said to emerge at first from the area of this church, and then to move in the direction of Frangokastello (1953, 283).

2. Date: V and T phases, detailed below.

3. Details and Measurements: Ag. Kharalampos has perhaps six phases, of which the first is speculative:

1. Five early Christian capitals built into façade and sides of church, including three marble Ionic capitals with crosses; marble column fr (Proconnesian?) built into foot of staircase. Andrianakis (1982, 33 and 1984, 73, 77) therefore suspects that there was a third LR church in the area, in addition to Ag. Nikitas and Ag. Astratigos (8.38). But the spolia could have been brought from the area of Ag. Nikitas which is a mere 200m away.
2. V chapel, now forming SE corner of present church; tiles look earlier V to M. Hahn. This phase is shown in the 1615 drawing of Frangokastello plain by Basilicata: single-aisled church with belltower.
3. VT phase, in which a N aisle was built beside the original church; V-style windows inserted into old B chapel, and V features on W façade.
4. 19th c. phase. The church was extended to its present size (11.60m x 8.20m), by doubling the length of the two existing aisles. This involved the rebuilding of the façade: the V elements over the door are misplaced. Building and decoration may be by the same craftsman as responsible for the 'Lower Preveli Monastery' built ca 1837; fine altar screen of 1841. Monastery built just W of church: peribolos wall and gates; fine cut blocks. The 19th c phase was a consequence of the activities of a refugee monk there, around 1821; he and a partner administered to the sick of the region (Papadhopetrakis 1888, 32). The doubling in size of the church in the late 1830s and the building of the monastery are probably part of one building phase. The church is named after a Cretan saint who lived 1723–1785. This is presumably the phase when the church acquired its new dedication.
5. Musket holes pierced in peribolos wall and extra height of wall built on N side with musket holes. Perhaps in 1867, when said to be headquarters of the T forces (Dhrakakis 1957: 9). That these were not subsequently blocked up shows that the monastery was already abandoned.
6. Crude carving over door in S side of peribolos with date of 1891. This date could perhaps refer to a phase of restoration.

The church is still in use, and is surrounded by recent graves (1950–1995). Gerola 1905–32, III.172; Andrianakis 1984, 73, 78–79; Andrianakis 1998, 28–30 (with excellent aerial photograph).

4. Icons: Left templo: Panagia, Christ, Panagia, and apostle; Ag. Kharalampos, with tamata. Right templo (dated 1841): Simeon with Nunc Dimittis on scroll; Panagia; Archangel Michael. Also one old wooden panel to Ag. Ioannis Khrysostomos.

5. Other Features: W of the church is a deserted double kamara house, with an adjacent large plastered threshing floor. The house seems to be built over earlier, LR?, structure and cistern (cistern red plaster internally); good LR sherds from round here.

Mill in bay E of Ag. Kharalampos: pit for large vertical wheel, ca 7m diameter.

6. Location:

1. Resources: Arable.
2. Visibility: Conspicuous position by sea.
4. Earlier significant structure: Spolia suggest one somewhere.

7. Explanation: None.

8. Recorded: 25.6.87; 4.7.88; 6.8.89; 7.8.89; 11.7.90; 13.7.90; 1.7.92; 6.9.96 (LFN); 21.9.00.

9. Additional References: None.

FK CH 9. AGIOS IOANNIS STO LAKKO (8.55); PLATE 21

1. Description: Chapel of Ag. Ioannis , 1200m SSE of Kapsodhasos, in a 'lakkos' or hollow with moisture in the plain on the 'East River'. The water-loving plant Vitex agnus castus grows along the N and W sides of the church. Olives planted S of the church (very young trees on the aerial of 1981; much taller by 1996 when the church first recorded for this book).

FK CH 2 Ag. Ioannis Prodhromos and the two villages can be seen from here, but nothing to the S can be seen because of the olives; FK CH 1 Ag. Theodhoros to the W is invisible for the same reason.

Ag. Ioannis sto Lakko is clearly visible from Patsianos and from the following churches: FK CH 2 Ag. Ioannis Prodhromos; FK CH 10 Prophitis Ilias; and FK CH 11 Ag Georgios.

2. Date: V (frescoes).

3. Details and Measurements: Church measures ca 6.50m x 3.75m, plus apse; Gothic vault; frescoed (Gerola 1961, 49 no. 226; Lassithiotakis 1971, 117; Andourakis 1978, 14–15). Walls chinked with tile.

The church includes several spolia, visible on the exterior of the church: two LR grey white marble Ionic capitals in NW corner of façade, and another on SW corner, all presumably Thasian, plus other reused blocks (cf. Andrianakis 1982, 33). The use of LR spolia is important in itself. It is possible, but no more, that their use might also indicate a LR basilica in this location.

There are two bacini holes on façade (the bacini could have been V or T); the four capitals inside the springs of vault do not all match, so could be reused.

4. Icons: Two icons each to Ag. Ioannis Prodhromos (Baptist) and Ag. Ioannis Theologos (Chrysostom).

5. Other Features: No other signs of earlier buildings on this spot; line of breccia cobbles running E of church might be old kaldirimi, but line does not appear on maps. The apparent lack of footpaths here is a mystery.

6. Location:

1. Resources: In water-rich arable.
4. Earlier significant structure: Spolia suggest one somewhere.

7. Explanation: None.

8. Recorded: 3.7.92 (LFN and SRFP); 5.9.96 (LFN).

9. Additional References: None.

FK CH 10. PROPHITIS ILIAS (8. 59, AND WITHIN SURVEY SITE OF SKALOTI PROPHITIS ILIAS 8.72); FIG. 2

1. Description: Chapel of Prophitis Ilias with graves, on ridge, 1km ESE of Kapsodhasos (8.51), but belongs to Skaloti (8.70). The church sits on the W hill of a larger site identified by the Survey (8.72). The church was previously accessible by a footpath and can now be reached on a car road. This area marks the eastern edge of the main section of the Frangokastello Plain.

The altitude of the church, 125 masl, is a reminder that churches to Prophitis Ilias need not be very high. Despite its relatively low height, the church affords a broad view of the plain: the Frangokastello fort; Patsianos (but not Kapsodhasos); FK CH 1 Ag. Theodhoros, FK CH 2 Ag. Ioannis Prodhromos, FK CH 7 Ag. Nikitas, FK CH 8 Ag. Kharalampos, FK CH 9 Ag. Ioannis sto Lakko; and possibly FK CH 5 Ag. Ioannis Vokolos are all visible from here. Skaloti is not visible from this church.

In this case, the area 'seen' by the church is named after it: the land below and to the SW of the church is called Aïlias.

2. Date: V (14th c. because of the frescoes).

3. Details and Measurements: Church: 6.32 x 3.90m. The church is 14th c. and has frescoes of 1335–6; it is not now whitewashed. It appears to have been roofed originally with stone 'tiles' which were removed (perhaps in the rebuilding of the roof) and dumped near the two arcosolia. Scaffold holes on S side of church; chisel marks on cut stones framing doorway. Walls built of uncoursed stone with some tile fragments (?Roman). Mortar very white with limestone grit.

In the church there are several LR spolia, perhaps from an LR basilica: the altar and its stand (impost capital marked with a cross); window pier with two half-columns projecting inward and outward with simplified Corinthian capital (cf. Orlandos 1952–6: II. 426, fig. 389). There could have been an LR church on this site, but we have no direct evidence for it.

Gerola 1905–32, II.334, IV.473; Gerola 1961, 49 no.230; Lassithiotakis 1971, 119–22; *AD* 29 Khron. (1973–4), 935–6, pl. 700c-d (rebuilding of roof); Andourakis 1978, 16–18; Andrianakis 1982, 33; Spatharakis 2001, 101–2.

4. Icons: Main icon of Prophitis Ilias painted on northern spur wall separating nave from apse.

5. Other Features: In the general area of the church, two arcosolium tombs W of church, now collapsed. There are a few mediaeval sherds near the church, but no walls or stone piles to suggest houses here.

On the E side of the W hill, on which the church sits, there were just enough stone piles and HR sherds to suggest a (small) ancient neighbourhood.

The sections exposed along the road to P. Ilias all contain a strange mixture of PH and VT sherds; there is other PH material in the area. The lack of VT structures, or even suggestive stone piles, is surprising given the amount of VT coarse ware here.

There is a spring with built well at the foot of the SE slopes of the W hill (with Prophitis Ilias), and the E hill. The pottery here looks H/R/LR-mediaeval, and dribbles down the terraces to the SE.

6. Location:
  1. Resources: Church is above a spring.
  3. Liminal location: Marks the E edge of the FK plain proper.
  4. Earlier significant structure: Spolia suggest one somewhere.

7. Explanation:

8. Recorded: 92; 5.9.96; 21.9.00.

9. Additional References: None.

FK CH 11. AGIOS GEORGIOS SKALOTIS (W OF 8.70 SKALOTI)

1. Description: Near the top of a low hill, with a revma below and to SE of church, now accessible by dirt road just before (W of) Skaloti. Stream bed has oleander and carob; thyme, *Poterium spinosum*, asphodeline also growing here. Green schist. Visible from here : church at Sterni (5.02); Thymiani Panagia (8.01); village of Komitadhes (8.02); church of Ag. Nektarios (constructed 1984); FK CH 2 Ag. Ioannis Prodhromos and general area of Pano Nero; FK CH 3 Ag. Pelagia; FK CH 10 Ag. Ioannis sto Lakko. Not visible from here: FK CH 10 Prophitis Ilias; Skaloti; Argoule. Ag. Georgios is less than 500m from FK CH 10 Prophitis Ilias.
  The church lies on a 'high' inland path linking the villages of Kapsodhasos and Skaloti.

2. Date: VT? (Gothic arch, build-up of soil along N wall.)

3. Details and Measurements: 5m95 E-W x 4m20 N-S; apse sticks out 80 cm. Door and window on S side. Porch built on S side. Interior whitewashed; no frescoes visible. Used to have Gothic arch, now difficult to make out since restorations. Altar is LR capital with cross on N side, and column; both whitewashed but presumably marble. Fragments of ceramic rooftiles outside.
  Ground level on the uphill (N) side of the church is at least 1m00 above floor level.

4. Icons: No templo in 1996 (restorations begun but not completed). New templo of 2001 has four icons, Ag. Georgios (with 1 tama), Mother of God, Khristos, Ag. Ioannis Prodhromos.

5. Other Features: Cemetery with separate enclosure wall built onto W side of church. Surnames are from Skaloti.

6. Location:
  2. Visibility: Early warning for the village of Skaloti, which is not visible at this point.
  3. Liminal location: Outermost edge of Skaloti village territory.
  4. Earlier significant structure: Spolia suggest one somewhere.

7. Explanation: None.

8. Recorded: 6.9.96; 21.9.00; 12.9.04.

9. Additional References: None.

FK CH 12. San Marco (built into 8.32 Frangokastello Fort)

Monanni's 'aerial' view of the castle in 1631 shows it with two two-storey buildings against the N and E walls, a central chapel, and a small entrance where the present SW doorway is. Some foundations of the internal buildings are probably still visible, but there is no trace of the church above ground.

References: Monanni 1631.

ICON STANDS

FK IK 1. Agios Ioannis Khrysostomos (near 8. 42 Patsianos); Fig. 3

1. Description: Metal icon stand painted white, at junction of the main E-W car road to the villages of Patsianos and Kapsodhasos with the road leading down to Frangokastello on the coast. The icon stand faces W.

2. Date: 1982.

3. Details and Measurements: Metal icon box with rounded roof and cross on top, on for metal legs with a pile of stone as base, plus two fragments of wooden beehive. Ag. Ioannis and 1982 painted on exterior in blue, in 'holy' script. Total H: 1m30.

4. Icons: One to Ag. Ioannis Khrystostomos, two to Panagia, one too dark to tell.

5. Other Contents: Oil lamps, incense, lighter, oil, embroidered cross picture, plastic lining, newspaper dated 17.8.03; no coins.

6. Location:
   3. Liminal location: Crossroads, also marked by six other signs: distances to Frangokastello and villages; Ministry of Culture sign to the actual fort of Frangokastello; E4 (official European trail); local hotels; etc, plus telephone pole with streetlight.

7. Explanation: None particularly for this icon stand, but people from Patsianos say that dhaimones lurk at crossroads; cf. pp. 29, 51, and 71–78 above.

8. Recorded: 2.10.03.

9. Additional References: None.

FK IK 2. (W of 8.18 Ag. Pelagia)

1. Description: Marble icon box, outside a new house W of FK CH 3 Ag. Pelagia, on the S side of the coastal car road.

2. Date: 1990s?

3. Details and Measurements: Marble icon box on concrete plinth on stone lump, facing W onto driveway outside house. Little tiles on pediment 'roof'; metal cross on top. Glass front of box broken; no icon inside. House is still inhabited (dog; chickens; car in driveway).

4. Icons: None.

5. Other Contents: None.

6. Location:
    3. Liminal location: Outside house.

7. Explanation: None.

8. Recorded: 2.10.03.

9. Additional References: None.

FK IK 3. Vranakis Memorial (between 8.18 FK CH 3 Ag. Pelagia and the Fort, 8.32)

1 .Description: On the N side of the coastal car road, a marble memorial to Kharalampos Vranakis, which is remarkable for two reasons: 1. no icon is included; 2. the memorial was erected by friends of the deceased (rather than kin). The Vranakis family is based in the village of Patsianos; family members own tourist establishments (hotel, taverna, etc.) on the coast near the road.

2. Date: After 1995 and before 2000.

3. Details and Measurements: Total H: 1m50. Upper part is marble plaque supported on two marble footings, with metal crucifix and two other metal attachments on either side of it, plus upper inscription. Plaque and footings sit on horizontal marble slab, above vertical marble-faced upright box member with inscribed marble plaque attached to it (= lower inscription). The whole thing is cemented into the ground with a smooth concrete area around it.

Text of inscriptions (all in capitals):

A. upper part:	Kharalampos l. Vranas
	Skotothike se trokhaio
	29.1.1995 eton 25

B. lower part:	Kheimonas 1995
	O Kharontas ekatevyke arga/
	tsi 29 tou Genari,/
	kai s'arpaxe alypeta apo/
	ti dhipli grami [sic] tou dhromou./
	san aetos ephyges psylla [sic] mas./
	Komatia [sic] exerizoses mesa/
	apo ti kardhia mas.
	Stolidhi tou mpaxe eisoune/
	sti parea./
	Phtera eikhes kai petouses/
	panda me glendia kai khares/
	ta neiata sou glendouses./
	Tsi limnes tou ouranou/
	n'anapafthi i psykhi sou./
	Ekia sti thesi pou ephylaxane/
	oi praxeis tsi zoi sou.
	I parea sou.

Translation:
Kharalampos I. Vranakis/ was killed in a traffic accident/29.1. 1995 aged 25.

Winter 1995
Kharon came down late/ on the 29th of January,/ and seized you without pity from the double line of the road.
Like an eagle you fled high above us/ and tore out pieces from within our hearts.

You were the flower of the garden among your friends./ You had wings and you flew,/always with fun and joy./ You took pleasure in your youth.

In the lakes of heaven/may your soul find rest,/ where the deeds of your life have kept a place for you.
        Your friends.

A. upper part: ΧΑΡΑΛΑΜΠΟΣ Ι. ΒΡΑΝΑΣ
                      ΣΚΟΤΩΘΗΚΕ ΣΕ ΤΡΟΧΑΙΟ
                      29.1.1995 ΕΤΩΝ 25

B. lower part: ΧΕΙΜΩΝΑΣ 1995

                      Ο ΧΑΡΟΝΤΑΣ ΕΚΑΤΕΒΥΚΕ ΑΡΓΑ
                      ΤΣΗ 29 ΤΟΥ ΓΕΝΑΡΗ
                      ΚΑΙ Σ'ΑΡΠΑΞΕ ΑΛΥΠΗΤΑ ΑΠΟ
                      ΤΗ ΔΙΠΛΗ ΓΡΑΜΗ ΤΟΥ ΔΡΟΜΟΥ.
                      ΣΑΝ ΑΕΤΟΣ ΕΦΥΓΕΣ ΨΥΛΛΑ ΜΑΣ
                      ΚΟΜΑΤΙΑ ΕΞΕΡΙΖΩΣΕΣ ΜΕΣΑ
                      ΑΠΟ ΤΗ ΚΑΡΔΙΑ ΜΑΣ.

                      ΣΤΟΛΙΔΙ ΤΟΥ ΜΒΑΞΕ ΕΙΣΟΥΝΕ
                      ΣΤΗ ΠΑΡΕΑ.
                      ΦΤΕΡΑ ΕΙΧΕΣ ΚΑΙ ΠΕΤΟΥΣΕΣ
                      ΠΑΝΤΑ ΜΕ ΓΛΕΝΤΙΑ ΚΑΙ ΧΑΡΕΣ
                      ΤΑ ΝΕΙΑΤΑ ΣΟΥ ΓΛΕΝΤΟΥΣΕΣ.

                      ΤΣΗ ΛΙΜΝΕΣ ΤΟΥ ΟΥΡΑΝΟΥ
                      Ν'ΑΝΑΠΑΥΘΗ Η ΨΥΧΗ ΣΟΥ.
                      ΕΚΙΑ ΣΤΗ ΘΕΣΗ ΠΟΥ ΕΦΥΛΑΞΑΝΕ
                      ΟΙ ΠΡΑΞΕΙΣ ΤΣΗ ΖΩΗ ΣΟΥ.

                      Η ΠΑΡΕΑ ΣΟΥ.

The lower inscription consists of two parts, prose and verse (two verses of four lines each). The text, though short, draws on Classical, Turkish, and Modern Greek tropes and terms: Kharon (originally the ancient ferryman who conveyed the dead across the River Styx to the underworld); baxes (garden), a Persian word which came in to Modern Greek through Ottoman Turkish bahçe; Cretan ekia, there (ekei in 'normal' mainstream Modern Greek); the word praxeis, also used for (the book of) Acts in the New Testament; and references to that fierce bird, the eagle. The spelling is occasionally incorrect. I am grateful to Peter Mackridge for helping me to translate the text, and to disentangle the prose and poetry.

4. Icons: None included; crucifix in upper part.

5. Other Contents: None.

6. Location:
   1. Resources: N side of the main car road through the coastal touristic area near the Venetian fort at Frangokastello.

7. Explanation:
3. Specific events and places: The place where a young man was killed in a car accident.

8. Recorded: 2.10.03.

9. Additional References: Cf. Plymakis 2001b, 80–83.

FK IK 4. Panagia, Ditch W (8.33)

1. Description: Blue metal icon stand between the W side of large irrigation ditch, and the E side of the dirt road running NNE along its W side. The junction of the ditch and the two dirt roads running along it is just N of the coastal car road, opposite the fort of Frangokastello. This icon stand faces W, away from the ditch.

2. Date: The ditch is present on aerial photographs of 1981; the icon stand is contemporary with or later than the ditch.

3. Details and Measurements: Metal icon box with rounded roof with cross on to, on metal legs (also blue) set into the ground. Total H: 1m20 not counting the cross.

4. Icons: One to Panagia; one too dark to tell.

5. Other Contents: Incense, two incense burners, oil, lighter, candle, cardboard, newspaper of 16.3.00; no coins.

6. Location:
   1. Resources: Near a major new feature (the ditch) changing the land use of the area.
   3. Liminal location: Crossroads.

7. Explanation: None.

8. Recorded: 2.10.03.

9. Additional References: None.

FK IK 5. Khristos o Theologos, Ditch E (8.33)

Description: Rusting icon stand between the E side of large irrigation ditch, and the W side of the dirt road running NNE along its E side. The junction of the ditch and the two dirt roads running along it is just N of the coastal car road, opposite the fort of Frangokastello. The icon stand faces E, away from the ditch. About 2m00 away is an electricity pole (DEH) with other electrical devices. A little farther away is a signpost marking the junction of two E4 routes gives walking times expressed in hours (Kallikrati, 4 hours; Asi Gonia 7 hours; Argyroupoli 9 hours; Khora Sphakion 4 hours; Loutro 7 hours).

2. Date: The ditch is present on aerial photographs of 1981; the icon stand is contemporary with or later than the ditch.

3. Details and Measurements: Metal icon box with pediment roof. Door rusted shut but eventually opened. Metal legs set into ground. Total H: 1m31.

4. Icons: Khristos o Theologos in centre; on left, Ag. Nik- (Nikolaos? Nikitas?); on right, icon with two people and a child.

5. Other Contents: Oil, two incense burners, newspaper of 17.1.02; no coins.

6. Location:
    1. Resources: Near a major new feature (the ditch) changing the land use of the area.
    3. Liminal location: Crossroads near ditch; also the junction of two E4 paths.

7. Explanation: None.

8. Recorded: 2.10.03.

9. Additional References: None.

BIBLIOGRAPHY

Adams, Ellen (2004). Power and Ritual in Neopalatial Crete: A Regional Comparison. *World Archaeology* 36.1, 26–42.

Alcock, Susan E. (1994). Minding the Gap in Hellenistic and Roman Greece. In Susan Alcock and Robin Osborne (eds.) *Placing the Gods. Sanctuaries and Sacred Space in Ancient Greece*, 247–261. Oxford, Clarendon.

Alcock, Susan E. (2001). The Reconfiguration of Memory in the Eastern Roman Empire. In Susan E. Alcock, Terence N. D'Altroy, Kathleen D. Morrison and Carla M. Sinopoli (eds.) *Empires: Perspectives from Archaeology and History*, 323–350. Cambridge, Cambridge University Press.

Alcock, Susan E. (2002). *Archaeologies of the Greek Past. Landscape, Monuments, and Memories.* Cambridge, Cambridge University Press.

Alcock, Susan E. and Robin Osborne (eds.) (1994). *Placing the Gods. Sanctuaries and Sacred Space in Ancient Greece.* Oxford, Clarendon.

Alexiou, Margaret 2002 (2nd edition, revised by Dimitrios Yatromanolakis and Panagiotis Roilos). *The Ritual Lament in Greek Tradition.* Lanham, MD/Oxford, Rowman & Littlefield.

Andourakis, Georgios B. (1978). Τοιχογραφημένοι βυζαντινοί ναοί τῆς Κρήτης. Athens, Andourakis.

Andrianakis, Mikhalis G. (1982). Ο νόμος Χανίων κατά την παλαιοχριστιανική περίοδο· κατάλογος μνημείων. *Khania 1982*: 22–49.

Andrianakis, Mikhalis G. (1984). Το Φραγκοκάστελο Σφακίων. *Arkhaiologia* 12, 72–80.

Andrianakis, Mikhalis G. (1998). *The Frangokastello at Sfakia.* Athens, Ministry of Culture, Archaeological Receipts Fund.

Ashmore, Wendy and Bernard Knapp (eds.) (1999). *Archaeologies of Landscape. Contemporary Perspectives.* Oxford, Basil Blackwell.

Asimakopoulou-Atzaka, Panagiota I. (1991). The Mosaic Pavements of the Aegean Islands during the Early Christian Period. *Corsi di Cultura sull' Arte Ravennate e Bizantina* 38, 33–65.

Atherden, Margaret and Jean Hall (1999). Human Impact on Vegetation in the White Mountains of Crete since AD 500. *The Holocene* 9.2, 183–193.

Barmpa-Pantzelios (n.d.). Τὸ τραγούδι τοῦ Δασκαλογιάννη, ed. Vasileios Laourdas (1947). Herakleion, Mourmel.

Basso, Keith H. (1996). Wisdom Sits in Places. Notes on a Western Apache Landscape. In Steven Feld and Keith H. Basso (eds.) *Senses of Place*, 53–90. Santa Fe (NM), School of American Research Press.

Bender, Barbara (ed.) (1993). *Landscape: Politics and Perspectives.* Oxford, Berg.

Bernières, Louis de (2004). *Birds without Wings.* London, Secker and Warburg.

Bevan, Andrew H., Charles Frederick, and Athanasia Krahtopoulou (2003). A Digital Mediterranean Countryside: GIS Approaches to the Spatial Structure of the Post-Medieval Landscape on Kythera (Greece). *Archeologia e Calcolatori* 14, 217–236.

Bickford-Smith, Roanden Albert H. (1898). *Cretan Sketches.* London, R. Bentley and Son.

Binford, Lewis R. (1978). *Nunamiut Ethnoarchaeology.* New York, Academic Press.

Bissinger, Manfred (1995). *Kreta: Byzantinische Wandmalerei. Münchener Arbeiten zur Kunstgeschichte und Archäologie* 4. Munich, Editio Maris.

Blackman, David, Keith Branigan, A. R. Doe, D. C. Homes, and John Bintliff (1977). An Archaeological Survey of the Lower Catchment of the Ayiofarango Valley. *Annual of the British School at Athens* 72, 13–84.

Blackman, David and Keith Branigan (1982). The Excavation of an Early Minoan Tholos Tomb at Ayia Kyriaki, Ayiofarango, Southern Crete. *Annual of the British School at Athens* 77, 1–57.

Boulay, Juliet du (1974). *Portrait of a Greek Mountain Village*. Oxford, Clarendon.

Bourchier, J. D. (1890). The Stronghold of the Sphakiotes. *The Fortnightly Review* 54, 186–201.

Bradley, Richard (ed.) (1996). *Sacred Geography*. World Archaeology 28.2. London, Routledge.

Bradley, Richard (1998). *The Significance of Monuments: On the Shaping of Human Experience in Neolithic and Bronze Age Europe*. London, Routledge.

Bradley, Richard (2000). *An Archaeology of Natural Places*. London, Routledge.

Brumfield, Allaire (2000). Agricultural and Rural Settlement in Ottoman Crete, 1669–1898. A Modern Site Survey. In Uzi Baram and Lynda Carroll (eds.) *A Historical Archaeology of the Ottoman Empire: Breaking New Ground*, 37–78. New York/London, Kluwer Academic/Plenum.

Bryer, Anthony and David Winfield (1985). *The Byzantine Monuments and Topography of the Pontos*. Dumbarton Oaks Studies 20. Washington, Dumbarton Oaks Research Library and Collection.

Buondelmonti, Cristoforo (1897 [1422]). *Descriptio Insule Crete,* ed. É. Legrand. *Description des îles de l'Archipel, par Christophe Buondelmonti*, Publications de l'École Spéciale des Langues Orientales Vivantes, sér. 4, vol. 14. Paris, Leroux (Repr. Amsterdam, Philo, 1974).

Buondelmonti, Cristoforo (1981 [1422]). *Descriptio Insule Crete*, ed. Marie-Anne van Spitael. Herakleion, Syllogos Politistikis Anaptyxeos.

Cameron, Pat (2003, 7th ed.). *Blue Guide to Crete*. London, A. and C. Black.

Carruthers, Mary (1998). *The Craft of Thought. Meditation, Rhetoric, and the Making of Images, 400–1200*. Oxford, Oxford University Press.

Carter, Joseph Coleman (1994). Sanctuaries in the *Chora* of Metaponto. In Susan E. Alcock and Robin Osborne (eds.) *Placing the Gods. Sanctuaries and Sacred Space in Ancient Greece*, 161–198. Oxford, Clarendon.

Castel, Jean-Yves (1980). *Atlas des Croix et Calvaires du Finistère*. Quimper, Société Archéologique du Finistère.

Chadwick, John (1976). *The Mycenaean World*. Cambridge, Cambridge University Press.

Chaniotis, Angelos (2005). Heiligtümer überregionaler Bedeutung auf Kreta. In Peter Funke (ed.), *Kult-Politik-Ethnos*. Stuttgart, Steiner.

Cherry, John F. (1986). Polities and Palaces: Some Problems in Minoan State Formation. In Colin Renfrew and John Cherry (eds.) *Peer Polity Interaction and Socio-political Change*, 19–45. Cambridge, Cambridge University Press.

Christides, Vassilios (1984). *The Conquest of Crete by the Arabs (ca. 824). A Turning Point in the Struggle between Byzantium and Islam*. Athens, Academy of Athens.

Coldstream, Nicolas (1976). Hero-cults in the Age of Homer. *Journal of Hellenic Studies* 96, 8–17.

Cole, Susan Guettel (1994). Demeter in the Ancient Greek City and its Countryside. In Susan Alcock and Robin Osborne (eds.) *Placing the Gods. Sanctuaries and Sacred Space in Ancient Greece*, 199–216. Oxford, Clarendon.

Cole, Susan Guettel (2004). *Landscapes, Gender, and Ritual Space: The Ancient Greek Experience*. London, University of California Press.

Cormack, Robin (1985). *Writing in Gold. Byzantine Society and its Icons*. London, George Philip.

Cormack, Robin (1990). Byzantine Aphrodisias: Changing the Symbolic Map of a City. *Proceedings of the Cambridge Philological Society* 36, 26–41.

Cormack, Robin (1997). *Painting the Soul. Icons, Death Masks, and Shrouds*. London, Reaktion.

Cormack, Robin (2000). *Byzantine Art*. Oxford, Oxford University Press.

Curuni, Spiridone Alessandro and Lucilla Donati (1987). *Creta bizantina*. Rome: Dipartimento di Storia dell'Architettura, Restauro e Conservazione dei Beni Architettonici dell'Università di Roma 'La Sapienza'.

Cyriacus of Ancona (1455 [2003]). *Later Travels*. Ed. and transl. by Edward Bodnar with Clive Foss. Cambridge, MA, Harvard University Press.

Damer, Seán (1988). Legless in Sfakiá: Drinking and Social Practice in Western Crete. *Journal of Modern Greek Studies* 6, 291–310.

Damer, Seán (1989). *Cretan Highlanders. The Making of the Sphakiot Legend.* Centre for Urban and Regional Research Discussion Paper 37. Glasgow, University of Glasgow.

Davies, Siriol (2004). Pylos Regional Archaeological Project, Part VI: Land and Settlement in Venetian Navarino. *Hesperia* 73, 59–120.

Dawkins, R. M. (1930). Folk-Memory in Crete. *Folklore* 41, 11–42.

Déceneux, Marc and Daniel Mingant (2001). *La Bretagne des Enclos et des Calvaires.* Rennes, Editions Ouest-France.

Deffner, Michael (n.d., ?1928). Ὁδοιπορικαὶ ἐντυπώσεις ἀπὸ τὴν Κρήτην. Athens, I. N. Sideri.

Dessenne, André (1949). Têtes Humaines. *Bulletin de Correspondance Hellénique* 73, 307–315.

Detorakis, Theocharis (1994). *History of Crete,* transl. by J. C. Davis.   Herakleion, no publisher.

Dhrakakis, M. E. (1957). Οἱ Κομιτάδες τῶν Σφακίων. *Kritiki Estia,* 6/71: 5–9, 6/72: 5–7, 7/73–4: 29–31, 7/75: 7–11.

Diacopoulos, Lita (2001). CRM and Heritage in Conflict: The Management and Conservation of Byzantine and Post-Byzantine Churches in Kythera, Greece. In M. M. Cotter, W. E. Boyd, and J. E. Gardiner (eds.). *Heritage Landscapes: Understanding Place and Communities,* 269–278. Lismore (New South Wales), Southern Cross University Press.

Diacopoulos, Lita (2004). The Archaeology of Modern Greece. In Effie Athanassopoulos and LuAnn Wandsnider (eds.). *Mediterranean Archaeological Landscapes. Current Issues,* 183–198. Philadelphia, University of Pennsylvania Museum of Archaeology and Anthropology.

Dimen, Muriel (1983). Servants and Sentries: Women, Power and Social Reproduction in Krióvrisi. *Journal of Modern Greek Studies* 1, 225–242.

Dinsmoor, William B. (1975 [reprint of 3rd ed. of 1950]). *The Architecture of Ancient Greece.* New York, Norton.

Doren, David McNeil (1981 [1974]). *Winds of Crete.* Athens, Efstathiadis.

Dubisch, Jill (1994–95). The Church of the Annunciation of Tinos and the Domestication of Institutional Space. In Eleutherios Pavlides and Susan Buck Sutton (eds.) *Constructed Meaning: Form and Process in Greek Architecture.* Modern Greek Studies Yearbook 10/11, 389–417. Minneapolis, MN, Modern Greek Studies Program.

Dubisch, Jill (1995). *In a Different Place: Pilgrimage, Gender and Politics at a Greek Island Shrine.* Princeton, Princeton University Press.

Erickson, Brice 2002. Aphrati and Kato Syme. Pottery, Continuity, and Cult in Late Archaic and Classical Crete. *Hesperia* 71, 41–90.

Fakinou, Eugenia (1992 [1982]). *Astradeni,* transl. by H. Criton. Athens, Kedros.

Fair, John, and Don Moxom (1993). *Abbotsbury and the Swannery, Stanbridge.* Dorset, Dovecote Press.

Faure, Paul (1979). Eglises crétoises sous roche – Εκκλησίες τῆς Κρήτης Μέσα σε Σπηλαιώδεις Κοιλότητες. *Kritologia* 9, 53–83.

Fielding, Xan (1953). *The Stronghold. An Account of the Four Seasons in the White Mountains of Crete.* London, Secker and Warburg.

Forbes, Hamish (1976). 'We Have a Little of Everything': The Ecological Basis of Some Agricultural Practices in Methana, Trizinia.   In Ernestine Friedl and Muriel Dimen (eds.) *Regional Variation in Modern Greece and Cyprus: Toward a Perspective on the Ethnography of Greece. Annals of the New York Academy of Sciences* 268, 236–250. New York, New York Academy of Sciences.

Fowden, Garth (1988). City and Mountain in Late Roman Attica. *Journal of Hellenic Studies* 108, 48-59.

Francis, Jane, Simon Price, Jennifer Moody, and Lucia Nixon (2000). Agiasmatsi: A Greek Cave Sanctuary in Sphakia, SW Crete. *Annual of the British School at Athens* 95, 429–471.

Freely, John (1991). *Strolling through Athens.* Harmondsworth, Penguin.

Gallas, Klaus, Klaus Wessel and Manolis Borboudakis (1983). *Byzantinisches Kreta.* Munich, Hirmer.

Gavrielides, Nicolas (1974). Fast Days and Feasting: Social and Ecological Implications of Visiting Patterns in a Greek Village of the Argolid. *Anthropological Quarterly* 47, 48–70.

Gennep, Arnold van (1960 [1909]). *The Rites of Passage,* transl. by Monika B. Vizedom and Gabrielle L. Caffee. London, Routledge and Kegan Paul.

Gerland, Ernst (1903–08). Histoire de la Noblesse Crétoise au Moyen Age. *Revue de l'Orient Latin* 10: 172–247, 11: 7–144.

Gerola, Giuseppe (1905–32). *Monumenti veneti nell' isola di Creta.* 4 vols. Venice, Istituto Veneto di Scienze, Lettere ed Arti.

Gerola, Giuseppe (1961). *Τοπογραφικὸς Κατάλογος τῶν Τοιχογραφημένων Ἐκκλησιῶν τῆς Κρήτης. Μετάφραση, πρόλογος, σημειώσεις Κ. Ε. Λασσιθιωτάκη.* Herakleion, no publisher.

Gerola, Giuseppe (1993). *Βενετικὰ Μνημεῖα τῆς Κρήτης (Ἐκκλησίες).* Transl. Stergios Spanakis. Sindhesmos Topikon Enoseon Dhimon kai Koinotiton Kritis. Herakleion, Typokreta.

Geronymakis, Kanakis (1996). *Κοινότης Ἀσφένδου Σφακίων.* Khania, Georvasakis.

Gosden, Chris and Gary Lock (1998). Prehistoric Histories. *World Archaeology* 30.1, 2–12.

Greco, Emmanuele, Thanassis Kalpaxis, Nikos Papadakis, Alain Schnapp, and Didier Viviers (1998). Travaux Menés en Collaboration avec l'Ecole Française en 1997. Itanos (Crète Orientale). *BCH* 122, 585–602.

Greco, Emmanuele, Thanassis Kalpaxis, Nikos Papadakis, Alain Schnapp, and Didier Viviers (2000). Travaux Menés en Collaboration avec l'Ecole Française en 1999. Itanos (Crète Orientale), *BCH* 124, 547–559.

Green, Sarah and Geoffrey King (2001). Seeing What You Know: Changing Constructions and Perceptions of Landscape in Epirus, Northwestern Greece, 1945 and 1990. *History and Anthropology* 12.3, 255–288.

Gregory, Timothy E. (n.d.). Churches, Landscape, and the Population of Northern Kythera in Byzantine and Early Modern Times, *A' Diethnes Synedhrio Kythiraïkon Meleton, 20–24 September 2000.* Kythira, Mythos kai Pragmatikotita, Eleft03ero Anoikto Panepistimio Dhimou Kythiron, 217–237.

Grove, A.T. (Dick) and Oliver Rackham (2001). *The Nature of Mediterranean Europe. An Ecological History.* New Haven, Yale University Press.

Gueguen, Alain (1993). *Croix et Calvaires de la Mayenne.* Laval (France), Société d'Archéologie et d'Histoire de la Mayenne.

Hallendy, Norman (2000). *Inuksuit. Silent Messengers of the Arctic.* London, British Museum Press.

Hansen, Maria Fabricius (2003). *The Eloquence of Appropriation. Prolegomena to an Understanding of Spolia in Early Christian Rome.* Rome, L'Erma di Bretschneider.

Hart, Laurie Kain (1992*). Time, Religion, and Social Experience in Rural Greece.* Lanham (MD), Rowman and Littlefield.

Hasluck, Frederick William (1929). *Christianity and Islam under the Sultans.* Oxford, Clarendon.

Heikell, Rod (1982). *Greek Waters Pilot.* Huntingdon, Imray Laurie Norie and Wilson.

Herzfeld, Michael (1985). *The Poetics of Manhood. Contest and Identity in a Cretan Mountain Village.* Princeton, Princeton University Press.

Herzfeld, Michael (1990a). Icons and Identity: Religious Orthodoxy and Social Practice in Rural Crete. *Anthropological Quarterly* 63: 109–121.

Herzfeld, Michael (1990b). Pride and Perjury: Time and the Oath in the Mountain Villages of Crete. *Man* n.s. 25, 305–322.

Herzfeld, Michael (1991). *A Place in History. Social and Monumental Time in a Cretan Town.* Princeton, Princeton University Press.

Hirschon, Renée (1983). Women, the Aged and Religious Activity: Oppositions and Complementarity in an Urban Locality. *Journal of Modern Greek Studies* 1, 113–129.

Hodkinson, Stephen and Hilary Hodkinson (1981). Mantineia and the Mantinike: Settlement and Society in a Greek Polis. *Annual of the British School at Athens* 76, 239–296.

Hood, Sinclair (1967). Some Ancient Sites in South-West Crete. *Annual of the British School at Athens* 62: 47–56.

Horden, Peregrine and Nicholas Purcell (2000). *The Corrupting Sea. A Study of Mediterranean History.* Oxford, Basil Blackwell.

Howe, Samuel Gridley (1825/1907). *Letters and Journals of Samuel Gridley Howe during the Greek Revolution.* 2 vols. London, Bodley Head.

Humphrey, Caroline (1995). Chiefly and Shamanist Landscapes in Mongolia. In Eric Hirsch and Michael O'Hanlon (eds.) *The Anthropology of Landscape. Perspectives on Place and Space*, 135–162. Oxford, Oxford University Press.

Jeffreys, Elizabeth (ed. and transl.) (1998). *Digenis Akritis. The Grottaferrata and Escorial Versions.* Cambridge, Cambridge University Press.

Jones, Donald M. (1999). *Peak Sanctuaries and Sacred Caves in Minoan Crete. A Comparison of Artifacts.* Jonsered, Paul Åströms Förlag

Jordan, Peter (2003). *Material Culture and Sacred Landscape. The Anthropology of the Siberian Khanty.* Walnut Creek, CA/Oxford, AltaMira.

Jost, Madeleine (1985). *Sanctuaires et Cultes d'Arcadie.* Ecole Française d'Athènes, Etudes Péloponnésiennes IX. Paris, Vrin.

Karakasidou, Anastasia N. (1997). *Fields of Wheat, Hills of Blood: Passages to Nationhood in Greek Macedonia 1870–1990.* Chicago, University of Chicago Press.

Kelaïdhis, Paris S. (1981). *Η Θυμιανή Παναγία στα Σφακιά*, Athens, Karavi kai Toxo.

Kelaïdhis, Paris S. (1982). *Αρχαίες Πόλεις στα Σφακιά.* Athens, Karavi kai Toxo.

Kelaïdhis, Paris S. (1983–4). *Ριζίτικα για τα Σφακιά,* 2 vols. Athens, Vardhinogiannis.

Kelaïdhis, Paris S. (2003). Η Αναβίωση Αθλητικών Αγώνων στον Άγιο Νικήτα. *Ta Sphakia* no. 103, 10.

Kelaïdhis, Stavros (2003 [1960]). *Στα Σφακιά του 1894.* Athens, Mitos.

Kenna, Margaret (1976). Houses, Fields, and Graves: Property and Ritual Obligation on a Greek Island. *Ethnology* 15, 21–37.

Kenna, Margaret (1984–85). Icons in Theory and Practice. *History of Religions* 24, 345–368.

Kenna, Margaret (1991). The Power of the Dead: Changes in the Construction and Care of Graves and Family Vaults on a Small Greek Island. *Journal of Mediterranean Studies* 1, 101–119.

Kenna, Margaret (1994–95). Where the Streets Have No Name. In Eleutherios Pavlides and Susan Buck Sutton (eds.) *Constructed Meaning: Form and Process in Greek Architecture.* Modern Greek Studies Yearbook, vol. 10/11, 439–461. Minneapolis (MN), Modern Greek Studies Program.

Kenna, Margaret (1995). Orthodox Theology and Local Practice in Contemporary Greece: Whose Tradition?. *Dialogos* 2, 42–53.

Kenna, Margaret (2001). *Greek Island Life: Fieldwork on Anafi.* London, Routledge.

Khaireti, Maria K. (1968). Ἡ ἀπογραφὴ τῶν ναῶν καὶ τῶν μονῶν τῆς περιοχῆς Χανίων τοῦ ἔτους 1637. *Epetiris tis Etaireias Vyzantinon Spoudhon* 36, 335–388.

Khatziphoti, I. M. (1986). *Τα Προσκυνητάρια των Ελληνικών Δρόμων.* Athens, Ekdhoseis Akritas.

Khrysoulaki-Paterou, K. (1986). *Λαογραφία των Σφακίων.* Athens, Lykhnos.

Kondylakis, Ioannes (1987 [1891]). *Patouchas.* Transl. Sotiroulla Syka-Karampetsou. Athens, Efstathiadhis.

Konstantinidhis, Dhim. (1975). Λαϊκὰ Ἀρχιτεκτονικὰ Στοιχεῖα τῆς Κρήτης. In *Pepragmena tou G' Dhiethnous Kritologikou Synedhriou (Rethymnon 18–23 September 1971)* 3: 199–206. Athens, [no publisher].

Koukoulis, Theodore (1997). Catalogue of Churches. In Christopher Mee and Hamish Forbes (eds.) *A Rough and Rocky Place: The Landscape and Settlement History of the Methana Peninsula, Greece,* 211–256. Liverpool, Liverpool University Press.

Kyriakidhou-Nestoros, Alki (1975). Σημάδια τοῦ τόπου η ἡ λογικὴ τοῦ ἑλληνικοῦ τοπίου. In Alki Kyriakidhou-Nestoros (ed.) *Laographika Meletimata,* 15–40. [Athens,] Olkos.

Lamprinakis, E. S. (1890). *Γεωγραφία τῆς Κρήτης.* Rethymnon, Kalaïzakis.

Lassithiotakis, Kostas E. (1971). Ἐκκλησίες τῆς Δυτικῆς Κρήτης. Ε΄. Ἐπαρχία Σφακίων. *KrChron* 23, 95–177.

Lee, Wayne E. (2001). The Pylos Regional Archaeological Project IV: Change and Material Culture in a Modern Greek Village in Messenia. *Hesperia* 70: 49–98.

Leontis, Artemis (1995). *Topographies of Hellenism.* Ithaca (NY), Cornell University Press.

Limbourg, Brothers (Pol, Jean, and Herman) (n.d. [ca 1415]). *Les Très Riches Heures du Duc de Berry. Le Calendrier.* Presented by Jean Porcher. Paris, Nomis.

Llewellyn Smith, Michael (1965). *The Great Island.* London, Allen Lane.

Llobera, Marcos (2001). Building Past Landscape Perception with GIS: Understanding Topographic Prominence. *Journal of Archaeological Science* 28, 1005–1014.

Löher, F. von (1877). *Kretische Gestade*. Bielefeld and Leipzig, Velhagen and Klasing.

López, Vidal and Ángel, Miguel (1995). *Gredos: Turismo, Deporte, y Aventura*. Ávila, Miján.

Machin, Barry (1983). St George and the Virgin: Cultural Codes, Religion and Attitudes to the Body in a Cretan Mountain Village. *Social Analysis* 14, 107–126.

Manouselis, Andreas (2003–2004). Στο Καψοδάσος Σφακίων. Ξαναχτιστική Ερειπομένη Εκκλησία. *Ta Sphakia* no. 107, 11.

Martin, Hervé (1983). La Fonction Polyvalente des Croix à la Fin du Moyen Age. *Annales de Bretagne et des Pays de l'Ouest* 90.2, 295–310.

Martin, Hervé and Louis Martin (1977). Croix Rurales et Sacralisation de l'Espace. Le Cas de la Bretagne au Moyen Age. *Archives de Sciences Sociales des Religions* 43/1: 23–38.

McInerney, Jeremy (1999). *The Folds of Parnassos. Land and Ethnicity in Ancient Phokis*. Austin (TX), University of Texas Press.

Mikelakis, Manos (2005). Ars Memoriae – Τέχνη της Μνήμης. Τα Παραδοσιακά και Νεότερα Εικονοστάσια-Προσκυνητάρια. *Arkhaiologia* 95 (June 2005), 92–97.

Miklosich, Franz, Ritter von and Joseph Müller (1860–90). *Acta et Diplomata Graeca medii aevi sacra et profana*. Vienna, Gerold.

Milner, Nicholas P. (1998). *An Epigraphical Survey in the Kibyra-Olbasa Region Conducted by A.S. Hall*. British Institute of Archaeology at Ankara Monograph 24. London, BIAA.

Monanni, Rector of Canea, description of Crete by (1631). VBM: MS Ital. VII.889(7798).

Moody, Jennifer, Harriet Robinson, Jane Francis, Lucia Nixon, and Lucy Wilson (2003). Ceramic Fabric Analysis and Survey Archaeology: The Sphakia Survey. *Annual of the British School at Athens* 98: 37–105.

Moody, Jennifer, Lucia Nixon, Simon Price and Oliver Rackham (1998). Surveying Poleis and Larger Sites in Sphakia. In William G. Cavanagh and M. Curtis (eds.), John Nicolas Coldstream and Alan W. Johnston (co-eds.) *Post-Minoan Crete*, 87–95. British School at Athens Studies 2. London, British School at Athens.

Morgan, Catherine (1994). The Evolution of a Sacred 'Landscape': Isthmia, Perachora, and the Early Corinthian State. In Susan E. Alcock and Robin Osborne (eds.) *Placing the Gods. Sanctuaries and Sacred Space in Ancient Greece*, 105–142. Oxford, Clarendon.

Morgan, Catherine (2003). *Early Greek States beyond the Polis*. London, Routledge.

Morgan, Gareth (1960). Cretan Poetry: Sources and Inspiration. *Kretika Khronika* 14, 7–192.

Morton, Jamie (2001). *The Role of the Physical Environment in Ancient Greek Seafaring*. Leiden, Brill.

Mourellos, I. D. (1950). Ἱστορία τῆς Κρήτης, 3 vols., 2nd edn. Herakleion, Erotokritos. (1st edn. 1931).

Murray, Priscilla M. and P. Nick Kardulias (1986). Modern Site Survey in the Southern Argolid. *Journal of Field Archaeology* 13, 21–41.

Murray, Priscilla M. and P. Nick Kardulias (2000). The Present as Past: An Ethnoarchaeological Study of Modern Sites in the Pikrodhafni Valley. In Susan Buck Sutton (ed.). *Contingent Countryside. Settlement, Economy and Land Use in the Southern Argolid since 1700*, 141–168. Stanford, Stanford University Press.

Myrivilis, Stratis 1959 [1955]. *The Mermaid Madonna [Η Παναγία Ἡ Γοργόνα]*. Transl. Abbott Rick. Athens, Efstathiadhis.

Nixon, Lucia (1991). Minoan Settlements and Greek Sanctuaries. In *Pepragmena tou 6. Dhiethnous Kritologikou Synedhriou*, vol. A2, 59–67. Khania, Chrysostomos.

Nixon, Lucia (1993). Review of John F. Cherry, Jack L. Davis, Eleni Mantzourani (eds.) (1991). *Landscape Archaeology as Long-Term History. Northern Keos in the Cycladic Islands from Earliest Settlements until Modern Times*, Monumenta Archaeologica 16. Los Angeles (CA), Institute of Archaeology, University of California. *Echos du monde classique/Classical Views* n.s. 12, 385–389.

Nixon, Lucia (1995). The Cults of Demeter and Kore. In Richard Hawley and Barbara Levick (eds.). *Women in Antiquity: New Assessments*, London, Routledge, 75–96.

Nixon, Lucia (1999). Women, Children, and Weaving. In Philip P. Betancourt, Vassos Karageorghis, Robert Laffineur, and Wolf-Dietrich Niemeier (eds.). *Meletemata. Studies in Aegean Archaeology presented to Malcolm H. Wiener as He Enters His 65th Year*, 561–567. Aegaeum 20. Liège, Université de Liège, Histoire de l'art et archéologie de la Grèce antique; Austin (TX), University of Texas at Austin, Program in Aegean Scripts and Prehistory.

Nixon, Lucia (2001). Seeing Voices and Changing Relationships: Film, Archaeological Reporting, and the Landscape of People in Sphakia. *American Journal of Archaeology* 105, 77–97.

Nixon, Lucia (2004). Chronologies of Desire and the Uses of Monuments: Eflatunpinar to Çatalhöyük and Beyond. In David Shankland (ed.) *Anthropology, Archaeology and Heritage in the Balkans and Anatolia, or The Life and Times of F.W. Hasluck (1878–1920)*. Istanbul, Isis, 99–118.

Nixon, Lucia in press. Investigating Minoan Sacred Landscapes. In Anna Lucia D'Agata and Aleydis Van de Moortel (eds.). *Festschrift for Geraldine C. Gesell*.

Nixon, Lucia and Simon Price (1990). The Size and Resources of Greek Cities. In Oswyn Murray and Simon Price (eds.), *The Greek City from Homer to Alexander*, 137–170. Oxford, Clarendon.

Nixon, Lucia and Simon Price (1995). *The Sphakia Survey, Methods and Results*. Oxford, Educational Technology Resources Centre [now Media Production Unit], 37 Wellington Square OX1 2JF (50 minute video tape).

Nixon, Lucia and Simon Price (2001). The Diachronic Analysis of Pastoralism through Comparative Variables. *Annual of the British School at Athens* 96, 395–424.

Nixon, Lucia, Jennifer Moody, and Oliver Rackham (1988). Archaeological Survey in Sphakia, Crete. *Echos du monde classique/Classical Views* 32 n.s. 7, 157–173. http://sphakia.classics.ox.ac.uk:591/emccv1988.html

Nixon, Lucia, Jennifer Moody, Simon Price, and Oliver Rackham (1989). Archaeological Survey in Sphakia, Crete. *Echos du monde classique/Classical Views* 33 n.s. 8, 201–215. http://sphakia.classics.ox.ac.uk:591/emccv1989html

Nixon, Lucia, Jennifer Moody, Simon Price, Oliver Rackham, and Vanna Niniou-Kindeli (1990). Archaeological Survey in Sphakia, Crete. *Echos du monde classique/Classical Views* 34 n.s. 9, 213–220. http://sphakia.classics.ox.ac.uk/emccv1990.html

Nixon, Lucia, Jennifer Moody, Simon Price, and Oliver Rackham (1994). Rural Settlement in Sphakia, Crete. In Panagiotis Dhoukellis and Lina G. Mendoni (eds.) *Structures rurales et sociétés antiques, Actes du colloque de Corfou 14–16 mai 1992*, 255–264. Annales littéraires de l'Université de Besançon 508. Paris, Les Belles Lettres.

Nixon, Lucia, Jennifer Moody, and Simon Price (2000). Settlement Patterns in Mediaeval and Post-Mediaeval Sphakia: Issues from the Environmental, Archaeological, & Historical Evidence, given at the *Mediaeval and Post-Mediaeval Greece Conference, Corfu, May 1998*. http://sphakia.classics.ox.ac.uk/bvtpaper.html

Nixon, Lucia, Jennifer Moody, Simon Price, and Oliver Rackham (2000). *The Sphakia Survey: Internet Edition* http://sphakia.classics.ox.ac.uk

Noiret, H. (1892). *Documents inédits pour servir à l'histoire de la domination vénitienne en Crète de 1380 à 1485*. Bibliothèque des Écoles françaises d'Athènes et de Rome 61. Paris.

[No author] (1999). Νικήτεια 99. *Ta Sphakia* no. 90, 1.

[No editor] (1996). I Bacini Murati Medievali, Problemi e Stato della Ricerca. *Atti XXVI Convegno internazionale della Ceramica, Albisola 28–30 May 1993*.

Nowicki, Krzysztof (1992). Report on Investigations in Greece VIII. Studies in 1991. *Archeologia* 43, 113–119.

Olivier, G.A. (1801). *Travels in the Ottoman Empire, Egypt and Persia*. 2 vols. London, Longman.

Orlandos, Anastasios K. (1952–56). Ἡ Ξυλόστεγος Παλαιοχριστιανικὴ Βασιλικὴ τῆς Μεσογειακῆς Λεκάνης. Athens, Vivliothiki tis en Athinais Arkhaiologikis Etaireias.

Pallas, Demetrios I. (1971). *Les Monuments Paléochrétiens de Grèce Découvertes de 1959 à 1973*. Rome, Pontificio Istituto di Archeologia Cristiana.

Panagiotakis, Nikolaos (1960). Θεοδώσιος ὁ Διάκονος καὶ τὸ Ποίημα τοῦ 'Ἅλωσις τῆς Κρήτης'. Kritiki Istoriki Vivliothiki Arith. 2. Herakleion, Ekdoseis Etairias [sic] Kritikon Istorikon Meleton.

Papadhimou, Dhimitri and Georgios Manousakis (1974). Ή Ελλάδα πού φεύγει. Athens, Olkos [unpaginated].

Papadhopetrakis, G. (1888). Ίστορία τῶν Σφακίων ἤτοι μέρος τῆς Κρητικῆς Ἱστορίας. Athens. (Reprinted Athens, Vardhinogiannis, 1971)

Papagrigorakis, Idomeneus (1959). Κρητικά Συμβόλαια ἐπὶ Τουρκοκρατίας. Kritiki Estia 7, part 77, 19–22; part 78, 19–23; part 79–80, 51–55; part 81–82, 51–55; part 84–85, 35–39.

Papalexandrou, Amy (2003). Memory Tattered and Torn: Spolia in the Heartland of Byzantine Hellenism. In Ruth M. Van Dyke and Susan E. Alcock (eds.) Archaeologies of Memory, 56–79. Oxford, Blackwell.

Parker, Robert (2005). Polytheism and Society at Athens. Oxford, Oxford University Press.

Parlamas, M. G. (1953). 'Ἀνέκδοτα ἔγγραφα ἐκ Σφακίων (1799-1832)'. KrChron 7: 235–257.

Pashley, Robert (1837). Travels in Crete (2 vols.). London, John Murray. (Reprinted 1970, Amsterdam, Hakkert).

Pavlides, Eleutherios and Susan Buck Sutton (1994–5). Introduction. In Eleutherios Pavlides and Susan Buck Sutton (eds.) Constructed Meaning: Form and Process in Greek Architecture. Modern Greek Studies Yearbook 10/11, 271–295. Minneapolis (MN), Modern Greek Studies Program.

Peatfield, Alan (1983). The Topography of Minoan Peak Sanctuaries. BSA 78, 273–280.

Peatfield, Alan (1992). Rural Ritual in Bronze Age Crete. Cambridge Archaeological Journal 2, 59–87.

Peatfield. Alan (1994). After the 'Big Bang' –What? Or Minoan Symbols and Shrines beyond Palatial Collapse. In Susan E. Alcock and Robin Osborne (eds.) Placing the Gods. Sanctuaries and Sacred Space in Ancient Greece, 19 –36. Oxford, Clarendon.

Pelekanidhis, Stylianos and Panagiota I. Atzaka (19744). Σύνταγμα τῶν Παλαιοχριστιανικῶν Ψηφιδωτῶν Δαπέδων τῆς Ελλάδος. 1. Thessaloniki, Kendron Vyzantinon Erevnon.

Peristerakis, Agesilaos (1991). Σφακιανά. Athens, Vasilopoulos.

Peters, Frances (2000). Two Traditions of Bronze Age Burial in the Stonehenge Landscape. Oxford Journal of Archaeology 19, 343–358.

Pichot, Daniel (2002). Le Village Eclaté. Habitat et Société dans les Campagnes de l'Ouest au Moyen Age. Rennes, Presses Universitaires de Rennes.

Platakis, Eleftherios (1979). Ἀγιώνυμα (καὶ τὰ συναφῆ) Σπήλαια τῆς Κρήτης. Kritologia 8, 5–18.

Plymakis, Andonios (2001a [revised edition of 1982]). Το Αγρίμι της Κρήτης. Khania, Georvasakis.

Plymakis, Andonios (2001b). Προσκυνητάρια στην Κρήτη. Khania, Kasimatis.

Plymakis, Andonios (2002a). Στ' Αγίου Πνευμάτου [sic] την Κόρφη. Khania, no publisher given.

Plymakis, Andonios (2002b). Σπήλαια στα Χανιά, vol. I. Mournies, Kasimatis.

Pococke, Richard (1743–45). A Description of the East, and Some Other Countries. London, Bowyer.

Polignac, François de (1995 [1984]). Cults, Territory, and the Origins of the Greek City-State, transl. by Janet Lloyd. Chicago, University of Chicago Press.

Polignac, François de (1994). Mediation, Competition, and Sovereignty: The Evolution of Rural Sanctuaries in Geometric Greece. In Susan E. Alcock and Robin Osborne (eds.) Placing the Gods. Sanctuaries and Sacred Space in Ancient Greece, 247–261. Oxford, Clarendon.

Politis, Nikolaos G. (1904). Μελέται περὶ τοῦ βίου καὶ τῆς γλώσσης τοῦ ἑλληνικοῦ λαοῦ· Παραδόσεις, 2 vols. Athens, Marasli (reprinted Athens, Ergani, 1965).

Prent, Mieke (2003). Glories of the Past in the Past: Ritual Activities at Palatial Ruins in Early Iron Age Crete. In Ruth M. Van Dyke and Susan E. Alcock (eds.) Archaeologies of Memory, 81–103. Oxford, Blackwell.

Price, Simon (1999). Religions of the Ancient Greeks. Cambridge, Cambridge University Press.

Price, Simon (2004). Local Mythologies in the Roman East. In Christopher Howgego, Volker Heuchert and Andrew Burnett (eds.) Coinage and Identity in the Roman Provinces, 115–124. Oxford, Oxford University Press.

Price, Simon and Lucia Nixon (2005). Ancient Greek Terraces and Terrace Walls: Evidence from Texts and Archaeological Survey. American Journal of Archaeology 109, 665-694.

Price, Simon, Tom Higham, Lucia Nixon and Jennifer Moody (2002). Relative Sea-level Changes in Crete: Reassessment of Radiocarbon Dates from Sphakia and West Crete. *Annual of the British School at Athens* 97, 171–200.

Rackham, Oliver and Jennifer Moody (1996). *The Making of the Cretan Landscape.* Manchester, Manchester University Press.

Randolph, B. (1687). *The Present State of the Islands in the Archipelago (or Arches).* Oxford, Clarendon Press.

Randsborg, Klavs (1995). *Hjörtspring. Warfare and Sacrifice in Early Europe.* Aarhus, Aarhus University Press.

Randsborg, Klavs (2002). *Kephallenia. Archaeology and History. The Ancient Greek Cities,* vols. 1 and 2. Acta Archaeologica 73.1 and 73.2, Supplementa IV.1 and 2. Copenhagen, Blackwell Munksgaard.

Raulin, V. (1869). *Description physique de l'île de Crète.* 2 vols. plus Atlas volume. Paris, Bertrand.

Redman, Charles (1978). *Social Archeology: Beyond Subsistence and Dating.* New York, Academic Press.

Renfrew, Colin and Paul Bahn (2000, 3rd ed.). *Archaeology: Theories, Methods, and Practice.* London, Thames and Hudson.

Rutkowski, Bogdan (1986). *The Cult Places of the Aegean.* New Haven and London, Yale University Press.

Saccopoulos, Christos A. (1986). Roadside Monuments in Greece. *Ekistics* 318–319.

Sakellarakis, Y. (1996). Minoan Religious Influence in the Aegean. The Case of Kythera. *Annual of the British School at Athens* 91: 81–99.

Sanders, Ian (1982). *Roman Crete.* Warminster, Aris and Phillips.

Sbonias, Kostas (2004). Accepting Diversity and Multiple Layers of Modern Greek Identity. The Implications for Cultural Resource Management in Greece. In Panagiotis Doukellis and Lina G. Mendoni (eds.), *Perception and Evaluation of Cultural Landscapes,* 117–135. Research Centre for Greek and Roman Antiquity, National Hellenic Research Foundation, Meletimata 38. Athens/Paris, De Boccard.

Schachter, Albert (1992). Policy, Cult, and the Placing of Greek Sanctuaries. In Albert Schachter and J. Bingen (eds.), *Le Sanctuaire Grec,* 1–57. *Entretiens sur l'Antiquité Classique* 37. Geneva, Fondation Hardt.

Semitecolo, G. (1639). *Descrizione del territorio della Canea.* Published by Dhimitra Spitha-Pimpli (1999). *Περιγραφή του Διαμερίσματος των Χανίων Ιερωνύμου Σεμιτέκολο του έτους 1639.* Khania, Spitha-Pimpli.

Seremetakis, Constantina Nadia (1991). *The Last Word: Women, Death, and Divination in Inner Mani.* Chicago, University of Chicago Press.

Shaw, Joseph W. (1977). Excavations at Kommos (Crete). *Hesperia* 46.3, 199–240.

Smith, Julia (1990). Oral and Written: Saint, Miracles, and Relics in Brittany, c. 850–1250. *Speculum* 65, 309–343.

Smith, R. R. R. and Christopher R. Ratté (1995). Archaeological Research at Aphrodisias in Caria, 1993. *American Journal of Archaeology* 99, 33–58.

Snodgrass, Anthony (1980). *Archaic Greece. The Age of Experiment.* London, Dent.

Soetens, Stephen, A. Sarris, K. Vansteenhuyse and S. Topouzi (2003). GIS Variations on a Cretan Theme: Minoan Peak Sanctuaries. In Karen P. Foster and Robert Laffineur (eds.) *METRON: Measuring the Aegean Bronze Age,* 483–488. Aegaeum 24. Liège, Université de Liège, Histoire de l'art et archéologie de la Grèce antique; Austin (TX), University of Texas at Austin, Program in Aegean Scripts and Prehistory.

Spanakis, Stergios (n.d.) [but no later than 1978]. *Κρήτη, 2. Δυτική Κρήτη.* Herakleion, Sphakianaki.

Spanakis, Stergios (2001). *Πόλεις και Χωριά της Κρήτης στο Πέρασμα των Αιώνων.* Herakleion, Dhetorakis.

Spatharakis, Iohannis (2001). *Dated Byzantine Wall Paintings of Crete.* Leiden, Alexandros.

Splinis, Petros Nikolaos (1999). Νικήτεια 1998. *Ta Sphakia* no. 89, 14.

Spratt, Thomas Abel Brimage (1865). *Travels and Researches in Crete,* 2 vols. London, John van Voorst.

Stavroulakis, Nicholas P. and Timothy J. DeVinney (1992). *Jewish Sites and Synagogues of Greece*. Athens, Talos Press.

Stevens, Wallace (1955). *Collected Poems*. London, Faber.

Stewart, Charles (1991). *Demons and the Devil*. Princeton, Princeton University Press.

Stewart, Charles (1997). Fields in Dreams: Anxiety, Experience, and the Limits of Social Constructionism in Modern Greek Dream Narratives. *American Ethnologist* 24, 877–894.

Stewart, Pamela J. and Andrew Strathern (eds.) (2003). *Landscape, Memory, and History: Anthropological Perspectives*. London, Routledge.

Stillman, William J. (1966 [1874]). *The Cretan Insurrection of 1866–68*. Reissued with notes by George Georgiades Arnakis as *An American Consul in a Cretan War*. Austin (TX), Center for Neo-Hellenic Studies.

Stillman, William J. (1976 [1867]). *Articles and Despatches from Crete*, ed. by George Georgiades Arnakis. Austin (TX), Centre for Neo-Hellenic Studies.

Strang, Veronica (1997). *Uncommon Ground: Cultural Landscapes*. Oxford, Berg.

Sutton, David (1998). *Memories Cast in Stone: the Relevance of the Past in Everyday Life*. Oxford, Berg.

Tapu Defter (ca. 1648). Tapu Defter 820 'Defter-i Hanya'. Istanbul: Başbakanlık (now Osmanlı) Arşivi.

Tilley, Chris (1994). *A Phenomenology of Landscape. Places, Paths and Monuments*. Oxford, Berg.

Tomadhakis, N. B. (1974).). *Ἱστορία τῆς ἐκκλησίας τῆς Κρήτης ἐπὶ Τουρκοκρατίας (1645–1898). I. Αἱ πηγαί*. Seira Dhiatrivon kai Meletimaton 18. Athens, Myrtidhis.

Tomadhakis, N. B. (1978). Ἐκκλησιαστικὰ Τοπωνύμια καὶ Ὀνόματα Μονῶν, Ναῶν (καὶ Εἰκόνων) τῆς Κρήτης. *Kritologia* 7, 17–48.

Tomadhakis, N. B. (1980). Περὶ τῆς ἐπισκοπῆς Καλάμονος καὶ τῆς μονῆς Ἁγίου Νικήτα (Φραγκοκάστελο) (Εἰδήσεις 1196 μ. Χρ.). *Promitheus o Pyrphoros* n.s. 4, part 20 (June-Aug.), 163–168.

Tomadhakis, N.B. (1983–84). Ο άγιος Ιωάννης ο ξένος και ερημίτης εν Κρήτη, 10ος – 11ος αιών. *Epetiris Etaireias Vyzantinon Spoudhon*, 46: 1–117.

Tomadhakis, N. B. (n.d. [ca 1965]). Σφακιά. *Megali Elliniki Enkyklopedia* 22: 658-9.

Travlos, John (1971). *Pictorial Dictionary of Ancient Athens*. New York, Praeger.

Triantaphyllidou-Baladié, G. (1988). *Το Εμπόριο και η Οικονομία της Κρήτης 1669–1795*. Herakleion, Vikelaia Vivliothiki.

Trivizas, Karolos and Elli Dhimitriou (2005). *Εικονοστάσια στο Ελληνικό Τοπίο*. Athens, Ekdoseis Kalendis.

Trivan (1644). ed. M. I. Manoussakas (1949). Ἡ παρὰ Τρίβαν ἀπογραφὴ τῆς Κρήτης (1644) καὶ ὁ δῆθεν κατάλογος τῶν Κρητικῶν οἴκων Κερκύρας. *KrChron* 3, 35–59.

Tsigakou, Fani-Maria (1981). *The Rediscovery of Greece*. New Rochelle, Caratzas.

Tsougarakis, Dimitris (1988). *Byzantine Crete from the 5th Century to the Venetian Conquest*. Athens, Basilopoulos.

Tsougarakis, Dimitri and Helen Angelomatis-Tsougarakis (2004). A Province under Byzantine, Venetian, and Ottoman Rule, A.D. 400–1898. Chapter 14 in Watrous et al. 2004, 359–439.

Tumasonis, Donald (1983). Some Aspects of Minoan Society: A View from Social Anthropology. In Olga Krzyszkowska and Lucia Nixon (eds.) *Minoan Society. Proceedings of the Cambridge Colloquium 1981*, 303–310. Bristol, Bristol Classical Press.

Ucko, Peter J. and Robert J. Layton (eds.) (1999). *The Archaeology and Anthropology of Landscape*. London, Routledge.

Van Dyke, Ruth M. and Susan E. Alcock (eds.) (2003). *Archaeologies of Memory*. Oxford, Blackwell.

Vallianos, Christophoros (1993). Settlements and Monuments of the Western Mesara: A.D. 961–1900. 237–240 in Livingstone Vance Watrous, Despoina Hatzi-Vallianou, Kevin Pope, Jennifer Shay, C.T. Shay, John Bennet, Demetrios Tsoungarakis, E. Angelomati-Tsoungaraki, Christophoros Vallianos, and Harriet Blitzer. A Survey of the Western Mesara Plain in Crete: Preliminary Report of the 1984, 1986, and 1987 Field Seasons. *Hesperia* 62, 191–248.

Vasilakis, Andonios S. (1989–90). Προϊστορικές Θέσεις στη Μονή Οδηγήτριας- Καλούς Λιμένες. *Kritiki Estia* 3, 11–79.

Vasilakis, Andonios S. (1992). Odigitria. In J. Wilson Myers, Eleanor Myers, and Gerald Cadogan (eds.), *Aerial Atlas of Ancient Crete*. London, Thames and Hudson, 213–215.

Vasilakis, Andonios S. (1999/2000). *Minoan Crete from Myth to History*. Transl. David Hardy. Athens, Adam Editions.

Vourdhoumpakis, Andreas P. (1939). 'Δύο ἀνέκδοτα ἔγγραφα ἐκ Σφακίων'. *Epetiris Etaireias Kritikon Spoudon,* 2: 256-262.

Vranousi, Era (1980). Βυζαντινὰ ἔγγραφα τῆς Μονῆς Πάτμου. Α΄. Αὐτοκρατορικά. Athens, Ethniko Idhrima Erevnon.

Wallace, Saro (2003). The Perpetuated Past: Re-use of Continuity in Material Culture and the Structuring of Identity in Early Iron Age Crete. *Annual of the British School at Athens* 98: 251–277.

Watrous, L. Vance (2001 [1994]). Review of Aegean Prehistory III: Crete from Earliest Prehistory through the Protopalatial Period. In Tracey Cullen (ed.) *Aegean Prehistory: A Review*. American Journal of Archaeology (AJA) Supplement 1, 157–223. Boston, Archaeological Institute of America. (= *AJA* 98: 695–753 plus Addendum: 1994–1999).

Watrous, L. Vance and Despoina Hadzi-Vallianou (2004). Palatial Rule and Collapse (Middle Minoan IB – Late Minoan IIIB). Chapter 10 in Watrous et al. 2004, 277–304.

Watrous, L. Vance, Despoina Hadzi-Vallianou, and Harriet Blitzer (eds.) (2004). *The Plain of Phaistos. Cycles of Social Complexity in the Mesara Region of Crete*. Los Angeles, Cotsen Institute of Archaeology.

Watson, Aaron (2001). Composing Avebury. *World Archaeology* 33.2, 296–314.

Waugh, Evelyn (1955). *Officers and Gentlemen: A Novel*. London, Chapman and Hall.

Whitelaw, Todd (1991). The Ethnoarchaeology of Recent Rural Settlement and Land Use in Northwest Keos. In John Cherry, Jack Davis, and Eleni Mantzourani (eds.) *Landscape Archaeology as Long-Term History. Northern Keos in the Cycladic Islands from Earliest Settlements until Modern Times*, 403–454. Monumenta Archaeologica 16. Los Angeles (CA), Institute of Archaeology, University of California.

Whittle, Alasdair (1995). Landscapes of the Mind (review of Tilley 1994). *Cambridge Archaeological Journal* 5, 323–4.

Whittow, Mark (1996). *The Making of Orthodox Byzantium, 600–1025*. London, Macmillan.

Williams, Caroline (1984). Hellenistic and Roman Buildings in the Mediaeval Walls of Mytilene. *Phoenix* 38, 31–76.

Wilson, Loraine (2000). *Crete. The White Mountains*. Milnthorpe, Cumbria, Cicerone Press.

Xanthoudides, Stephanos (1924). *The Vaulted Tombs of Mesará*, transl. J.P. Droop with preface by Sir Arthur Evans. London, University Press of Liverpool/Hodder and Stoughton.

Xanthoudides, Stephanos (1939a). Ἡ ἐνετοκρατία ἐν Κρήτῃ καὶ οἱ κατὰ τῶν Ἐνετῶν ἀγῶνες τῶν Κρητῶν. Texte und Forschungen zur byzantinisch-neugriechischen Philologie, 34. Athens, Verlag der "Byzantinisch-neugriechischen Jahrbücher".

Xanthoudides, Stephanos (1939b). 'Τὸ δίπλωμα (προβελέγιον) τῶν Σκορδιλῶν Κρήτης'. *Epetiris Etaireias Kritikon Spoudhon* 2: 299–312.

Younger, John and Paul Rehak (2001). Neopalatial, Final Palatial, and Postpalatial Crete. In Tracey Cullen (ed.) *Aegean Prehistory: A Review*. American Journal of Archaeology (AJA) Supplement 1, 383–473. Boston, Archaeological Institute of America. (= *AJA* 102: 91–173 plus Addendum: 1998–1999).

Zarinebaf, Fariba, John Bennett, and Jack L. Davis (2005). *A Historical and Economic Geography of Ottoman Greece. The Southwestern Morea in the 18th Century*. Hesperia Suppl. 34. American School of Classical Studies at Athens.

Zinovieff, Sofka (2004). *Eurydice Street. A Place in Athens*. London, Granta Books.

INDEX

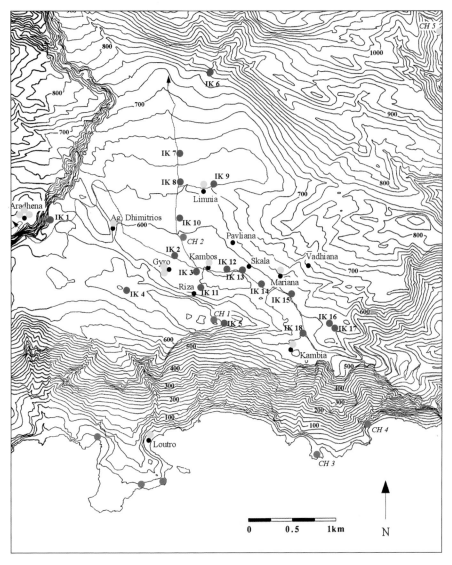

- ● icon stands
- ● settlements
- ● outlying churches
- ● village churches

PLATE 1: Map of Anopoli with churches, settlements, icon stands, and main car roads; the map includes all of Region 4, part of Region 5, and the extreme eastern edge of Region 3. The map joins PLATE 6.

● icon stands   ● outlying churches

● settlements   ● village churches

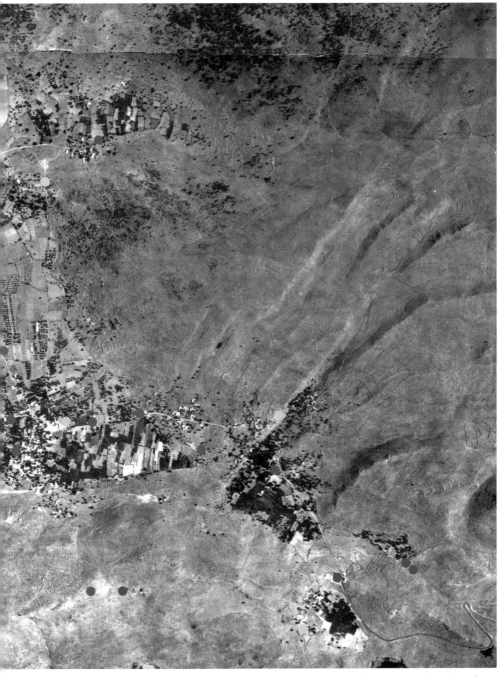

PLATE 2: Aerial photograph of Anopoli: churches, settlements, and icon stands (photograph courtesy of the Greek Ministry of Land Use, Settlement, and the Environment, negative numbers 136448 and 136450). July 1981.

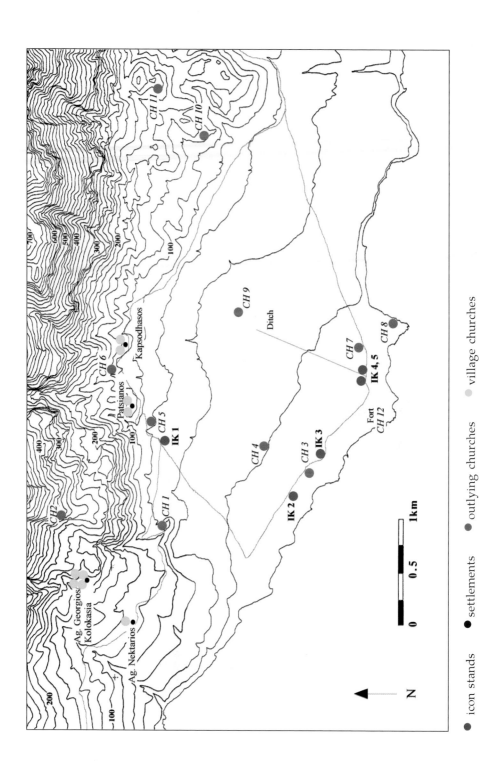

PLATE 3: Map of Frangokastello: churches, villages, icon stands, and main car roads.

● icon stands   ● settlements   ● outlying churches   ● village churches

● icon stands ● settlements ● outlying churches ● village churches

PLATE 4: Aerial photograph of Frangokastello: churches, settlements, and icon stands (photograph courtesy of the Greek Ministry of Land Use, Settlement, and the Environment, negative number 136500). July 1981.

PLATE 5: Ag. Pavlos (3.01) on the shore below the village of Ag. Ioannis, looking north. July 1989.

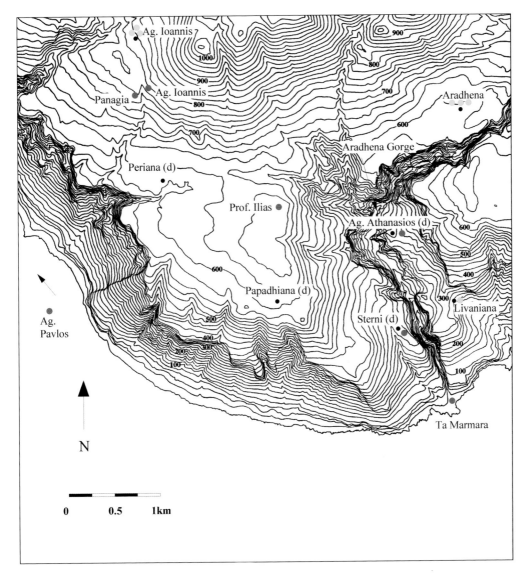

Ag. Ioannis

1000

900

800

Panagia
Ag. Ioannis
800

700

900

800

700

600

Aradhena

Aradhena Gorge

Periana (d)

Prof. Ilias

Ag. Athanasios (d)

600

500

400

600

Papadhiana (d)

300

Livaniana

Ag.
Pavlos

500

Sterni (d)

200

400
300
200
100

100

N

Ta Marmara

N

0   0.5   1km

PLATE 6: Map of Region 3 and part of Regions 4 and 5, with settlements and churches. The map joins PLATE 1.

PLATE 7: AN CH 1. Beacon church of Ag. Aikaterini on top of the Anopolis Ridge, and church of Panagia at the edge of Kampia (4.52), neighbourhood of Anopoli, looking west. July 1988.

PLATE 8: AN CH 4. Closer view of church (Ag. Paraskevi) and icon stand at Glyka Nera, looking northwest. June 1992.

PLATE 9: AN CH 4. Church (Ag. Paraskevi) and icon stand at Glyka Nera, from the sea looking northwest. September 1998.

Plate 10: AN IK 2. Icon stand of Ag. Eirini Khrysovalantou, general view looking northwest. September 1996.

Plate 11: AN IK 2. Ag. Eirini Khrysovalantou, close-up of interior, February 1997.

PLATE 12: AN IK 4. Icon stand of Ag. Georgios ('fridge'), looking southwest, with concrete sheepshed in background. August 1996.

PLATE 13: Anna Kantounaki beside AN IK 9. Icon stand of Ag. Panteleimon, outside her new house in Limnia (4.33), Anopoli. September 1996.

PLATE 14: AN IK 11. Icon stand of Ag. Georgios built into fence outside house in Kampos(4.19), Anopoli. September 1998.

PLATE 15: Icon stands AN IK 16 and 17 (Panagia) with church of Panagia at Mariana (4.56), Anopoli, looking northwest. February 1997.

PLATE 16: FK CH 2. Beacon church of Ag. Ioannis Prodhromos, distant view, looking northwest up to Patsianos Kephala (8.30). July 1990.

PLATE 17: FK CH 2. Ag. Ioannis Prodhromos, closer view, looking southeast and down to the shore at Frangokastello. September 2004.

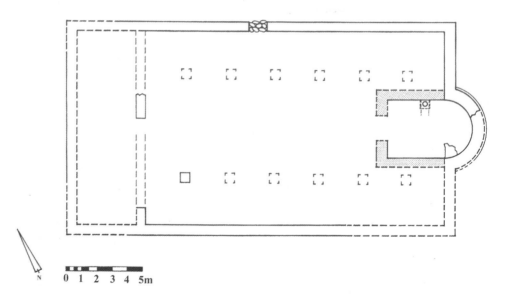

0 1 2 3 4 5m

PLATE 18: Plan of FK CH 4. Ag. Astratigos, built over Late Roman basilica (drawn by Scott Donovan).

PLATE 19: FK CH 7. Ag. Nikitas and excavated area of Late Roman basilica, looking east. In distance, new entrance gate to church enclosure, with palms. September 2000.

PLATE 20: FK CH 7. Ag. Nikitas, festival in September 2004.

Plate 21: FK CH 9. Ag. Ioannis sto Lakko with Late Roman marble spolia built into southwest corner. July 1992.